She Left Me the Gun

Emma Brockes writes for the *Guardian Weekend* magazine and contributes to the *New York Times*, *Vogue*, *Harper's Bazaar* and *Elle*. She is the winner of two British Press Awards (Young Journalist of the Year and Feature Writer of the Year), and while at Oxford she won the Philip Geddes Memorial Prize for Journalism. She is the author of one previous book – *What Would Barbra Do?* – about her love of musicals. She lives in New York.

by the same author

What Would Barbra Do?

SHE LEFT ME THE GUN

My Mother's Life Before Me

EMMA BROCKES

faber and faber

First published in this edition in 2013
by Faber and Faber Limited
Bloomsbury House,
74–77 Great Russell Street,
London WC1B 3DA
This export edition first published in 2013

Typeset by Faber and Faber Ltd

Printed in the UK by CPI Group (UK) Ltd, Croydon, CR0 4YY

Extract from *The Beauty of the Husband: A Fictional Essay in 29 Tangos*
by Anne Carson, published by Jonathan Cape. Reprinted by permission of
The Random House Group Limited

A CIP record for this book
is available from the British Library

ISBN 978–0–571–27584–7

2 4 6 8 10 9 7 5 3 1

For my dad, Johnny

A wound gives off its own light
surgeons say.
If all the lamps in the house were turned out
you could dress this wound
by what shines from it.

ANNE CARSON, *The Beauty of the Husband*

Contents

'We three' and Bonza the dog. It annoyed my mother that, in the only photo of her and her parents in existence, you couldn't see her face.

Preface

My grandmother thought she was marrying someone vibrant and exciting, a man with wavy hair and tremendous energy. He was a talented carpenter, a talented artist, a convicted murderer and a very bad poet. He spent his working life as an engine driver and down the gold mines, and when he met my grandmother, sometime in the early 1930s, he was probably employed at the railway station she passed through en route to her office training course.

My mother said two things about this man: that he was 'very clever', and that he was 'very peculiar'. She also said he had a faulty sense of humour – he liked slapstick – which was her backhanded way of calling him Afrikaans. I gather he was vain about his European origins.

At the time my grandparents met, my grandmother was being courted by someone else, a man called Trevor, or 'Bessie Everett's brother Trevor' as the family on that side remembers him, which is to say, as a known quantity. Nice Trevor, boring Trevor; I picture him in a cardigan, smoking a pipe and reading the less interesting bits of the daily newspaper. By all accounts, my grandmother and Trevor only stepped out a few times. The fact he still rates a mention, some seventy years on, is because in the story that follows Trevor became the shining symbol of what might have been.

She was called Sarah Doubell, and like everyone who dies

young, is supposed to have been beautiful. She had long dark hair, pale skin, big brown eyes and slender ankles. She would get 'stopped on buses', said her older sister Kathy, and asked out by men of superior backgrounds. Before they moved to the coast, her family had been skilled labourers on the ostrich farms, and in group photos, where her siblings look solid, agrarian folk in stout boots and triangular smocks, Sarah seems always to be in floaty dresses and unsuitable footwear. She didn't marry Trevor. She married the other man, at the Babanango Court House, in the presence of her sister Johanna and her brother-in-law Charlie, and moved to a cinder-block house somewhere out in the country. They came into town for the birth of the baby.

There is a single photo of that brief family, sitting on a picnic mat outside in the sun, the father in a shirt and tie, the mother in a pretty dress and the baby in a bonnet looking up at her father. A bulldog pants in the foreground. '"We Three" and Bonza,' Sarah has written on the back, the 'We Three' in inverted commas, as if she is poking affectionate fun at them, a conspiracy of happiness against the rest of the world. I assume they were happy and that my grandmother didn't know about her husband's murder conviction. Which is a shame. It would have been useful information to have had when, as she lay dying, she was deciding whom to leave my two-year-old mother with.

For a few years after her death, Sarah's family stayed in touch with the husband. They were relieved to hear he'd remarried. And then one day he was gone. It was almost forty years before the family tracked down the baby, by which time she was living in London and married to my dad. Her cousin

Gloria, Kathy's daughter, sent her a letter introducing herself as a member of her mother's family and asking where she had been all those years. I wonder now how my mother replied.

My mother didn't talk much about her past when I was growing up. I knew she had emigrated to England from South Africa in 1960 and, in the intervening years, had been back twice. I had met none of her seven siblings and could name probably half of my sixteen first cousins. There were a few stories: about her childhood, her work, her friends, which for the most part she made sound fun. She also hinted at another history, behind the official version, which sounded less fun and which for a long time I was happy to ignore. It was only when she was dying that she told me anything specific. When she was in her mid-twenties, she said, she'd had her father arrested. There had been a highly publicised court case, during which he had defended himself, cross-examining his own children in the witness box and destroying them one by one. Her stepmother had covered for him. He had been found not guilty.

I was calm as she told me this, as I had not been on the one previous occasion she had tried to bring it up. Along with everything else going on, I filed it away to think about later, but as tends to happen, later came sooner than expected.

Six months after my mother's death, I flew from London to Johannesburg to try to piece together the missing portions of her life. It is a virtue, we are told, to face things, although given the choice I would go for denial every time – if denying a thing meant not knowing it. But the choice, it turns out, is not between knowing a thing and not knowing it, but between knowing and half knowing it, which is no choice at all.

Even after I discovered the real story, I was still evasive about it, to myself and others. When someone suggested, during the course of writing this book, that I read the 'clinical literature', I was outraged. I didn't want my mother reduced to the level of case study. I didn't want to lump her in with all those terrible people moaning on about themselves, going on talk shows to weep and wail. I objected to the language they used: 'survivors', as they sometimes called themselves, seemed to me to be a term that only underlined their victimhood. The notion of 'survivordom' had, in any case, become so prized in the culture, so absolving of all behaviour the initial trauma gave rise to – so completely, narcissistically inviting – that those without very much to survive these days rummage around until they come up with something.

'Hard-hearted Hannah' my mother sometimes called me. Mimics frequently get the style but not the heart of a performance right.

Above all, I didn't want to give up the memory I had of her and replace it with something skewed and pathologised. My greatest fear, when I started this, was that I would undo all her good work. Finally, one day, during the endless displacement activities one undertakes while writing a book, I bought a research paper online. It was a study by Canadian psychologists into the parenting deficits of women with 'girl children' who had in their own childhoods been the victims of extreme sexual and physical violence. There were the well-known repeated behavioural patterns. There were high instances of alcohol and drug dependency. It was the interviews with women who had not gone on to abuse their own children that shook me the most, however. Excerpts from these women's interviews catalogued the worry they had about over-protecting their children. They saw danger everywhere; they talked about the suspicion every male who came into contact with their daughters fell under, including their husbands, and the strain this put on their relationships. They talked about the intense pressure they felt to control the environment around their children and of the need to make their children invincible. In the most heartbreaking terms, they talked about the desire to keep them safe without making them crazy. Meanwhile, they had no way of helping themselves.

My mother wasn't a great one for asking for help. She would rather do something herself than have someone else do it for her. Towards the end of her life, she reluctantly accepted she might need some practical assistance, without ever quite relinquishing the upper hand. When a nurse came from the hospice, my mother extracted her life story and started ringing letting agents on her behalf. When neighbours came round with soup and fans, she smiled as if doing them a favour.

An enormous effort went into maintaining this idea she had of herself, and of me, and there were times when I thought I could see the mechanism at work. It had a hint of the burlesque about it, all her positive thinking. As a child, it annoyed me. 'OK, OK,' I thought, 'I get it.' Her genius as a parent, of course, was that I didn't get it at all. If the landscape that eventually emerged can be visualised as the bleakest thing I know – a British beach in winter – she stood around me like a windbreak so that all I saw was colours.

A therapist once described my mother's background in relation to my own as the elephant in the room, a characterisation I reacted strongly against at the time. And my dad did too, when I told him. I have no idea what my mother did with the elephant, but most of the time it wasn't in the room with us. And so, while I strain to find an explanation for just how a person can live one kind of life to the age of almost thirty and then, witness-protection-like, cut that life off and begin again, I have no real answer. Friendship helped. And humour. Beyond that, all I can say is, it was an effort of will.

She never got any credit for it. Her aim – to protect me from being poisoned by the poison in her system – depended for its success on its invisibility. 'One day I will tell you the story of my life,' she said, 'and you will be amazed.' She never did, not really, although I think she wanted to. So I went to find out for myself. It's amazing. Here it is.

Mum, two years old, with her father, Jimmy, in Zululand.

I

If You Think That's Aggressive, Then You Really Haven't Lived

My mother first tried to tell me about her life when I was about ten years old. I was sitting at the table doing homework or a drawing; she was standing at the grill cooking sausages. Every now and then the fat from the meat would catch and a flame leap out.

She had been threatening some kind of revelation for years. 'One day I will tell you the story of my life,' she said, 'and you will be amazed.'

I had looked at her in amazement. The story of her life was she was born, she had me, ten years passed, end of story.

'Tell me now,' I'd said.

'I'll tell you when you're older.'

A second later, I'd considered saying 'Am I old enough now?' but the joke hadn't seemed worth it. Anything constituting a Life Story would deviate from the norm in ways that could only embarrass me.

I knew, of course, that she had come from South Africa and had left behind a large family: seven half-siblings, eight if you included a boy who'd died, ten if you counted the rumour of twins. 'You should have been a twin,' said my mother whenever I did something brilliant, like open my mouth or walk across a room. 'I hoped you'd be twins, with auburn hair. You could have been. Twins run in the family on both sides.'

And, 'My stepmother was pregnant with twins, once.' There were no twins among her siblings.

She always referred to her like this, as 'my stepmother', and unlike her siblings, for whom she provided short but vivid character sketches, and even her father, who featured in the odd story, Marjorie was a blank. As for her real mother's family, all she would say was, 'Strong women, strong genes,' and give me one of her looks – a cross between Nobody Knows the Trouble I've Seen and Abandon All Hope Ye Who Enter Here – that shut down the possibility of further discussion.

It wasn't evident from her accent that she came from elsewhere. In fact, years later, a colleague answering my phone at work said afterwards, 'Your mother has the poshest voice I've ever heard.' I couldn't hear it, but I could see it written down, in the letters she drafted on the backs of old gas bills. It was there in words like 'satisfactory' (great English compliment) and 'peculiar' (huge insult). 'Diana,' she wrote to her friend Joan in 1997, 'such a pretty girl, but such a sad life.' She was imperiously English to her friends and erstwhile family in South Africa, but to me, at home, she was caustic about the English. The worst insult she could muster was, 'You're so English.'

I was English. I was more than English, I was from the Home Counties. I played tennis in white clothing. I went to Brownies. I didn't ride a horse – my mother thought horses an unnecessary complication – but I did everything else commensurate in those parts with being a nice girl. This was important to my mother, although she couldn't help hinting, now and then, at how tame it all was.

'Call that sun?' she said, when the English sun came out.

'Call that rain?' When I got bitten by a red ant at Sports Day, my mother inspected the dot while I started to sniffle. 'For goodness' sake. All that fuss over such a tiny little thing.' Where she came from, any ant worth its salt would kill you.

Among the crimes of the English: coldness, snobbery, boarding schools, 'tradition', the royals, hypocrisy, fat ankles, waste and dessert, or 'pudding', as they called it, a word she thought redolent of the entire race. 'The English', she said, 'are a people who cook their fruit.' It was her greatest fear that she and my dad would die in a plane crash and I would wind up in boarding school alone, eating stewed prunes and getting more English by the day.

If I'd had my wits about me I might have said, 'Oh, right, because white South Africans are so beloved the world over.' But it didn't occur to me. It didn't occur to me until an absurdly late stage that we might, in fact, be separate people.

Above all, she said, the English never talked about anything. Not like us. We talked about everything. We talked a blue streak around the things we didn't talk about.

My parents met at work in the 1960s, at the law firm where my dad was doing his articles and my mum was a bookkeeper. In the late 1970s, when I was a few years old, we moved out of the city to a village an hour away. Ours was the corner house, opposite the tennis club and a five-minute walk from the station.

It was a gentle kind of place, leafy and green, with the customary features of a nice English village: a closely mown cricket pitch, lots of pubs and antiques shops, a war memorial on the high street and, in the far distance, a line of wooded hills that on autumn days caught the sun and made the village postcard-pretty. It was emphatically not the kind of place where people had Life Stories. Life *stages* perhaps, incremental steps through increasingly boring sets of circumstances; for example, we used to live in London and now we lived in Buckinghamshire. It was also very safe. There was no police report in our local newspaper, but if there had been, it would have been full of minor acts of vandalism and dustbins blowing over in high winds. There was the occasional parking violation when the bowls club had a tournament, and two men were arrested, once, for doing something in the public toilets the paper struggled to find words for. 'What about the women and children!' thundered a Tory councillor, causing my dad to look up mildly from his newspaper at breakfast. 'What has it got to do with the women and children?'

(When my mother read the newspaper, it was with a pen in one hand, so that when she came across a photo of a pompous-looking public official – if he was smiling – she could absent-mindedly black out one of his teeth. Helmut Kohl, François Mitterrand, Ronald Reagan all lost teeth this way. 'Your mother's been at the newspaper again,' my father would sigh.)

She was in many ways a typical resident. She went to yoga in the village hall. She stood in line at the post office. She made friends with the lady on the deli counter in Budgens and had a nice relationship with the lovely family who lived next door to us. Their young boys would come round to look at the fish in our pond. Every year I made her a home-made birthday card that depicted scenes from family life. She tacked them up on the kitchen wall, where they faded with each passing summer. I found them recently, seven in all, a memoir of my mother's existence in the village. There she is, wonkily drawn in her yoga gear, surrounded by me, my dad, two cats and the fish.

At the same time, it pleased her, I think, to be at a slight angle to the culture; someone who had adopted the role of a Buckinghamshire mum but who had at her disposal various super powers – powers she had decided, on balance, to keep under her hat. (I used to think this an attitude unique to my mother, until I moved to America and realised it is the standard expat consolation: in my case – a British person in New York – looking around and thinking, 'You people have no idea about the true nature of reality when you don't know what an Eccles cake is or how to get to Watford.')

In my mother's case, it was a question of style. She was very much against the English way of disguising one's intentions. One never knew what they were thinking, she said – or rather, one always knew what they were thinking but they never came out and said it.

She loved to tell the story of how, soon after moving in, she was sanding the banisters one day when a man came to the door, canvassing for the Conservatives. 'He just ASSUMED,' she raged then and for years afterwards, 'he just ASSUMED I WAS TORY.' She wasn't Tory, but she wasn't consistently liberal, either. She disapproved of people having children out of wedlock. When a child-molester storyline surfaced on TV, she would argue for castration, execution and various other medieval solutions to the problem, while my father and I sat in uncomfortable silence. She was not, by and large, in favour of silence.

Even her gardening was loud. When my parents bought the house, the garden had been a denuded quarter acre which my mother set about Africanising. She planted pampas grass and mint. She let the grass grow wild around the swing by the shed. Along the back fence, she put in fast-growing dogwoods.

'It's to hide your ugly house,' she said sweetly when our other neighbour complained. After that, whenever my mother was out weeding and found a snail, she would lob it, grenade-like, over the fence into the old lady's salad patch.

'That's very aggressive,' said my father, who is English and a lawyer. If he ever threw a snail, it would be by accident.

'Ha!' said my mother, and gave him the look: If You Think That's Aggressive, Then You Really Haven't Lived.

When it works, the only child/parent bond is a singular dynamic. Being an only child is a bit like being Spanish: you have your dinner late, you go to bed late and from all the grown-up parties you get dragged to you wind up eating a lot of hors d'oeuvres. Your parents talk to you as if you were an adult, and when they're not talking to you, you have no one to talk to. So you listen.

By the time I was eight, I knew that olives stuffed with anchovies were not pukey but 'an acquired taste'. I knew that Mr X who lived down the road was not a blameless old codger but a 'mean shit' who didn't let his wife have the heating on during the day. I knew that Tawny Owl was too scared to drive after dark and that this rendered her useless, not only as a leader within the Girl Guide movement but as a human being generally. Later, I knew which of my friends' parents had appealed against their twelve-plus results and with what success, and I knew, from a particularly fruitful session at the bathroom door, what my own results were before being officially told. When a classmate was off sick from school for the fourth day running, my mother and I speculated that she and her family were actually in Hawaii, in crisis talks over the marriage. We blamed the dad. 'He's decidedly odd,' said my mother, 'don't you think?'

My mother would never admit to being homesick for South Africa, but she was, occasionally, nostalgic for London. She would, she said, have liked me to have grown up in a more mixed environment. There was only one black person in the village when I was growing up, a man who worked in the library and who was not only black but 'gay to boot'.

'Shame,' she said when we passed him in the street. She never lowered her voice when she made these assessments. 'Shame,' she would say when she saw someone fat, smiling broadly at them in pity. 'It must be glandular.'

'How do you know he's gay?' I asked. My mother gave me the look: Woman of the World in a Town Full of Hicks.

'It's the way he walks,' she said. 'Among other things.'

I knew a few details from her childhood. My mother loved to tell stories and there were some dazzling set pieces I begged her to tell me again and again. She had grown up in a series of small towns and remote villages, 'out in the bundu' of what was then Zululand, now KwaZulu-Natal, so that most of her stories involved near-deadly encounters with the wildlife and weather. There were hailstones the size of golf balls. There was lightning to strike you dead as you were crossing a field. Those snakes that weren't hanging from trees waiting to drop down her back were fighting scorpions for the deeds to the toe end of her slippers.

She told me about her aunty Johanna, cracking eggs into a bowl one day and releasing with the final egg a mass of tiny black snakes into the yellow mixture. A cobra had laid its eggs next to the hens' in the hen house. She told me about her brother Mike and the practical jokes he had played on her. From the earliest age, just as I knew the rules about lying and stealing, I knew what a bad idea it was to leave a dead snake in someone's bed as a joke, because its partner might come looking for it. Some snakes, she said, mate for life.

As a consequence, if I ever went to Africa, I said, it would be on condition I could wear a balaclava, dungarees, Wellington boots and some kind of headgear. I pictured myself walking down a jungle path dressed in something halfway between a beekeeper's outfit and what you might wear to weld metal.

'You couldn't,' she said. 'You'd be too hot.'

'I still would, though.'

'It wouldn't be *practical*.'

We didn't go. Instead, every year or so, my dad and I watched as my mother raised the possibility and then talked herself out of it. There were the politics, she said; this was the mid-1980s, when every night on the news we watched footage of government Casspirs going into the townships. There were family politics, too. If we stayed with one, it would upset the others. If we stayed in a hotel, it would upset them all. You have no idea, she said, how a family that size operates.

Anyway, she said, if we went anywhere long-haul, she would rather go to Australia. We didn't go to Australia. Although the money was there and my dad was willing, I got the impression we didn't go because, at some level of my mother's thinking, going to Australia meant flying over

Africa. It is quite an achievement, in a village in England, to feel that evasive action is being taken to avoid the southern hemisphere, but that's how it was.

Instead we went to France and Spain. We went to Cornwall at half-term. I went on school trips to Somerset and to Brownie camp in Liverpool. 'I'll be glad when you're back,' said my mother, face clenched, seeing me off at the coach. I thought the scene demanded tears and began, experimentally, to sniffle. 'For goodness' sake,' said my mother, relaxing into irritation. 'It's enough now.'

Among her stories, there was one which made me vaguely uncomfortable. I couldn't put my finger on it at the time, but I see now what it was: the threat of withheld information. It came with one of her looks, the one I didn't like: a kind of sideways swipe of the eyes, like windows on a computer desktop hastily minimising.

Nonetheless, it was a very good story. After my mother had arrived in England, but before she had met my dad, she had gone to see a healer, a retired postman and 'humble little man', she would say (as if we were royalty), who lived in a council flat in Tottenham. She didn't believe in all of that; on the other hand, you never know, and so, on the recommendation of a friend whose back he'd fixed, she went to see Mr Trevor.

His visions came out in flashes over tea. She would have one child, he said, a girl with long fingers like a starfish (true). She would face a fork in the road one day, and depending on which branch she took, be either very happy or slightly less happy (the former, I hope). At some point in the session, Mr Trevor came over peculiar and in a horrible voice said, 'Is that dirt or a birthmark?'

'That was your father,' he said, coming to. Her father was dead and had in any case never been to England. Mr Trevor couldn't possibly have delivered his mail.

Whenever she told this story, she would lift her hair and show me, at the nape of her neck, a strawberry-coloured birthmark that had survived her father's best efforts to scrub it off. Those were always the words he would use, she said.

Letters came in from her siblings occasionally; nothing for years and then a fifteen-page blockbuster written entirely in capitals. She would leave it on the kitchen table for me, for when I got home from school. 'Read it to me,' she said, and I would.

To me, her siblings had a kind of mythical status, partly for the glamour all large families hold for only children, and partly for their complete and utter absence from our lives. When my mother talked about them, it was as though they were people she had known a long time ago and had once been very fond of. There was the one she called her best friend. There was one who was her conscience. There were two she hardly knew. There was one who'd died of whooping cough as a child, whose small white coffin she remembered walking behind. There was one who was very charming but whom you had to keep an eye on. There were two she called her babies – 'Fay was my baby, Steve was my baby' – whom she'd brought up, more or less, when her stepmother's hands were full.

There were no photos of these people around the house, but she did once dig out a cardboard box from the garage to show me some old, sepia-coloured photos from an even earlier era.

This, she said, was before her mother had died and her father remarried and had so many more children.

There were three or four in the set, small, white-bordered and faded with age. One was of my mother as a baby, standing in a hot-looking crib, clutching hold of the bars. In another she was standing, waving, in a garden. On the back, my grandmother Sarah had written, 'Pauline on her 2nd birthday.' There were two further photos in the set: my mother as a toddler, with fat little legs and scrunched-down socks, standing beside a fresh grave, the soil still exposed; and in the same position on a different day – the grave already looked older. Someone had written on the back, 'Pauline arranging flowers on her mother's grave,' but who that was she had no idea. 'Shame,' said my mother, when she showed me the photos, 'poor little thing,' as if it was not her we were looking at but someone entirely unrelated to either of us.

Mum putting flowers on her own mother's grave.

I remember asking her once if we had any heirlooms. It was a word I'd picked up from a friend while tiptoeing around her parents' formal drawing room one day, where we weren't allowed to play. My friend had pointed out various spindly-legged chairs and silver trinkets which had been her granny's and which, she said importantly, would be hers one day. I had gone back to my own house and, while my mother considered the question, had looked around for something old to cherish.

'What about this?' I said. It was a green cigar box in thick, heavy glass with a brass hinge.

'For goodness' sake,' said my mother. She didn't know where it came from, and anyway, it was hideous.

We didn't have heirlooms, she said, because she could only fit so much into her trunk, and besides, her mother had died when she was two, what did I want? I was goading her a little, I knew it. Our peculiarities were annoying me that day. Of this particular friend of mine's mother, my own mother had been known to say, 'I don't know why she's so pleased with herself. They made their money in gin.'

Actually there were a few things she could have pointed out to me. There was a tiny porcelain teacup, the sole sur-viving item from a doll's tea service, with a depiction of the young Queen, then Princess Elizabeth, on the side. There was a glass beaded necklace. And there was a portrait of her moth-er, Sarah, that hung above the TV in the lounge. It was blown up from a black-and-white photo and painted over in colour, in the style of the times. The colours were a little off – the lips too bright, the skin too pale; she looked consumptive, which is in fact what she was. My mother didn't mention these items in the talk about heirlooms. They must have struck her as a mean inheritance, the pitiful remains of a long dead young woman, and when I thought about it later, I was sorry for asking. Later still, I thought about the painting and where she had chosen to hang it; whenever my mother raised her eyes from the TV, she met her own mother's gaze.

In fact, there was something my mother wanted me to have by way of an heirloom. It had come over on the boat with her in an old-fashioned trunk, the kind with its ribs on the outside. 'All my worldly goods,' she would say, and when one of these things surfaced in the course of daily life, a moment would be taken, as before an item recovered from Christ's tomb.

Before I moved countries myself and understood the pull of sentiment over practicality, I thought her packing choices eccentric. So no overcoat, although she was sailing into an English winter, but a six-piece dinner service. The complete works of Jane Austen, minus *Mansfield Park*. A bespoke two-piece suit in oatmeal with brown trim. A tapestry she had done, even though she wasn't arty, of a seventeenth-century English drawing-room scene in which someone played the harpsichord and someone else the lute. And at the bottom of her trunk, wrapped in a pair of knickers, her handgun. Getting it through customs undetected was her first triumph in the new country.

The gun was kept in a secret drawer beneath the bookcase in the downstairs guest bedroom, the most secure of the improvised safes in the house. In my parents' bedroom, a decoy tumble dryer contained some gold and silver necklaces under a pile of citrus-coloured T-shirts and a towelling tracksuit we called aquamarine. Outside the bathroom, in the cavity between two plastic buckets which served as a fortified laundry basket, were my mother's gold bracelets. For a while, she stashed things in the ash collector beneath an unused fireplace in the dining room, but couldn't shake the fear she would die suddenly and we would forget what she had buried there, sending it up in smoke. I forget what she buried there. Not the rings we called knuckle-dusters, with huge semi-precious stones – topaz, amethyst, tourmaline – on tiny gold and silver mounts. They weren't valuable or even wearable, but they were very pretty, and most of them had been given to her by friends or sent in padded envelopes across vast distances of space and time by relatives who thought she should have them. The person they'd belonged to must have died, but who that was I don't know.

The secret drawer, which she had designed herself after liaising with the carpenter, was where she kept her most precious items: her naturalisation papers; a list of how much I weighed during the first six months of my life; various documents testifying to her abilities as a bookkeeper; and the gun.

'Remember it's here,' she said, the one time she showed it to me. 'And remember my jewels. Don't let your father's second wife get her hands on them.'

'Ha!' called my dad from the hallway. 'I should be so lucky.'

My mother smiled. 'You'll miss me when I'm gone.'

It was smaller than I'd imagined, silver with a pearl handle, like something a highwayman might proffer through a frilly sleeve during a slightly fey hold-up. I knew it was illegal, but gun licensing wasn't the issue then it is now and it struck me as naughty in the order of, say, a white lie, rather than something genuinely criminal, like dropping litter in the street or parking on the double yellow lines outside Threshers. She had it, she said, because 'everybody had one'. I think she saw it as a jaunty take on the whole stuffy English notion of inheritance – just the thing for a woman to bequeath to her only daughter. My dad hated having it in the house and threatened, once, to throw it in the local arm of the Grand Union Canal.

'You'll do no such thing!' my mother raged. 'I'm very fond of that gun.'

It was about a year after this that she stood in the kitchen cooking the sausages, face flushed from the heat pulsing out of the grill. My dad was watching TV in the next room. 'Go and change,' she had said when he had come in from work, as she said every night. Without turning and in a voice so harsh and strange she sounded like a medium channelling an angry spirit, she said, 'My father was a violent alcoholic and a paedophile who . . .'. The rest is lost, however, because at the first whiff of trouble I burst loudly into tears like a cartoon baby.

Something unthinkable happened then. My mother, who at the slightest hint of distress on my part would mobilise armies to eliminate the cause, who routinely threatened to kill people on my behalf and who felt, I always thought, short-changed that I never gave her an opportunity to show me exactly what she could do in this area, didn't move across the floor to console me, but stood staring disconsolately into the mouth of the grill. 'Your father cried, too, when I told him,' she said, and I could see there was consolation in this, her sense of being surrounded by weaklings. Abruptly I switched off the tears. My dad came in. We ate dinner as normal. We didn't talk about it again for fifteen years.

Except that we did, of course. 'The absence from conversation of a known quantity is a very strong presence,' wrote Margaret Atwood in *Negotiating with the Dead*, 'as the Victorians realised about sex.'

'Don't get kidnapped,' said my mother, whenever I left the house. 'Don't get abducted. Don't get raped and murdered.'

'I'm only going to the shop,' I said, or later, over the phone from London, 'to the office/Manchester/the loo.'

'So?' she said. 'They have murderers in Manchester, don't they?'

About once a week, she rang after a sleepless night, and we went through the routine.

'I had a sleepless night.'

'What?'

'Someone broke into the house in the night and snatched you away.'

Or:

'Someone ran away with you on your way home from work.'

Or, simply:

'Your dirty washing.' The more ludicrous the cause, the better. Once, a personal best, a sleepless night about my flatmate's dirty washing. I told him by way of a boast, 'Look how much my mother loves me, so much she loses sleep over whether *you* have clean clothes or not.' I remember he giggled rather nervously.

Only occasionally her comic tone faltered. In the car on the way back from Oxford one day: 'Don't be cross with me – I had a sleepless night.'

I was instantly furious. 'For God's sake,' I said. 'It was one date. ONE DATE.'

My mother looked at me ruefully. 'I thought he might cut you up and put you under the floorboards.' This referred to a recent case in the news in which a man from Oxford had murdered his girlfriend and, folding her like a ventriloquist's doll, stuffed her in a suitcase under his bed. The floorboards part was a flourish I think she got from Jack the Ripper.

'I'm not going to tell you anything if this is how you behave.'

Her contrition evaporated. A warning look. 'People get abducted, don't they? People get murdered.' And there it was in the car with us, the huge mauve silence at the edge of the known world. 'These things happen.'

'Not to me they don't.'

She looked at me then with every ounce of love in her system.

'No, not to you.'

Mum, her sister Fay (in huge hipster glasses) and Fay's ex-husband, Frank, in Trafalgar Square before I was born.

2

South Africa, 1932–60

The official reason my mother gave for leaving was politics. 'I couldn't stand the politics,' she said and pointed to March 1960, when sixty-nine people had been killed in Sharpeville while protesting against apartheid. She had been to a couple of meetings, she said, and had to decide whether to stay and commit or leave altogether. This was the story as she told it.

No one in her family had ever been to England. Her father's ancestry was Dutch. Her mother's, she said, had been French. But like most English-speaking white people in the colony, she had grown up thinking of England as a point of origin. She was a great reader and had ploughed her way through the nineteenth-century English novels. She identified strongly with Jane Eyre, even more so with Bertha Mason and not at all with Cathy, in *Wuthering Heights*, who she thought made a spectacle of herself, carrying on like that at the window. She would have sympathised with Virginia Woolf's put-down of Katherine Mansfield, who was said to have appeared in ghost form after her death, which Woolf thought typical of the woman: to be caught leading such a 'cheap posthumous life'. Her favourite Austen heroine was Elizabeth Bennet for what she saw as her keen lack of hysteria.

I knew she had been born in Durban, in her aunty Kathy's house, and that when she was two years old her mother had died of tuberculosis. I also knew that around the age of five her father had remarried. But of his second wife – where they met, who her family was or anything much about her beyond her name, Marjorie – I knew nothing. My mother had no sympathy for her, although her life would seem to have been hard. She was pregnant for more or less a decade after marrying my grandfather, and my mother, like many eldest children in a family that size, was put in the position of surrogate parent to some of her half-siblings.

She never called them 'half'. She called them 'my brothers and sisters'.

If it struck me as odd that we never saw or heard from them, I didn't dwell on it. Like most children, the life my parents led before I was born was a rumour I didn't believe in. When I gave her childhood any thought at all, I thought it sounded kind of fun; like *Cider with Rosie*, but with deadlier wildlife.

My mother was tall, slim, not athletic exactly but aware of her own strength. She was very blonde as a child, and no matter what she did with her hair, couldn't get it to curl. This was the era of Shirley Temple, and my mother presented it to me as the tragedy of her childhood: lank hair. But she had large brown eyes and high cheekbones, and one day, as she left the schoolyard, two little boys shouted after her, 'We love you, we love you!'

Maths was her subject. She worked hard at school, each week competing for first place with a girl called Stella, but whereas Stella was gifted, said my mother, she had to work for it. She gave me a meaningful look. 'Oh, cut it out,' I thought. She

'We love you, we love you!' Eight-year-old mum with her brother, Michael.

wanted to be a nurse, but the teacher took her aside and said nonsense, you should be a doctor. Since most of her schooling took place in English-speaking Natal, in the south-east of the country, she never learnt Afrikaans – which didn't stop her, years later, startling Dutch guests around the pool in Majorca by trying to use it to engage them in small talk, while I slid behind my paperback and pretended to be Spanish.

She sometimes referred to her father as Jimmy. He had worked in the gold mines or as an engine driver, and she was rather proud of the latter; of the two jobs, it's the one she chose to list as his profession on her marriage certificate. She showed me a poem he had written once, which he had given to her when she left South Africa. It was called 'Salutation to the Dawn' and was full of soppy descriptions of the sky and wildlife. 'He probably copied it out of a book,' she said bitterly, a rare break in tone. Most of her recollections ran along jollier lines.

She told me her brother knew Tarzan, and I believed her. (My dad tried to rival this claim by saying his brother knew Kermit the Frog, but this I did not believe. His brother lived forty miles away in London and Kermit, as everyone knew, lived in New York, with Miss Piggy.)

She told me of various capers involving the family dogs. One was killed at a picnic when a scorpion bit him on the nose. Another, Caesar, was killed when a neighbour threw out a piece of steak for him, studded with glass. My mother couldn't remember why. At one point they had a Great Dane, who adopted a baby chick from the yard when its mother abandoned it. They called the chick Tarzan and let it sleep in the crook of the dog's giant forelegs. When they put food out for the dog, Tarzan would hop onto the side of the bowl and eat with him.

'What happened to Tarzan?' I said. My mother looked blank.

'I can't remember. We probably ate him.'

It didn't occur to me until much later that the moral of most of my mother's stories was look lively or die.

She told me about Flora the maid. They were poor, said my mother, but they were still white and so despite having nothing, a succession of black women roaming the countryside with even less installed themselves in the kitchen and started work in the hope of eventual remuneration. 'Poor things,' said my mother. She remembered Flora in particular. She had been abandoned by her husband and had gone round the bend. Every day, she dragged the gramophone out into the yard and wedged it beneath the peach tree, which she climbed to scan the horizon for her lost love, while Tony, my mother's little brother, stood sentry at the base of the tree. 'Tony, where's my husband?' Flora wailed. 'Tony, where's my huuuuuusband?!' – it was a great catchphrase of my youth – while the gramophone played 'If I had wings like an angel / over these prison walls I would fly.'

There was a single story my mother told from the period between her mother dying and her father remarrying. It wasn't even a story, just an image. They were living out in the wilderness somewhere, her father working night shifts in the mine, and he would leave her at dusk with an oil lamp burning. She was five years old. At some point in the night the lamp would burn out. 'And I would be alone, in the dark.'

Mum as a baby with her father, Jimmy.

She didn't become a doctor. She left school at sixteen and got an entry-level job as a clerk in an office. She had never been to the city before, and the night before her first day she asked her father, who'd grown up in Johannesburg, if he would accompany her the next morning. He said he wouldn't and instead drew her a map of how to get from the bus station to her office. She spent her first lunch hour riding up and down the escalators in a department store. She had never seen anything so amazing in her life, she said.

When she was seventeen, her stepmother had another baby, a boy called Steven who was premature and cried and cried, said my mother; she remembered rocking him for hours and watching the soft, unformed top of his skull move in and out as he wailed. 'Fay was my baby, Steve was my baby.' She sang to Steve endlessly, which is why, she said, he could never hold a tune later on in life.

In her early twenties she moved into a flat-share in the city with a girl she'd met at work called Joan. They went out on the town; my mother took to painting a beauty spot on her face, until she got caught in a rainstorm going to visit her family one day and it streaked. Her brothers fell about laughing: 'Is that beauty spot washable?'

She changed jobs. She studied for an office-management certificate. For a while she worked at Unterhalter's Mattress Works ('Enjoy your repose with Rosey-Doze'). Eventually she got a job as a bookkeeper at one of the country's biggest law firms, where she encountered someone whose name would ring down through my childhood. Sima Sosnovik could have been a heroine from Tolstoy. She worked from a glass office overlooking the bookkeeping pool, whence she plucked my

*Like a heroine from a movie, Sima Sosnovik, my mother's mentor
and friend.*

mother and groomed her for stardom. It is the only time I
heard my mother give credit for her life to anyone else, except
in the most general sense to the 'good genes' she inherited
from her mother's side. 'She saw something in me,' said my
mother. 'She saw something in me and she saved me.'

Her first line to my mother, repeated down the years as if
from a classic movie and to be imagined in a Russian accent,

was, 'You do your work as if you expect it to be checked.' My mother was mortified. It lit a personality trait in her that would last the rest of her life. There was never a penny unaccounted for in her transactions. Her cheque book was fanatically balanced. She kept records of everything: how long the water filter had been in the jug; how many times the semi-perishable plastic bowl had been used in the washing machine. In her address book, she kept a record of every birth, death, divorce and remarriage in the family she never saw or spoke to. She would look up, suddenly, from the sink and say, 'It's my brother John's birthday today.'

'I have an elephantine memory,' she sighed. The curse of brilliance.

Sosnovik was the head of accounts, a title which, said my mother, if she hadn't moved to London would surely have been hers one day. I have a photo of this woman, posing on the deck of a ship sometime in the 1930s. She is elegant in a pencil skirt, cigarette in one hand and with wavy red hair. She looks like Norma Shearer. Sima Sosnovik.

'What happened to her?' I said once. It was dangerous to veer off the chosen path of my mother's story and her face clouded instantly. 'She died,' she said. End of discussion.

It wasn't long after this that my mother saw the ad in the newspaper, a 'once in a lifetime' special offer: a one-way passage to England, a week in a hostel in Earl's Court and tickets to a West End show, for £5 all in. She took it as a sign, resigned from her job, sold all her furniture and sailed that November. After a two-week voyage the ship docked at Southampton, where a telegram was waiting for her at the

Union Castle office. It was from her stepmother, who, after filling her in on her siblings' goings-on over the past fortnight, informed her that while she was at sea, her father had dropped dead of a brain haemorrhage. He had been buried when she was somewhere around the Azores. All she would say of that first winter in London was that it was very cold and she found the people peculiar.

That was the story as my mother told it. Since then, she had seen her family a handful of times. Fay, her sister, had come to stay before I was born, with her then-husband Frank. There was a photo of them festooned with pigeons in Trafalgar Square, Fay wearing insane Eric Morecambe-style glasses, my mother grinning and even Frank looking quite jolly. He had disgraced himself on that trip, said my mother, by refusing to travel on the Underground and demanding his dinner at the same time every night. My mother did an impression of him: 'Faith, where are my boiled eggs?' Frank was English, of course.

And her brother Mike had come, before I was born, to play against England in the South African hockey team. He was in goal. My mother had shown him and his teammates around London, and when they asked her a question she didn't know – 'Is Marble Arch really made out of marble?' – she just made it up. When I was a year old, my mother had a gigantic row with her in-laws, scooped me up and fled back to South Africa for a month. There was a photo from that trip of a round, pasty-faced baby, ears sticking out at right angles, surrounded by cousins I didn't recognise.

'Weren't you worried?' I said once, pointing at my ears.

'Don't you criticise my child,' said my mother fiercely and repeated the story of Debbie, who'd been pregnant at the same time as my mother, but whereas Debbie's baby 'looked like a pig', I was beautiful. 'She just couldn't see it!' My mother looked freshly amazed every time.

Among the photos from that trip there was one of my mother with her aunty Kathy. Kathy was very old by then, sitting beside my mother with Uncle Dick, her husband, on somebody's porch wicker furniture. My mother spoke very highly of Kathy, whom, after that one and only meeting, she identified as the source of various sterling traits in the family. 'Aunty Kathy', she said, 'had a very sharp tongue.'

It was Kathy who told my mother what had happened in the immediate aftermath of Sarah's death: that efforts to adopt her had been made by Sarah's sisters, but that her father had rejected them. That they had kept track of him for a few years and had been relieved to hear he'd remarried. That Kathy had sent his new wife some little vests for the child, and that she had them sent back, with a note saying they weren't in need of charity. Then the family disappeared.

Kathy spent years trying to find her late sister's baby. Another sister, Johanna, even named my mother sole heir to her and Charlie's farm, as if the convention of an advantageous will to draw people out of obscurity like a magnet might summon her back to them. But when Johanna died, some years later, my mother failed to materialise. When Kathy retired from the search, her daughter Gloria, a year older than my mother and born in the same bed, took it up.

It was Gloria who finally tracked my mother down to London, by which time she was in her thirties and married to my dad. Gloria sent her a letter, introducing herself as a member of her mother's family and asking, 'Hey, what happened? We've been looking for you for thirty years. Someone left you a farm . . .'

My mother stared blankly when she said this and shrugged at the shame of it all. She couldn't blame her mother for picking her father. 'He was the exciting choice,' she said helplessly. If you were twenty-two and had a shortened life expectancy, you wouldn't marry a man called Trevor, either.

'What happened to the farm?' I said.

'It went to someone else.'

My mother's friends during those early years in London were a circle of gay men, who became like substitute family. During school holidays, we drove down in her Mini to see them: my godfather Len, Bob and Nick, Ken and David, Willy and Barry, Edward – 'dear Edward' – Roger, and Kenneth. They were mainly artists and architects. They had large abstract paintings on their walls and Eames chairs in their living rooms. When they came to see us in the village, my mother's voice took on an arch tone, as if her life here was a bizarre experiment she would one day abandon. She always said of these friends that they expected her to spoil me – the only child born a month shy of her forty-third birthday. 'They thought you'd be a brat,' she said. I don't know what gave them that idea. Perhaps it was the decor in the living room, where photos of me taken every year from age two and a half upwards ran across the length of one wall and which uncharitable friends called The Shrine.

'Rogue's gallery,' she said.

For the rest of the school holidays, we hung out at home. We went to the shops and to the bottle bank one town over. My mother worried I would be lonely without siblings and organised copious play dates and activities. For her sake I suffered Scrabble, although it bored me, and for mine she suffered Snakes and Ladders, although as a game that turned entirely on luck, it offended her principles. 'You make your own luck,' she said. And, 'Sufficient unto the day.' And, 'Don't scratch, you'll make it worse.' One summer she taught me canasta and we created vast, sprawling games across the kitchen table. We had a whale of a time.

'Did they feed you?' she said, when I came back from a sleepover. 'What did they feed you? Who else was there? What were the sleeping arrangements?'

'Who's your best?' she would say and name two of my friends. 'Which would you rather?'

I once heard Nigel Nicholson tell a story on the radio of an encounter he'd had as a child with Virginia Woolf. She had asked him about his teacher, and he had given her a bland description, enough to fob off most adults, to which she had replied impatiently, 'Yes, but what sort of *shoes* does she wear?' My mother was like that. 'Did you see . . .? What did you see? What do you think . . .? Which would you rather . . .?' Motivation established, then came judgement. My mother's judgements were arbitrary and final. Cremation over burial. Charlotte Brontë over Emily. France over Italy. Spain over

France. 'Slob,' she once said of the mother of a schoolfriend of mine whom I'd reported seeing dump clean laundry from the machine straight onto the floor. 'What a slob that woman is.'

One day I walked in from school to an atmosphere so tense you could almost smell it; there was something sharp and filmy in the air, like petrol. My mother was at her usual post, on a bar stool by the sink.

'What?' I said. She turned to look at me so strangely.

'Mike died.'

'Oh.'

Her brother Mike was seven years her junior, the next one down and a great athlete. In the event of her and my father dying, she'd said once, I'd go and live with Mike. I'd been quite looking forward to it. Now he had collapsed with a heart attack at the mine, in his forties, fit as a fiddle, with three young children and a wife.

My mother glared and turned away so I wouldn't see her cry. I carried on standing in the doorway, neat in my school uniform, worried about my maths homework, dental checkup in the diary, tennis coaching, swimming coaching, rehearsals for the school play, dance class, piano practice, Latin verb revision on my mind, and before she turned away, I thought, the look on her face was unmistakable: this child has nothing to do with me. She didn't go back for the funeral.

And then a cousin came to stay; an actual blood relative, the daughter of my mother's sister Fay. Her name was Victoria and she was three and a half years older than me. She had long blonde hair and was very pretty. We got on in a low-key kind of way. She wanted to be a vet and spent most of the trip in

Mike, Mum's younger brother and 'best friend' in the family.

the tack shop on the high street, talking to the woman about horses. She told us about the time her pet rat died and she dissected it to see how it worked, pinned out the skin and laid out the bones. It was a startlingly unsentimental thing for a child to do. My mother blinked when she told us this, as one does when confronted, unexpectedly, with one's own reflection.

Because of the age gap, my mother arranged a play date for her niece with older siblings of a friend of mine. It didn't go well. They teased her about something – her accent or her shyness. Anyway, my mother got wind of it and never let it go. It gave her immense satisfaction when these girls grew up, and 'despite all their advantages', didn't go to university or amount to anything much beyond marriage. She persecuted their mother with news of my progress – would literally stalk her down the high street into every shop, until she had her cornered in the post office, whereupon she pinned her flat against the wall and made her listen to my exam results. Or Victoria's exam results; my cousin did become a vet, after seven years of training. My mother could wait. She was in it for the long game. You worked hard, time passed, the wheel eventually turned.

One of the things my mother admired about her niece was her good manners, which she thought important in a child. To that end she policed a strict no-swearing zone around me while I was growing up, so strict in fact that I remember the two occasions when it was broken. 'It's not big and it's not clever,' she said, when I expressed a reluctance to go to Brownies and prefaced it with the words, 'Oh my God.' And then we were walking down a London street with my godfather one day when it started to rain. 'It's pissing it down,' he said, and received a look from my mother to turn a man to stone.

Years later, she was driving me to school when a car cut in front of us at the roundabout by the garden centre. I was in my teens by then. 'What a cunt!' said my mother airily, and gave me a sly look. 'What?' she said, feigning surprise as my jaw hit the floor. 'Didn't you know your mother had a filthy mouth?' She had tried her best, she said. If I wasn't well-spoken after all these years, there was nothing more she could do. 'It's enough now.'

It was an attitude she wanted me to inherit; not quite stiff up-per lip, which she considered too English, but a less repressed version of that. Whining was not permissible. Undervaluing oneself was not permissible. 'For goodness' sake,' she said, when I had the temerity to suggest I might have to slip down a grade in tennis coaching. 'Of course you can do it, you're my child, aren't you?' (I feel a pressure from beyond the grave to point out that I held my place in the top stream.) I wasn't much interested in inheriting an attitude. I was entering a ma-terialistic phase. My mother showed me the things she had brought over on the boat with her: the trunk in the garage, with her name and cabin number on the side; all the books; and the dinner service. She had me try on the bespoke suit, but it was too big. I read her copy of *Gone with the Wind*, which she said her best friend in Johannesburg had given to her. 'To Dear Pauline,' it said on the flyleaf. 'God Bless! All my love, Joan, December 16th 1956' – my mother's birthday. My mother looked sentimental at the mention of Joan. And then there was the gun.

Of everything she brought over with her it was the item she most wanted me to have. 'This will be yours one day,' she said, long before those kinds of conversations were necessary. In the end, however, the price of a gesture can be too high to bear. In 1990, a gun amnesty was declared in Britain, and my mother decided that, after all, it might get me into trouble. Reluctantly, she laid it in a box like a dead pet and drove it to the police station. By the time she got back she'd cheered up. The female desk sergeant had squealed when she opened the box and called out her fellow officers from the back room. It was the only contribution to the amnesty they'd had.

'They were completely intrigued,' said my mother, beaming. 'I suppose I don't look the type.'

I still have the trunk and I still have the dinner service. The bespoke suit went down in a freak sewing accident in the mid-1990s. I am not, on the whole, sentimental about the gun.

Me and Mum in the late seventies.

3

Chasing the Train

One evening in 2003 the phone rang and I answered it. Over a bad line, my cousin Victoria said she had a message for my mother from her own mother: Fay was poised to book a flight to England from South Africa and wanted my mother to green-light it. I put my hand over the mouthpiece and walked from the hallway into the living room, where my mother sat in a chair by the window, blanket over her legs, feet poking out of the end in thick woolly socks. Outside in the heatwave the trees towered and loomed. I passed on the message.

'Absolutely not,' said my mother.

She had been off-colour for a while. There was a persistent skin irritation that wouldn't go away, even with antibiotics. She was uncharacteristically listless, then nauseous, and finally breathless. She lost interest in pretty much everything except going out every morning to feed the birds in the garden and reading the newspaper. It took her the best part of a day to get through it.

Much later, my dad and I tried to trace back the symptoms – the tiredness and coughing, the misdiagnoses (asthma, bronchitis) – to work out how long she'd been ill. Well over a year, we thought. Since her mother had died from TB, she'd been confident, when we finally went in for the biopsy, that that's what it was. I think she was even a little consoled by this, a connection to the woman she had never known and of whom no living person had a single memory. The diagnosis of lung cancer seemed unfair when my mother hadn't smoked for thirty years.

I took the phone round the corner and in a low voice said to my cousin that Fay's offer was appreciated but that my mother was too tired for visitors. My cousin disappeared from the line and came back a moment later to say her mother understood. I went back into the living room, passed my mother the phone, and the sisters spoke to each other for a few minutes. Then my mother said goodbye and hung up. I went back into the kitchen to make cocktails.

We were working our way through the *Savoy Hotel Cocktail Book* that summer, which is why, for years afterwards, I had orange liqueur and Tia Maria and angostura bitters in my cupboard, up there with the baking soda and other things I never use. I'd had an idea we'd start at A and work through, but by mid-June this was looking ambitious. There were too many ingredients and the exercise, conceived of in the absence of any better ideas on how to ritualise the end, threatened to furnish me with a tragic coda at the funeral: 'We only got to Sea Breezes!' (An epitaph she would have loved, by the way.)

Because I was in charge, my mother drank from a glass. Left to her own devices, she would drink from a washed-out old yoghurt pot, silver foil still stuck to the rim. It was the kind of ostentatious economy she loved, right up there with reusing unfranked stamps or folding a single sheet of loo paper in half. She poured her first yoghurt pot at nine in the morning.

'Here,' I said, handing her a White Russian.

'Cheers.'

We sat and looked out through the living-room window. Every now and then the breeze would lift and a great hiss and surge of light seem to fill every frequency.

'It's so peaceful,' she said. 'It's so peaceful here.'

When my dad came in from work, she looked up and smiled. 'Go and change.'

There was something we were supposed to be doing, during those dozy afternoons and long empty mornings, which we had emphatically been failing to do. My mother always said that, given the choice, she would rather go down the long slow decline route than run-down-by-a-bus. That way, when the time came, she'd have had a chance to have put her affairs in order. But now we were here and it wasn't appealing. It seemed absurd at this stage to ruin what time we had left with painful and long-avoided subjects, although 'what time we had left' was a cliché we were finding hard to make meaningful. I had taken semi-leave from work, and the sense of time running out had been replaced with the peculiar drag of being home on a weekday, with its echo of sick days off school. It felt like this period would go on in slow motion for ever.

'Is there anything you want to do today?' I asked in the morning, and my mother's eyes flitted.

'No,' she said. 'I don't think so.'

In the evening, another phone call, another sister, another 3,000 miles away. This one didn't offer to visit. 'Sensible woman,' said my mother.

We were trying to be disciplined about crackpot remedies. Some free reflexology at the hospital, a rosary I bought in Camden Passage for a joke. In a moment of weakness, I'd been to Holland and Barrett for pills that promised to restore a full head of hair in record time.

'Do I have to?' she'd said when I handed her one. I was horrified. My mother loved nothing better than to contrive a minor discomfort for herself, for the pleasure she got from overcoming it. 'Too many pills,' she said in a small voice.

'Of course you don't have to,' I said briskly, and packed them away.

Every morning, either my dad or I – whichever of us had slept overnight in the downstairs bedroom in the single bed next to hers – helped her up and we hobbled through the kitchen to the living room. At lunchtime, I manoeuvred her into the car and we drove the two blocks to the high street, where we sat in the window of the Chinese restaurant. We'd been going there for years; my mother always asked after the owner's children. The place was empty, and he solicitously and diplomatically took our order.

'I'm surprised it pays them to stay open,' I said.

'Yes.'

For a change, one day I drove us to a pub halfway between our village and the next. We used to go there for a treat on the last day of school. Under-twelves weren't allowed in, but my mother said if I was quiet, no one would object. We'd stopped going when they changed beer suppliers to a brand she didn't like and the ham in the ham sandwiches went from dry-cured (right) to honey-glazed (wrong), so this was a sentimental gesture, of sorts. We sat in the garden.

'Beats working, doesn't it?' called my mother to the couple at the next table. It was the hottest day of the year so far and she looked startling in a heavy wool jacket, black skullcap, which she preferred to a wig, and red T-shirt I had given her with Che Guevara on the front. The couple turned in alarm. Tormenting the English was one of my mother's favourite pastimes, but there was something off in her tone that day; it had none of the usual archness – was almost beseeching – and where normally I would have cringed, I thought, 'Answer her, you fuckers.'

'Yes,' they said, eventually. My mother turned away and, relaxing for a moment, tilted her face skywards as a flower tracks the sun. 'Lovely,' she said. After lunch, we crossed the garden in a feat of horizontal rock-climbing: table to chair to wall to drainpipe, into the pub and across endless carpeted space to the toilet. 'Phew!' said my mother, hanging onto the door handle. 'I thought we'd never make it.'

I drove us back the long way. Down the road that ran parallel to the railway, along which we had driven to school every day for ten years. When we coincided with a train, she'd speed up to race it until I squealed and made her slow down again. Up the hill, round the lane by St Mary's, past the RAF base, and then I pulled in at a place where I used to go swimming. We sat in the car in front of a squat 1970s building.

'Do you remember . . .?' I said.

'Yes,' she said vaguely. I had the sense she was indulging me.

In the evening, I sat beside her in the living room, holding her hand. 'Look,' I said. There was a pattern on one of her fingernails, a corrugated effect like the ghost of an old infection. 'Is that a new thing?'

'I don't know,' said my mother. 'Funny.'

'I'll get us another drink.' She smiled at me.

'If anyone tries to stop you, call a policeman.'

If the first cocktail didn't work, I reverted to rum and coke. After two rounds I started to scale back the measures. We got stuck on pina coladas for a week before tiring of them. The margaritas came out like lighter fuel. But the White Russians were perfect, the Kahlua thick and syrupy, the texture of cough medicine. When I poured in the milk, it came up, like sludge, from the bottom of the glass.

My mother was sitting on a stool at the kitchen table. I was standing behind her, rubbing lavender oil into what remained of her hair. It had come back a little curly and appeared now in fine grey swirls on her scalp, like a weather map depicting a hurricane. As I applied the oil, I saw the strawberry birthmark at her hairline. 'Stimulates regrowth' is what it said on the bottle, but it was just a nice sensation. I had to stop it from flooding the neck of her jersey.

'Lovely,' she said.

There was no preamble. It appears in my memory out of nowhere, as it had done the first time, although this time my mother's voice was less harsh. When all else failed, she said, she had her father arrested. The case had gone to the High Court. He had defended himself and cross-examined his own children in the witness box, destroying them one by one. He had been found not guilty. She didn't say what the charge was, beyond that the action was triggered by a pattern repeating itself. What had happened to her had been happening to Fay, her sister, the one she called her baby, and she wouldn't stand for it any longer. My mother was twenty-four; her sister was twelve. She gave me the last of the heavy-weather looks, a worn out version of an old favourite, Woman of Destiny Considers Her Life. I managed to squeak out a question this time: how was he found not guilty?

My mother looked bitter and by way of an answer repeated something the prosecutor had said to her about her stepmother: 'If that woman isn't careful, I'll have her up as an accessory.' She had lied in the witness box or retracted her statement; some kind of U-turn which contributed to the collapse of the case. The prosecutor was furious with her, said my mother.

After the verdict, her father had come up to her in the courtroom and, grinning, said, 'Aren't you proud of me?' My mother said it was the most shocking moment of her life.

She had gone back to her apartment and had tried to decide what to do. She had dragged her siblings through a horrifically public ordeal, which had failed. She had been personally defeated. The worst thing about it, she said, was worrying that people at work would find out. It had been in the newspapers.

It occurred to her that she had two options: to carry on living, or to kill herself. We sat side by side at the kitchen table. I put my head on my arm. In an odd way, I was less disturbed by the information itself than by the fact of its eleventh-hour revelation. It seemed to me incredible that, behind all those hints and intimations, all those years of comic threats and camp overreactions which I had come to see, more or less, as a flourish of character, an actual solid event had existed. Occasionally over the years I had wondered which would be worse: to discover that something terrible *had* happened, or that not very much had happened at all and that either my mother or

I had concocted a drama from nothing. As she spoke, a tiny part of me was relieved that neither of us had turned out to be mad.

I was also incredulous. Deathbed revelations weren't something people had. That my mother, who would ring me at work with the newsflash that she'd found the socks she was looking for, that the thermal vests she'd ordered for my dad had arrived, that a woman we knew slightly had walked past the house and her ankles were huge, and whom I rang back with the news I'd had tuna for lunch, had managed to keep this from me was extraordinary.

There was no time to think about it. I knew, dimly, that it would come back at some stage and demand to be thought about. But right then, alongside the daily effort of not looking forward, not looking back was relatively easy. Only once, and for a second, did I have any real understanding of what she had told me – that to her this was not an ancient grievance, easily back-burnered. It was a few days later. She was walking through the door from the kitchen to the hallway. A thought occurred to her in that instant that she articulated to me, sitting at the kitchen table, and that in the face of stiff competition still constitutes I think the most shocking moment of *my* life.

She looked at me and said, with something like surprise and as if it had only just occurred to her, 'I think I have come to terms with it.' Not 'came', but 'come'. As if, in all those years of village life, in the market, at the tennis club, in the midst of our mild existence, a process had been ongoing, another reality alive to her in which she'd been wholly alone.

For the space of an afternoon she had sat in her apartment and weighed up her options. If she lived, she said, she had to be sure she could meet two conditions: one, that she would never be intimidated again; and two, that she would be happy. She may very well have done this. But – and I knew this instantly – the recollection had a tailored quality to it that suggested the scene had been worked on. It bore all the hallmarks of my mother's philosophy: that it's not what happens to you that matters so much as the story you choose to tell afterwards – even if the only person you tell is yourself.

A few days later I asked her, as a joke, if there were any skeletons in the closet. She gave the appearance of thinking about it. 'No,' she said, and tilting her face upwards adopted her most theatrically innocent look. 'I don't think so.' Oh, God.

She died at 7.20 p.m. on a warm summer evening, in the downstairs guest bedroom of our house. All that talk of 'putting one's affairs in order' had fallen away to this: 'You and your dad must stick together.' I had told her we would. She had tried, then, to counsel me about her own death. 'You'll be sore afterwards . . .' This was too much, even for my mother, and she looked away. I was furious that she should even try such a thing, such a piece of existential masochism, just as I'd been furious when, well into her illness and unsteady on her feet, she had insisted on going out every morning to feed the birds. I had wanted to scream at her, 'Stop it, it's over, you can't bluff your way through this one.' Then she had stopped going out and complained of being in pain, and I longed for the old bravado.

She was adamant that no one should come to the funeral; just my dad and me and the woman from the humanist society who, when she visited a few days after the death, seemed taken aback by the stringency of my mother's wishes. My dad and I wavered. There were my mother's friends from London; there were the parents of my own friends, who'd become her friends; there were neighbours and friends from the village. All summer they'd dropped in with offers of help: portable fans to disperse the heat, ideas on how to get her to eat. We owed them a funeral. An elderly woman called Hazel whom I knew by sight but had never spoken to stopped me in the street and asked if I needed help going through my mother's wardrobe. 'It can be hard,' she said. We got all the way to Hazel, buoyed by the idea we were doing the right thing, before stopping and helplessly scrapping the list.

The humanist looked at me. (I thought she'd be woollier, but she was actually quite stern. 'Mum would have liked her,' we said afterwards, hopefully.) It's not that she didn't have friends, I said. It's that she didn't want . . . she didn't like the idea of people gathering in these circumstances. I knew exactly how my mother felt about this: that being the only dead person in the room would put her at a decided disadvantage.

Mr Quigley, the undertaker, had come for her that night in formal dress, accompanied by his daughter, who was very young and very grave, wearing what looked like a man's black suit and standing behind her father, staring respectfully at her shoes. The undertaker had explained we might want to wait in the living room and shut the door; the removal of the body could be upsetting.

My dad and I did as he instructed, milling awkwardly in the middle of the room. Her glasses were still on the window-sill, on top of a shiny-backed crime novel, from the library.

Twenty-seven versions of my own face stared down at me from The Shrine. There was a sharp bump against the door. Something in my brain lifted up and resettled. The turn from the hallway to the porch was tight and I couldn't imagine how they'd make it, or how two slight-looking people, an old man and a girl, could manage the load. (Mr Quigley may not have been old, but that's how he seemed, in his gentle formality.)

We opened the door and went out into the hallway. The porch opened onto the warm summer night. Mr Quigley and his daughter re-emerged from the darkness, and when we shook their hands, I noticed the girl's watch, which was huge, like something you'd wear to go diving in. 'My mother will be fascinated by all this,' I thought.

On the day of the funeral it started to rain, the first rain of summer. 'Hammy to the end,' I thought. We honoured her wishes and kept the guest list to two.

My grandmother, Sarah Doubell.

4

London–Buckinghamshire–London

The shift is instantaneous. It is as if, the day after her death, a van pulls up outside my house and men start unloading luggage onto the pavement.

'Oi,' I say. 'Hang on a sec. None of that's mine.'

'Sorry, love,' says the man. 'Someone has to have it.'

What can I say? 'OK. Bring it in.'

My dad and I had never talked about it. He could hardly get a word in with my mother around, although in the last year of her life a subtle change had started to occur. Whereas usually when I rang home she gave my dad five minutes on the line before swooping in and taking over, as she got sicker and less able to follow the conversation the balance had tilted. My dad's portion of the phone call got longer and longer, while my mother's dwindled. I would tell him jokes and stories from my day that I hadn't told her. He would laugh, and I would know, in the background, she was hearing it and registering the change. I knew how awful this was, but I kept on doing it. I was punishing her for leaving me.

As a result, my dad and I have never really talked about anything serious, certainly not about her history. She was the gatekeeper and she kept the gates shut.

I don't have the heft for this. I can't get lids off jars. I get drunk on half a shandy. My mother, who could get the lid off anything and metabolised alcohol like water, would be appalled by this admission, it being worse in her view to admit to a weakness than to have one in the first place. 'Go and ask the man,' she would say when I was little, trying to get me to overcome my Englishness. I didn't want to ask the man. I would rather do without than ask the man. How I became a journalist, when all you do all day is ask the man, I have no idea. And yet despite being a journalist, I have never so much as fed her name into a search engine. All I have, after her death, are the stories she told and the stories she threatened to tell but didn't.

It had delighted my mother when I went into journalism. 'I'd have been proud, of course, if you'd been a maths genius,' she said airily, 'but it wouldn't have been my *preference*.' She bored the neighbours rigid with details of my life. She once got into a fight with someone in the village who suggested, mildly, that I was an odd choice to send to Israel to interview Ariel Sharon – twenty-five years old and bereft of any knowledge, let alone specialism in Middle Eastern politics. (In fact, so wholly unthreatening a proposition was I that Sharon, showing me around his farm, picked an orange from his orchard and, after peeling it, fed a piece of it into my mouth like a baby bird, while I tried to arrange a response around the giant size of my freak-out. Such are the dividends of knowing nothing.)

'She seemed an odd choice,' said the man in the village, and my mother snapped, 'I'd like to see you do better.' In the newsagent's, she furtively moved stock so that copies of the *Guardian*, where I worked, covered copies of the *Telegraph*, where I didn't.

Lurid threats were made as to what, precisely, would befall my employers if anything befell me.

The year before she died I won an award, and my mother considered her legacy: 'Some people write novels or paint beautiful paintings,' she sighed. 'I created you.'

Now I sit in my flat in London and turn on my computer. 'I will be professional about this,' I think. I will do all the things you do in the early stages of a story: flip between websites, jump up for snacks, write words at crazy angles in your note-book and hope they'll never come before a judge, not least because you've drawn a little house with a chimney and smoke coming out of it in the middle of the page, confident that if it looks like action it will generate results, or at least the mo-mentum to achieve them down the line. It will be a matter of lists and itineraries. I am suddenly cheerful. Some cups of tea, some common sense and who knows what harm might be un-done?

I had asked my dad, groping for a language – any language – in which to talk about these things we'd never talked about, if she had said much to him.

'There was something about a trial?' I said, as we sat in the kitchen not long after the funeral. We were drinking red wine from the box on the counter. Apart from cocktails, which were different, I wouldn't drink much when I was at home. I drank plenty in town, but at home I instinctively avoided it. I might have a glass of champagne at Christmas, but I wouldn't join my parents in wine at the table. 'It's good you don't drink too much,' said my mother occasionally. 'Not like your mother.'

'That's not true,' I'd say angrily. I wouldn't take her up on it, she who never asked for help nor confessed to a need. It was too late, by then, to change my idea of her. Now it's just me and my dad, drinking a glass of red wine like ordinary people.

'Yes,' he said. 'She mentioned it, a long time ago.' And he repeated the quote she had given me, which the prosecutor had said of her stepmother: 'If that woman isn't careful, I'll have her up as an accessory.' There had been some kind of abuse – violence and worse – and that's all he knew, too. Like a veteran returning from the First World War, my mother had maintained, in her marriage as in her life, a hard line on revisiting the past. My dad had respected that. I said something like, 'Obviously her dad was a weirdo.' My dad said something like, 'That would be putting it mildly.' We reached the limit of what either of us was able to say.

The day after her death I had rung her sister Fay in Johannesburg, a conversation I remember less for its content than for the fact I made the call on my mobile phone. Peak hour, long distance, on a mobile. 'You must be mad!' my mother would have said. I had been calling my friends all day, getting two seconds into the conversation and then losing it. 'Did you know I was crying all the way through that phone call?' my friend Merope said later, although I hadn't heard her through my own crying. Later, much later, my friend Pooly said, 'After I spoke to you I had to go home from work.' My friend Dave picked up the call in a bar: 'Hold on, hold on, I'm going outside,' he said. I told him the news. Dave had come up to see us a few weeks before, when my mum could barely open her eyes. Now he said, 'I'm standing on a traffic island in the middle of the street and there are tears just streaming down my face.'

Unlike these calls, neither my aunt nor I cried, and Fay didn't try to console me. We didn't know each other, after all, although I had the sense we were striving to live up to the same steely ideal. 'Dying just isn't the sort of thing my mother would do,' I said glibly, and Fay laughed.

'No, it isn't.' My aunt told me a bit about her life, her grown-up children and grandchildren, her routine. Like all my mother's siblings, she wasn't married and hadn't been for a long time. Every morning, she told me, she got up at the crack of dawn to go out and feed the birds in her garden.

'That's so funny,' I said. 'My mum does that, too.'

'Your mother had a lot of time for Fay,' said my dad in the kitchen that evening.

'I'd like to go there,' I said, 'to South Africa, to see them.' It had only been a week and already – with no siblings, no aunts, no uncles, no cousins, no one I had common cause with except for my dad – I was tired of my face being the only reminder. He said that sounded like a good idea.

'I offered to go,' said my dad. 'But Mum always said no.'

The South African national archive has a searchable database, broken down into seven geographical regions. Search terms return on a single line with a date, shelf reference and archive locator, indicating the whereabouts of the paperwork. Civil trials, criminal trials, land disputes, naturalisations and probate going back to the nineteenth century all seem to be held on the system, which I defy anyone to spend five minutes on and fail, guiltily, to have the response I did: say what you like about the British Empire, they knew how to keep records.

Her maiden name had, at one time, been relatively common in those parts and so pages of unrelated data come up – old wills and estate disputes, applications for citizenship, bail hearings – before I recognise the name of one of my aunts. Below it is the name of another aunt, and then a third. It is only a record of their divorces, but they are such hypothetical figures to me that, even though by now I have spoken to Fay on the phone and seen letters from the others, their names in the archive strike me as the first decisive proof – official proof – that they actually exist.

A few pages on, and there he is: my grandfather, unmistakable with his unusual middle name, Mauritz, the Dutch version of Maurice. There is a single line of description – 'Criminal case. Regina vs. James Mauritz DeKiewit' –and a date two years before my mother emigrated. A trial had taken place. Something terrible had happened. We weren't all caught in a hideous misunderstanding. I stare at it for a long time before printing it out.

Then, for good measure, I run the name through the other regional databases. To my surprise, my grandfather's name returns a second match, in a remote depository in Pietermaritzburg, 300 miles south of Johannesburg. I ring my dad.

'Do you know anything about a murder?' I say.

'No,' he says innocently. 'What murder?' (Like a human GPS, my dad, after thirty years of marriage to my mum, is used to mapping a vague context onto thoughts that start in the middle and work outwards.)

'Before all the other stuff.'

I tell him what I've found: my grandfather's name alongside two others in a murder trial.

'Ma never mentioned it.' He is thoughtful. 'Maybe it's not him.'

'I will send away for the papers,' I say.

'Be careful,' says my dad.

'What?' I scoff. 'It's hardly dangerous. Everyone in this story is dead.'

'No,' he says. 'I mean, be careful how much of this you want to know.'

I think about it afterwards, what I am doing and why. The stronger reaction, I think, would be to walk away, to honour the firewall my mother put between her past and my present and to carry on with my life. But I can't. In those days and weeks after her death it is all I can think about. While she was alive, it was none of my business. Now, unless I make it my business, it will follow her into oblivion. By way of explanation, I return in my mind to something that happened in high school. When I was fifteen or so, a brief craze for Ouija boards swept the school, and every lunchtime for a month girls gathered around home-made boards to commune with the dead. The dead had three fixed qualities: omniscience, omnipresence and they were all men, which is weird. You'd think it'd be like calling home from college, when your dad picks up the phone and has three seconds of secure airtime before your mother, scattering furniture, touches down to snatch the receiver from his hand.

Most of the spirits we called up introduced themselves as Bert or Arthur and in reply to the question 'Where are you?' – or rather, 'WHERE ARE YOU?', bellowed at the penny as if it were an antique listening device – spelt out A-Y-L-E-S-B-U-R-Y C-E-M-E-T-E-R-Y, whereupon someone in the circle burst into tears and said it was her grandfather.

Two significant things happened during these sessions.

The first has nothing to do with my larger point, but is worth repeating for the benefit of sceptics. To test the authenticity of the exercise, those in the circle asked the spirits things only they knew about themselves: pets' names, middle names, and then Lizzy Shute suggested bra sizes. She was a big girl, as were two of the others around the board that day, and there was much clapping and screaming from the crowd as the penny divined their CC and D cups. I will never forget the agonising journey undertaken by Bert or Arthur to describe my 28AA. My point is this: for those who doubt the reality of the afterlife, don't you think, if I had been pushing that penny, I might at least have given myself a B cup?

There were strict protocols surrounding Ouija. At the end of each session, you had politely to ask, 'Please can we leave now?' and wait for the spirit to release you. There were rumours of people who hadn't broken the connection cleanly and, like a phone bill that keeps running, had accrued a vast and unhealthy debt to the Other Side, causing them to throw themselves from buildings and become teenage mothers. The craze eventually ended when the deputy head, looking grimmer than anyone had ever seen him – grimmer than when Michelle Leyland fell out of the coach on the way back from Germany, grimmer than when Joanna Fretwell told Mrs Stone the PE teacher to fuck off – visited every classroom in turn and said words I forget but which impressed us deeply at the time. We were nice girls. We stopped.

And here is my second point: twelve years later, in the wake of my mother's death, it occurs to me that despite everyone's best efforts, a connection has failed to be severed.

Politely it has been asked, 'Please may we leave now?' and the request has been denied. I won't have it any longer. The time for politeness has passed.

From a list of researchers provided by the Pietermaritzburg archive, I choose a man with the most English-sounding name and email to ask if he'll photocopy papers for me. He replies promptly with details of a Barclays bank account in Worthing. Typical Brit, I think. Keeping a toehold in England in case he ever has to flee.

Two weeks later, a large buff envelope drops onto the mat before work. I put it on the table, and that evening, when I get home, I stand by the window and tear it open. The top page is divided into two halves: English on the left-hand side, Afrikaans on the right. Under the heading 'Preparatory Examinations' there are three names, one of which is my grandfather's. Then: 'charged with the offence of MURDER'. The capitalisation strikes me as histrionic. The case was prosecuted by a William Scott Bigby on behalf of His Majesty the King, and the three men, 'hereinafter called the Accused', were 'now or lately prisoners in the gaol at Ladysmith'.

I glance down the page. In the bottom left-hand corner is something I recognise instantly. Apart from the poem, the only other thing of her father's that my mother kept was his copy of *The Rubaiyat of Omar Khayyam*. He had signed it, I remembered, on the flyleaf. I go to the bookcase, pull it out and, returning to the window, hold it up against the charge sheet. Under a heading of previous convictions, there is a single entry for housebreaking and theft, with a twelve-month suspended sentence. 'I admit the previous conviction,' the murderer has written, signing his name underneath. The signatures are the same.

I read on. The murder was of an old man and took place in the course of a robbery. The three accomplices had identified the remoteness of the farm and the vulnerability of the victim and struck without mercy. It was, said the judge, unforgivably brutal. He had considered applying the death penalty, then relented and gave each of the men ten years with hard labour.

There follows a thick sheaf of paperwork, most of it depositions by witnesses. The three men had been spotted at the railway station and by various labourers on the road up to the farm. When they were caught, they were in possession of a firearm and the old man's money. There were no details of how much of that decade-long jail term was served, but my grandfather must have been released early. I look at the date of sentencing. My mother was born six years later.

I have no idea if my mother knew about the murder. I have a dim recollection of her telling me her father had been to jail once, but for what I don't know – although I have an even dimmer memory of her saying he was fired from various jobs and locations for 'interfering' with children he had access to.

In any case, any doubts I had about going to South Africa are resolved by this paperwork. It is one thing to have a researcher photocopy and send me pre-trial notes from the murder; the murder is impersonal. But the idea of someone providing a similar service for the second trial – of potentially reading my mother's testimony in the action she brought against her father before I do – is unthinkable. I will have to go to Pretoria and read whatever is in the archives for myself.

Journeys like these should take months of planning – trips to travel agents, consultations of maps and with shamans – but ten minutes on the Internet and it's done: flights, hotel, even an email to a man who used to work with my mother at the law firm in Johannesburg. He writes back instantly to say he remembers her well and would be delighted to have lunch when I come in the new year. I feel vaguely embarrassed; after all these years, is this all there is to it?

I ring the South African consulate to ask about visas, and they suggest something that hasn't occurred to me: that if my mother's paperwork is in order, I can apply for dual citizenship. I have a visceral reaction, followed by a second, guiltier one. I put the phone down and ring my friend Pooly. 'They offered me a passport,' I say.

She bursts out laughing. 'And?'

'I know it's a new era and all, but –'

'What?'

'Ugh. "South African passport holder." Makes me feel physically sick.'

At the weekends I go home to Buckinghamshire, out on the Friday night train and back again on Sunday. It is a journey I've done hundreds of times. Now it turns into a cliché – woman looks through train window at familiar landscape made alien by sad thoughts about death. My memory of those months from July to September is reduced almost entirely to being on the train every weekend, watching the bleached walls of the council estate go from ash grey in the sun to pewter in the rain, and the derelict lots, with their mountains of scrap metal, burnish and blacken. The new Wembley stadium is being built in the distance and gets higher each week. London bleeds into the suburbs and then the green belt: the spire at Harrow, the allotments, the back end of the private school, the pub garden. My favourite part of the journey comes forty minutes in, when the train emerges from tree-covered escarpments into a clearing with views across the valley. It looks like the opening scene from a Jane Austen adaptation. My spirits soar. I am two stops from home.

Before my mother died I would round the corner and see her head in the window, and she, eagle-eyed, waiting, would wave. The window looks blank now. Friday night passes somehow and then, on Saturday, while the weather holds, my dad and I go on long walks. We go along the canal for the first time since I was a child. We go up the hill behind Chequers, and I climb over the fence to the summit. There are sheep up there, and we wonder who they belong to. You can see right down into the prime minister's residence. We joke about snipers. We go across the fields by the air-force base, yellow stubble underfoot, dry hay in the air, and across the cricket field behind the station. We don't talk much, just walk and stop at the pub for lunch or a drink.

We go all the way along the ridge to the beacon at Ivinghoe. The weather is on the turn by then and it is blustery enough to hold out your arms and lean into the wind. One weekend, we go the steep way up the hill behind the house where we scattered her ashes. On a clear day you can see across the

Thames Valley from here, all the way to County Hall.

One Sunday, my father and I drive over to Henley to take his parents out for lunch. It is the first time we've seen them since my mother's death, and although they are kind, they don't mention her, either her death or the fact of her ever having lived. I think how she would have loved this; confirmation of what she had been saying for the best part of thirty years, about the English generally and her in-laws in particular: 'My family are weird, God knows, but this lot are weirder.'

During the week, I walk to work instead of taking the bus. It is better to be moving; sitting still risks opening the door to reflection. I retreat to the most ordinary of memories: standing in line for the park-and-ride in Oxford, waiting for the bus, boarding and sitting in it. That's the entire memory. My mother is in a blue three-quarter-length coat, a brown cashmere scarf my father's brother gave her for Christmas and Ecco shoes, in which she has put neon-green laces. I don't know why I remembered it, beyond that I must have been happy, anticipating the day we would spend together, looking at colleges before I filled out my university application forms.

There is another, more complicated image I keep looping on. Six months earlier, my mother had come up to London to help me buy a sofa. It was one of those early-spring days of freak heatwave, and London was smouldering. There were roadworks everywhere. My mother had worn a coat too warm for the day, a padded green jacket with a brooch in the shape of a fox on the collar. I told myself she had merely failed to look at the forecast, although she wasn't eating enough then to stay warm. All morning we walked up and down the Tottenham Court Road, getting nowhere. Heal's was too expensive. Everything in Furniture Village was dark and heavy, with a cheap finish. There was nothing in Habitat.

By mid-afternoon, we were exhausted and my mother was keen to get back. She was late for the train, and with half the Underground shut for track maintenance, we waited in the heat outside Edgware Road for the replacement bus service to Marylebone. We should have taken a taxi. I wish we had. I thought the satisfaction of doing it the hard way would outweigh the discomfort, but on the bus halfway there I saw I'd miscalculated. As we shuddered and lurched down the Marylebone Road, the air boiling around us, I saw something like panic cross my mother's face, followed by regret for letting the side down. We got to the station so late that, after leaving me at the barrier, she had literally to sprint the length of the platform to catch the departing train. I watched her run with a sudden, leaden awareness that everything – the heat, the panic, the retreating figure in a jacket too warm for the day – was something I would remember, when remembering became necessary. It was the last of the ordinary days.

One Friday evening, I don't take the train. I stay in London and go to the launch of my godfather's art show, where an old friend of my mother's hands me an envelope. It is photos of her he found and thought I might like to have, from an early holiday they took in Portugal or Spain. I've heard about these holidays. On one, my mother and godfather read *Portnoy's Complaint* on the beach and both cried. On another, her long hair bleached blonde by the sun, men followed her

through the streets of Lisbon, clicking their fingers and pro-
positioning her. This was 'before Portugal opened up', she
would say grandly, and how much it annoyed my godfather
had delighted her.

'I'm not doing anything,' she had said innocently, when he
hissed at her to stop.

I have never seen these photos before, although I've seen
one of her from a few years earlier, just before she left South
Africa, when she was a bridesmaid at her friend Denise's wedding. She had looked slightly spinsterish then, with a terrible
1950s hairdo and unflattering bridesmaid's garb. In these she
is modern, sleek, with an almost cat-like expression. There is a
startling shot of her standing in a black ankle-length negligée
on a vine-strewn terrace. The negligée is transparent and she
isn't wearing anything underneath. I have a surge of primness;
for God's sake, mother, put some clothes on. I wonder if she
is having a breakdown. I study her face. She looks coy, as she
always did in photos, but pleased with herself, serene. In another photo, she stands on the beach in a jaunty orange tunic,
feet firmly planted in the sand, bag swinging, my godfather
standing beside her in a pair of swimming trunks. I have a
dizzying sense of the largeness of the life led before I came
along.

One rainy autumn day, I take the train to a town an hour
outside London. My mother's cousin Gloria and her husband
Cyrille are in England, visiting their daughter and son-in-
law. It was Gloria who sent my mother the painting and the
teacup, the little items from her mother's estate, and it was
Gloria's mother, Kathy, who spent all those years trying to
track my mother down. Gloria grew up with the legend of her

disappeared cousin, and when she catches sight of me in the station car park, her eyes fill with tears. 'Oh, my heart could just break.'

Gloria is small and ferociously family-orientated. Years earlier, she and Cyrille came to stay with us for a few weeks. I remember them as kind, generous people – the personific-ation of the good side of the family. Gloria remembers that trip primarily for my mother's short temper. My mother was very fond of Gloria; she was a link to her own mother, which didn't stop her shouting at her cousin for taking too long to get ready and then laughing at the old-ladyish rain hood she put on.

'She had such a sharp tongue!' says Gloria, over tea in her daughter's house. 'Just like my mother.' At seventy, Gloria is still reeling from some of the sharper things her mother said to her over the years.

Gloria does not have a sharp tongue. She is infinitely kind. She is involved in a church group. I see her do a brave thing now, which is, knowing my mother's feelings about religion and correctly intuiting mine, to say, 'I know you don't want to hear this, luvvie, but Jesus does love you.'

Gloria is the memory of that side of the family, and as we settle in for the afternoon, she tells me about it. I have never heard any of this and am fascinated. The first Doubell any-one can remember, says Gloria, is Bebe, said to have fled from France to England after killing a man in a boxing match, and from there on to Africa, sometime in the early nineteenth century. Several generations later, his descendants boiled down to eight siblings: Daniel, Samuel, Benjamin, Francis, Jo-hanna, Anna, Kathleen – Gloria's mother – and the youngest, my grandmother, Sarah Salmiena Magdalena Doubell. She gave birth to my mother in her sister Kathy's house, attended by Dr Boulle, the railway physician, and his midwife, Sister Cave. I burst into laughter. 'Boulle and Cave?' I say.

Gloria laughs. 'Yes.'

'They should have had a magic act.'

Gloria was delivered by the same duo, in the same bed, in the back bedroom of the house she grew up in. 'Oh, my mother loved your grandmother,' she says. 'Sarah was the baby of the family. It broke my mother's heart when she died.'

Gloria remembers clearly the first time she met my mother. It was at the airport in Durban. My mother had flown down there from Johannesburg at the tail end of her trip in 1977. She would be meeting members of her mother's family for the first time. When she spotted Gloria across the concourse, she had to sit down on her suitcase abruptly; her legs buckled under her.

'When I think of what happened . . .' says Gloria, tearfully. 'She had a terrible life.'

'But I don't think she did, Gloria!' I say in astonishment. I've never had to defend my mother's happiness before. It is strange to hear a rival view of her. 'I think she knew how to be happy.' It is also strange to be talking like this, around forbidden sbujects and in my mother's absence. I wonder if she'd be angry.

Gloria urges me to come and visit them in Durban when I arrive in January, and I say that I will. She gives me food for the train. On the way back, I look out of the window and think of the pride with which she related the family history. I think of her unquestioning concern and generosity towards me. And I think of her mother, Kathy, who my own mother admired so much. Whatever else happened, I think, the baby who became my mother had, at least, been born into love.

'All her life my mother asked,' Gloria had said before I left, 'all her life she asked, "Where's Pauline? What happened to Pauline? I wonder where Pauline is now?"'

Mum and Dad on their wedding day, outside Kensington registry office.

5

Departure

My dad is coming with me to the newspaper library at Colindale. It is winter. London is frozen beneath a sheet of black ice. I have decided to do some research before leaving, to get a head start on what I'll find in the archives in Pretoria. This is less a journalistic than a therapeutic urge; if there are going to be surprises, I'd like to confront them in stages.

It is a nondescript building deep in the northern suburbs, known to journalists and family-tree enthusiasts for its extraordinary archive of practically every newspaper – certainly every colonial title – from inception to the present day. There are two I want to skim through in particular, one a defunct Johannesburg tabloid, the other a broadsheet. We order up rolls of microfilm covering the year in question – the year of my grandfather's trial – and dividing them between us, sit in a windowless research room at neighbouring machines. The only sound is the whir and click as the pages scroll by.

I sometimes think you could publish an alternative history of a place just by compiling its newspaper headlines – the dialogue a country has with itself, at least those in the country who are permitted to speak. In 1957, the year my grandfather appeared in court, the South African newspapers were full of the country's then main preoccupations: weather, wildlife, Whitehall and crime. I scroll through January, and then February.

It is the year Agatha Christie publishes the *4.50 from Paddington*. London is fog-bound. For those who can afford it, you can fly from London to Johannesburg in twelve hours on the new Vickers VC10. Readers follow the misfortune and recovery of a woman in the Cape, 'bitten by her own Christmas dinner'. In the courts, a man is let off for throwing a hunting knife at his wife, and a woman is granted a divorce from her husband because he looks 'like a hobo'. On the inside pages, women are advised they can choose from a variety of knitting machines. I change reels; the microfilm whirrs.

'Anything?' I say to my dad.

'Not yet.'

Five Killed by Huge Hailstones
Shot Himself While Joking
Bees Attack Children
Snake in Letter Box
Attacked by Circus Bear
Killed by Crocodile
Cake Sale for Shark Victims

South Africa in the 1950s is a parochial country, riven with colonial insecurity. 'SA Women Equal to Other Women Abroad', reads one headline; another, with exquisite defensiveness, 'Afrikaners Don't Like Only Slap Stick'.

At the same time, it is struggling with a problem that is endemic in the colony and across white Africa.

Like the Puritans who went to America, Dutch settlers in South Africa in the seventeenth century were devout Calvinists in pursuit of religious utopia, and the culture they formed was narrow and repressed. It is hard not to read the behaviour that followed – the drinking, the violence – as a kind of manic release, the inevitable counterweight to all that fanaticism, except that when the empire-building Brits turned up a hundred years later, they weren't religious yet went the same way – all those notorious 'shooting incidents' in Kenya and Rhodesia, the Happy Valley mob drinking themselves into oblivion night after night. My mother said it was because England sent out its scum to the colonies (she didn't hold it against the Dutch, for some reason). What can you expect, she said, of a people who came only to exploit, who arrived in South Africa with nothing and suddenly found themselves part of a master race?

In an editorial that year, 1957, the Pretoria Society of Alcoholism estimates there are between 40,000–80,000 alcoholics in white South Africa – one in fifty of the population – compared to 20,000 in Holland (one in 550), putting the problem at almost ten times the severity of the European country. It estimates that 27 million gallons of alcohol are consumed in South Africa every year. The mining communities are a particular problem. The editorial touts the latest treatment orthodoxy, which is to keep bad cases in their own homes, rather than sending them to rehab. There is a quote from the minister of labour, Jan de Klerk, who says, 'With our small European population it is important that every person must realise his full labour potential and it is not necessary for me to tell you what effect the misuse of alcohol could have on our military ability.'

Of the two newspapers, I'm surprised to find it's the tabloid that's vaguely left-wing. I didn't know that in late-1950s South Africa a newspaper was even allowed to refer in its editorial to 'this sham apartheid'.

After years of discrimination by the British colonial government, under which black South Africans were denied the vote and the right to sit in parliament, the system of racial segregation was formalised and extended in 1948, with the election of the Afrikaner National Party under Daniel Malan. Every baby born was issued with an identity card stating his or her race, one that governed every aspect of the life he or she would lead. A slew of laws followed, including, in 1949, the Prohibition of Mixed Marriages Act and, a year later, the Immorality Act, which banned sexual relations between the races. In 1950, the Group Areas Act dictated where each race could live, paving the way to forced removals of black South Africans from the economic centres to remote regions of the country. The Bantu Education Act of 1953 segregated schooling and ensured black South Africans were kept under-educated and fit only for menial work. In 1957, in the run-up to the following year's general election, there is some hope in the newspaper that the National Party under Johannes Strijdom might lose out to the more moderate – although still pro-white rule – United Party, but the Nats win by a landslide.

The film whizzes by; my eyes water.

First Female Dentist
First Female Barrister
First Negro Air-Hostess
Englishman to Become Ghana Citizen
Non-Whites to See Play

Towards the end of that year, South Africa gives asylum to Dutch immigrants fleeing unrest in Indonesia. With brilliant, understated panic, the headline confronts the possibility that 'Refugees May Not Be White'.

'Anything?'

'Not yet.'

There is the saga of a woman who poisoned her husband because she 'felt like giving him a slow death'. There is the long-running story of Lana Turner's daughter being taken into care. Somewhere in there I stumble on what has become my favourite headline of all time: 'Pensioner Forced to Make Cocoa at Gunpoint'.

By the end of the afternoon, I have a notepad full of useless headlines from a strange, brittle culture, confronting such questions of the day as, 'Have Our Men No Respect for Their Womenfolk?' and 'How Old Must a Typist Be?' Either I missed the story in the blizzard of information, have the wrong newspapers, or – the thought resurfaces – there is nothing to find.

My dad, also empty-handed, says, 'Oh, love, I'm sorry.'

My mother told me she had been to a therapist once, when she first arrived in London. It hadn't worked out and she didn't try again, which she probably should have. That winter, I go to see one, too. I tell her I'm a journalist, gearing up to fly to South Africa to meet my mother's family for the first time and to bring up potentially painful subjects that they may or may not have talked about before. I am interested in her advice not as therapist to patient but as professional to professional; I don't want to give anyone a breakdown.

She opens her mouth to respond, but before she can get a word out, and to our great mutual surprise, I burst into tears, angrily retract them, drag my arm across my face and through great hacking sobs suck a large plug of snot back up my nose. She nudges a box of tissues in my direction.

'Ugh, I can't believe I did that,' I say. She looks at me kindly. After I recover, she says it's possible no one will want to talk to me. She suggests I observe boundaries and take my cues from the people I'm speaking to. At the end of the session she recommends I come back next week. I tell her I'll be in touch.

I start reading a history of the country. I buy maps and look at Johannesburg's one-way system, wondering if I'll have the gumption to tackle it. I try to amend my expectations of the city, which are as outdated, I know, as my mother's Dickensian vision of London before she got here. When I think of Johannesburg, I think of a small, bustling city, full of elegant apartment blocks and racially segregated park benches, with the occasional snake making its way down the street.

Not long before leaving, I put in place what I consider to be a brilliant psychological safety net. If there is something you don't want to do, I have discovered, the trick is to find something you want to do even less and then to oscillate between the two, thanking God at each stage that you're not doing the other one. Schedule an unnecessary eye operation. Start reading John Fowles's *The Magus*. Before leaving London, I agree to a book deadline I know I can't meet. I'll work towards it in the mornings, and when I shut my computer at noon, I think, the relief will be so great it will carry me unscathed through the rest of the day.

One evening, a few months before I leave, the phone in my flat rings. A South African voice asks if it's me.

'Yes,' I say.

'It's your mother's friend, Joan,' she says. 'I haven't heard from her for months. I'm worried.'

Oh God. I knew about Joan, of course. She was my mother's oldest friend; in their twenties they had worked together in Johannesburg and shared a flat. Joan had even visited once, when I was young. My mother let me take the day off school to meet her, an unprecedented honour. Joan was travelling through England with a friend, and the four of us drove to the pub for lunch. While the three adults ate, I played outside on the adventure playground in the rain. I remember my mother was in a bad mood afterwards, banging around the house, exuding sour air.

To my shame, I hadn't called Joan to tell her the news. My dad and I had divided up the phone calls so that I had called my friends, he had called his parents and my mum's friends in London, and I had called Fay, the only member of my mother's family I had a reliable number for. I just hadn't considered my mother's South African friends.

'Oh, Joan. I'm so sorry. I should have rung you months ago. She died in July.'

There is a low, almost animal-like moan. She and my mother had corresponded faithfully for forty years; my mother had always referred to her with the deepest affection. I knew all of this and yet, when I told Joan down the line that her old friend was dead, I was stunned when she started to cry.

'We were friends when we were girls,' she says. 'Oh, I loved her.'

Joan is too upset to talk, and after telling her of my forthcoming trip, which she tearfully receives as wonderful news,

I apologise again for my negligence and hang up. Afterwards, I'm shaken. I have never given my mother's friends from South Africa much thought. Unlike the letters that came in from her siblings, her friends' letters were conventional, scandal-free, uninteresting to a child. I have certainly never considered them as equivalent to my own friendships. For the first time I do the maths and realise my mother was twenty-eight when she came to England, the same age I am as I go back the other way. I try to imagine leaving England tomorrow and not seeing anyone I know for years and then decades, keeping in touch only by letter and the occasional phone call. What was she thinking? The only other people who cried like Joan on news of my mother's death were my own best friends.

Belatedly, I go to my mother's address book. My mother kept two, one for England – a neat and orderly catalogue of colleagues, hairdressers, contractors, decorators – and one for South Africa, which doubled up as an informal encyclopedia of old friends and family. I had found it in the top drawer of a desk in the living room. It is falling apart at the seams, has tape around the spine and is so livid with crossings out that the contents look like hieroglyphics.

I turn the pages carefully. Here are birth dates, death dates, name and address changes – all the annotations reflecting the complicated evolution of a large family, and a dysfunctional one at that. I see that a great many arrows were needed when her brother, Tony, married his own son's mother-in-law. When Scientology briefly ripped through the family, my mother hesitated long and hard over how to represent her sister's discovery she was the reincarnation of a First World

War cavalry soldier. Eventually, she settled for a faint question mark above her name.

Next to Mike's entry, in my mother's careful hand: 'died, 5/10'.

Further back under M, something that shocks me: a series of addresses – Banket Street, Hillbrow; Trafford Close, Germiston – under 'Mum'. For later addresses, she amends this to 'Mother'. Marjorie's death date is not recorded.

I find a number for Denise, my mother's other regular correspondent, with whom she became friends around the same time she met Joan. They travelled to work on the bus together. I call Denise to tell her the news. She cries, too.

While my mother was ill, I scrubbed all of her voice-mail messages from all of my phones. I didn't want to be ambushed after she was gone, but you can't foresee everything. One weekend that winter, a book arrives from the village bookshop, addressed to my mother and with a note attached apologising for the delay and hoping she enjoys it. It's a true-crime book, about Leopold and Loeb. I remember her talking about it. She was fascinated by the case, how the two strove to commit the perfect kidnap and murder and how it went wrong. I look at the note from the bookseller and experience a milder form of the vertigo I felt when they removed her from the house. It seems a matter of philosophical principle: if actions take place in the world predicated on the assumption of one's continuing existence, must one not, at some level, continue to exist?

I don't go back to the therapist. I tell myself I have things under control. I carry on walking to work instead of taking the bus. After work I go out and I stay out. I'm wound so tight that at a bar with friends one evening I bring my teeth down on the side of a wine glass and a large, clean piece of it snaps off in my mouth. I put it down on the table and carry on talking.

In November and December, everything comes at once, as it always has: my birthday, my mother's birthday, Christmas, my dad's birthday. For her birthday, my dad and I go up the hill behind the house to the place where we scattered the ashes. It is a frozen December day, the earth rising in icy ribs beneath our feet. There is no view from the top; just white-grey mist as far as one can see.

For Christmas we have a brilliant idea. I'm often in LA for work, and Christmas there is as outlandishly far removed from our idea of Christmas as you can get. Christmas at home meant turkey and trimmings, the open fire my mother liked to light in the morning and keep going all day, maybe a walk to the village. This year, my dad and I take the ten-hour flight to the west coast of America and check into a hotel opposite the beach, on Ocean Avenue. On Christmas Day we go to the movies, twice. (LA being a movie town, every cinema is full, mostly with big family groups. It's surprisingly festive.) We have hot dogs for Christmas dinner and walk beside the Pacific, along Venice beach.

As a journalist, you discover quite quickly that the question 'What did you feel?' doesn't get you very far. 'What did you see?' is the more useful question. And so, while I can't remember what I felt that Christmas, I remember what I saw. I remember thinking about the importance of seeing new things; that whatever else the coming trip might or might not achieve, it would at least serve to generate fresh memories, to unseat the things I saw in my head when I closed my eyes or stared through a bus window or did anything that permitted my mind to go slack and default to that same set of images. Even if I had a wretched time in South Africa, I thought, each wretched new memory would be a welcome brick in the wall between me and the things I saw: a head that couldn't hold itself upright; two eyes opening and slowly closing again; the closeness of a room on a warm summer evening, when the energy shifted and the air seemed to part.

I am hung-over that morning. All week I have been seeing friends to say goodbye. As a leaving gift, my friend Susannah gives me a copy of Mary Wollstonecraft's *A Vindication of the Rights of Woman* and a miniature bottle of Tabasco sauce which, in the event of disaster, seem obliquely to cover all bases.

The night before, a friend came round, and we worked our way through the best part of a bottle of vodka until she was sick on my wood-effect flooring and I passed out on the sofa. On the way to the airport, I rest my head against the condensation-slick window and try to steady my brain while London churns by.

'You could change your flight,' says my dad, loyally.

'I'll be OK.'

We are going to the airport via the cattery, where the cat has been billeted since Christmas. Our cat is used to a five-star cat spa with central heating and an evening lecture programme, but that was for the two weeks when we went on holiday and this is for months, while my dad sells the house. 'Arm-and-a-leg job,' we had said, at the prospect of sending her to the usual place. 'Second mortgage.' Instead, we put her out on a farm. My mother would have been horrified, and we knew it. We haven't seen Mogs since December and so, guiltily, we drive out to see her before my afternoon flight. She was my mum's cat more than ours; I want to say goodbye.

'Do you think she still knows us?' At the back of the cage, the cat cringes and glowers. I sprinkle my fingers in her sullen face. 'Mogs!' She glares. The farmer looks away.

In the car again on the way to the airport, my dad passes me his mobile and asks if I'd mind ringing his parents to say goodbye. It is my dad's stepmother who answers. My heart sinks. She was the main inspiration for my mother's rants about English people, how cold they are, how incapable of saying anything to each other that mattered.

'Hello,' I say.

'Oh, Emmy, hello.' The diminutive, so at odds with the tenor of our relationship, had driven my mother crazy. It was blatant hypocrisy, and besides, she hadn't authorised it. I wonder now if, back in the day, it had been offered as a tentative gesture of intimacy, which my mother had rejected as too little, too late. The lines had been drawn by then; each had decided who the other was: my mother, in the eyes of her father-in-law's wife, a horrendous loudmouth with a superiority complex based, as far as she could tell, on absolutely nothing. Where in the world did this woman come from? Who were her family? And my mother, for her part, saw a woman who 'rejected my child', as she liked to say, looking martyred, and who was, despite all her airs and graces, 'only a farmer's daughter'.

I didn't feel particularly rejected, but speaking to my dad's stepmother was always a trial. She had a knack on the phone of communicating a lack of interest so profound it was amazing she could summon the will to breathe. And so, when she says on the phone that day, 'How are you feeling about your trip?' I am amazed. Feelings haven't been reported between us in either direction for as long as I've lived. Frazzled, freaked, hung-over, I answer honestly for once. 'Pretty nervous, actually.'

'Well,' she says, kindly, 'of course you are. It's only to be expected.'

Mum in her early twenties with her brother Michael,
and her brother Steven just visible behind.

6

At the Archive

I have friends who, on visiting Israel for the first time, came back to report experiencing a powerful deliverance, a sense of recognition which at the extreme end is recognised by psychiatrists as Jerusalem Syndrome: when previously balanced people set foot in the Holy Land and become instantly psychotic. (Lesser versions of this take place when Western teenagers set foot in India, Africa or anywhere you can buy beads.) I had half wondered whether I'd have a similar reaction when I touched down in Johannesburg. Instead, to my relief, I have no reaction at all.

For the first time in six months, I'm in a place with no cues, no reminders. It is raining when I arrive; a mild English rain, not the African downpour my mother had threatened. In the early morning drizzle a taxi takes me through suburbs that look like Milton Keynes or Houston to an aggressively bland hotel in the north of the city.

I have been deliberately hazy about my arrival date. I want space to acclimatise before the pressure of a meeting. I am aware that what I'm doing is unfair, unethical, possibly unforgivable: flying halfway around the world to bother other people's parents with questions I had been too afraid to ask my own. I'm also aware of the licence I have. I'm the bereaved; I can do whatever I like and no one can say anything.

The hotel room is dimly lit and perfectly climate controlled, the only distinguishing detail a note on my bed left by the hotel management advising me against leaving the premises alone on foot. My mother would have had a fit.

'Is it safe there?' I go through the old catechism, in my head now.

'Of course it's safe. It's a hotel, there's a lock on the door.'

'But if there's a fire you can still get out?'

I remove the note, lie down and sleep for several hours with sudden, weightless abandon. Heaven, I think, might very well be a version of the high-end business hotel.

When I wake up, it's still raining. I go downstairs and walk gingerly out into the parking lot. Nothing happens. I turn left and walk down a pavement running alongside the highway. There are glass-and-chrome business parks on either side and a well-manicured strip of grass down the middle, where black men in overalls are either sleeping or touting for work. They look like figures drawn on a laminate sheet, overlaid from a different reality entirely. They emphatically fail to molest me when I pass.

At the end of the street is a shopping mall, where I revel in the triumph of finding the adaptor plug I need and in the price of the sushi in Yo! Sushi, where even the purple plates are under a pound. By the time I get back to the room I'm euphoric. I have managed, in defiance of the hotel's instructions, to walk along a road without incident. I pick up the phone and, looking in my notebook, turn to the first number on my list.

'Oh, my darling!' Joan's voice bursts down the line as if released from a can. 'Where even are you? In your hotel room?! Oh, I can't bear it – what would your mother say? I'll get Ted to drive over THIS INSTANT and pick you up –'

'Oh, Joan, that's lovely of you but –'

'– I can have the spare room all ready. It's a bit cluttered, but alone in your hotel room and is it even safe there? Oh, I'm almost crying, I –' a muffle as her hand goes over the mouthpiece – 'in her hotel room, yes I've told her, oh, I can't bear it –'

'Joan, it's the Crowne Plaza.'

A howl down the telephone. 'How much must it be costing!'

I am out of sync, generationally, with Joan's children because my mother had me so late. There is more than a twenty-year age gap between Joan's daughter Jennifer and me. 'Dear Aunty Paul,' wrote Jennifer to my mother once a year on her birthday. I reassure Joan I am happy in the hotel and arrange to meet her in two days' time. I turn to the next number on my list.

The phone rings for a long time before someone picks up.

'Hello?' The voice is faint. My heart drops as if the cable snapped.

Fay and I have spoken several times by now; there should be no taboo in it. But ringing from a distance of a few miles seems a different proposition to ringing her from England. Those conversations were distant, logistical, hampered by a bad line. Now, I'm nervous. It occurs to me it's possible I'm about to embarrass myself. I have come all this way to claim a connection everyone else involved might think expired long ago.

'Fay, it's Emma.'

'Emma!' Her voice soars. 'Are you here?'

'I'm here!'

'Where are you?'

My aunt does not object to me being in a hotel; boundaries are being observed, as are certain formal preliminaries necessary when white South Africans of a certain age encounter anyone, of any age, from anywhere else.

I ask after her daughter, Victoria, and after telling me where she is and how she's doing, my aunt assures me unbidden that her children were brought up to respect all human life. When her son was thirty-six, she says, he thanked his mother for teaching him to see everyone as equal, so that while some of his contemporaries are struggling to adjust to the new South Africa, he is not. When she herself goes on holiday, says my aunt, Maria, her maid, stays in the house and sleeps in the guest room like anyone else.

'It's just so wonderful you're here,' she says. Her voice is low and quiet. There is an urgency to the conversation that was absent from the previous ones.

'I'm glad I'm here.'

Fay doesn't know precisely where all her siblings are, but there is a chain of command through which they can, if necessary, be reached and which is how news of my mother's death spread. She tells me some family news, which I receive like a drink of water after crossing a desert. Since leaving Johannesburg, her sister Doreen has sold all her furniture and practically become a nomad. 'I couldn't,' says Fay. 'I need the – what's the word? Security.'

'What about Tony?' I ask.

'Tony is Tony. He means well. It just doesn't always come out right.'

'And Steven?'

'Steven is Steven.'

I sit on the edge of the bed in the gathering gloom. The only light in the room is from the spots above the minibar and the glowing LED of the alarm clock. My aunt tells me about these people I have heard of all my life, whose characters, like those from a novel, I am familiar with as archetypes: Arty, Sporty, Sneaky, Fighty, Saintly, Baby and Dead – although the designations overlap. By the sound of it everyone is a bit fighty and more than one is dead. 'Fay was my baby, Steve was my baby.' Out of all of them, Fay, I think, is the one who will tell me what I want to know.

'You know your mother was called Pauline before she changed it to Paula?' says my aunt.

'Yes, I know.'

Fay says this was because 'the first thing she did when she got off the boat in England was to buy a pair of shoes, and the label in them said Paula, so that's what she called herself'. I laugh indulgently. There is nothing in the Story of How I Arrived on These Shores about this. Besides, my mother would never have named herself after a pair of shoes. She changed her name because she'd always thought 'Pauline' was soppy.

Fay tells me my mother used to take her to the central library in Johannesburg when she was a little girl. She made her read *Anne of Green Gables*. 'Me too,' I say.

She tells me the story of Derek, an old boyfriend of my mother's who once visited the house and made a profound impression on the younger siblings. He owned a station wagon – no one could understand why my mother didn't marry him. She and Derek were going to a dance. When he came to the door, says my aunt, my mother stepped out in an exquisite navy dress with a white collar. Everyone gasped. And then, crossing the room, she caught the dress on a baby's wicker pram belonging to Fay and it ripped. Fay was seven; it was just after Christmas. My mother didn't shout, says Fay, which made her feel even worse. 'I remember it so clearly. It was such a beautiful dress. I don't remember Derek at all. But I remember that dress. She looked so beautiful. I felt terrible when it ripped.'

Several times, we push up against the boundaries of what can and cannot be said, buffeting and retreating like a boat trying to dock in bad weather. When I say, tentatively, that I find it useful to write things down sometimes, I sense her bristle and withdraw.

I tell my aunt I need a few days to settle in, and we arrange to meet at the weekend. I will stay over at her house on Saturday night and we'll have Sunday to catch up. She asks what I'd like to eat and should she buy yoghurts, 'or yoggies, as your mother used to call them. I can just hear her saying it.' So can I. A chill passes through me. 'Yoghurt would be lovely,' I say.

Towards the end of the conversation, my aunt says, 'I feel terrible, I never knew her mother's name.' I sometimes forget they had different mothers, or any mothers at all, so absent from my mother's narrative was her stepmother. Fay has barely mentioned Marjorie either.

'Her mother's name was Sarah,' I say.

'Sarah!' says my aunt. We are so desperate for signs. 'I had a plant called Sarah once. I gave it to my sister Doreen to look after. She killed it, of course.'

Fay asks me what I'm doing the following day. 'Oh,' I say vaguely, 'this and that.'

That evening in the hotel bar I take out my journal. It was given to me by my friend Merope as a leaving present, with an inscription on the flyleaf: 'I am your South Africa book. Be nice and write clever thoughts in me.' If she hadn't given it to me, I'm not sure I'd be keeping much of a record. Despite my journalistic camouflage, I'm going about this whole thing while looking through my fingers, as if watching a scary scene in a horror movie. It's not that I want to *find out* what happened so much as to *have found out*, in the same way, I think, that my mother didn't want to tell me so much as to *have already told*.

The bar is off to one side of the lobby, furnished in dark wood and with the TV tuned to an American sports channel. Lone businessmen sit, jackets off, ties loosened, craning up at the telly. I order a double vodka tonic, and feeling pleased with myself, record the day's events: the buying of the phone adaptor ('panic, panic over'); how much my lunch at Yo! Sushi cost (£5); my miraculous walk along the highway. I note my aunt's determined 'nothing surprises me' outlook and the strange, feverish tone of our conversation. I write joyfully of Joan's *joie de vivre*.

In a separate notebook I keep all the names, numbers and addresses, the evolving to-do lists and impressions scribbled at angles to be transcribed later. It is these notes, unthinkingly produced, that, looking back, strike me as the truer record of what happened.

Given the choice, I would rather see things written down first; you can control the flow of information just by looking up and don't have to do anything particular with your face. The thing I had concealed from my aunt is that I am not going to sleep late or wander around the neighbourhood acclimatising the following day. I am going to hire a car and driver from the front desk and go to the national archive in Pretoria. Taking no chances – I don't imagine it's a popular route – I plan for the trip as if driving myself. I study the map and in the second notebook scrawl: 'Hamilton Street, Arcadia, via Mears, Jeppe, Beatrix, right into Savage, right into Hamilton.' If all goes to plan, I'll photocopy the paperwork, take it back to the hotel, and with a large drink in hand, read it at my leisure.

The next morning is overcast again. There is a women's health conference on in the hotel and you can't wait at the elevators or stand in line at the breakfast buffet without over-hearing women wearing laminated badges loudly discussing chlamydia. Outside the foyer, security men in yellow vests mill redundantly around.

When the maroon BMW pulls up, I shake hands with the driver, who introduces himself as Paul, and say I will need him all day; after he drops me at the address in Pretoria, he will have three hours to kill before coming to collect me. While speaking, I monitor myself for signs of condescension, over-compensation, madam syndrome, visible race or class guilt, or any other tonal imperfections, while wondering if he is rip-ping me off. The rate is so high it is practically Western. Paul nods and we get into the car.

Pretoria, the capital, is not known for its charm; Johannes-burg has the charm, the guile and energy, although I have yet to see any of it. We pull off an arterial road into a leafy car park and Paul lets me out. He promises to be back at the al-located time.

I don't match the profile, I suppose. I am too young to be here in the middle of a weekday, a lone female arriving at the guard hut eccentrically on foot. The two men in the booth eye me suspiciously. I slide my passport across the counter. They will see it, I think. They will see I am bringing unruly emotions into what is, after all, a library environment and they will not let me in.

'Purpose of visit?' says the man.

'Family tree.' He looks down at my passport and back up at me. Then he waves me through, towards the double airlock doors.

The routine is reassuringly familiar. As at Colindale, I check my bag and jacket and go into the reading room with my pens in a plastic bag, as if for an exam. The smell hits me first: old paper, plastic book covers, more than one patron whose last shower was not quite recent enough. The comforting smell of every public library in the world.

The reading room is low-tech, a card-index system in one corner, a bank of photocopiers against the wall. The only decor is a Soviet-style poster of a woman raising her fist to the sky, under a slogan for the country's biggest trade union. The procedure seems to be to fill in a slip, then wait in your seat until your order is brought up from the vaults. Every now and then a woman with a grey bun wheels a trolley across the floor, unloads a pile of ledgers and leaves again, whereupon elderly men in khaki shorts fly over from all corners of the reading room to raid what she's left, like beetles carrying off cubes of sugar.

I have no expectation of finding anything. That the numbers in my notepad might correspond with a physical object in this building or in the vaults under it seems to me as improbable as stumbling on a message in a bottle which, when unfurled, has your own name upon it. Not just your name, but your family's darkest secrets, typed up by a third party and signed by witnesses. It seems outrageous that such a thing might exist, under cover of neutrality, on cool, indifferent paper and on a shelf with other papers just like it. Calmly, I sit and wait, and while I wait, I watch these quiet, elderly people grazing over open ledgers. Some of them have put on ties and jackets to come here. Good, kind people, I think, researching their family trees to pass on to their grandchildren and redeem in themselves a sense of continuity and purpose.

The first shock is that a file matching my request comes up from the vaults. The second shock is logistical. When I walk over to the table and find it, I see that photocopying it will be out of the question. It's a huge ledger, labelled on the spine with a single year and containing every court case heard in the district in that period. It's too overstuffed to fit on the copier. I haul it back to the table and, looking at the clock, see I have two hours to transcribe whatever I find by hand.

I have no month to go by and start paging through from the beginning. It is like playing a game of Russian roulette, each page containing the split-second possibility of an explosion in my face. A couple of breaking and enterings. A Mrs Potgeiter molested in her own home. A long legal debate on what does and does not constitute rape. Mrs Potgeiter's assailant got twenty-five years, but he was black, and it becomes apparent, after thirty or so pages, that the only successfully prosecuted trials were ones such as this; the legalistic relish for the black man attacking the white woman rises up off the pages like mist. I am so engrossed in Mrs Potgeiter and her troubles that when, three-quarters of the way in, I turn a page and see my mother's name, I don't keel off my chair, but take it as more or less part of the continuum.

Three words leap out of the summary page: 'incest' and 'not guilty'.

My mother never used that first word. I've never even used it in my head. I look up to see if anyone is watching me. I look down at the page again.

I take in the name of the prosecutor, Britz, and the defendant, acting 'for himself'. The case has been brought, I see, not in my mother's name, but in my aunt's. Of course. At twenty-four, my mother was too old to be medically useful. I do the maths. Fay was twelve.

There is a faint cough. I look up to find a man in the national costume of his people – khaki shorts, khaki shirt, khaki knee-length socks with a comb tucked into them – craning in my direction. In an avuncular sort of way he asks what I am doing here. 'Family tree,' I say, and give him a look I hope communicates just how happy it would make me to see him go down, Leonard Bast-like, in a shelving accident. 'Well, if you need any help,' he says, and writes his email address on a scrap of paper.

I return to the ledger. It takes me a few moments to figure out what I am reading. There seem to be two charge sheets and two cover sheets recording verdicts from two different trials. In one, my grandfather is found guilty; in the other, not guilty. They are separated by a period of several months. I finally figure out what this signifies: the passage of the case from its preliminary hearing at the local court – the

South African equivalent of a committal hearing in front of a magistrate, held to determine whether there is sufficient evidence in the case for a full criminal trial – to the High Court in Johannesburg. He was found guilty at the first hearing and not guilty at the second. I flip the pages back and forth. Guilty/not guilty. Guilty/not guilty. On such words entire life histories turn.

I flip the page and the first hearing begins. There is a list of witnesses, with my mother's name near the bottom. I see that her brother Tony is on the list, and her sister Doreen, but no sign of Mike. Her stepmother is the first witness.

A few pages in there is a diagram depicting a cross-section of the human body, beneath the name of the twelve-year-old, with arrows alongside which a court surgeon has signed. It takes a moment for me to make sense of it. Oh, injuries. I look up from the page.

Over the next two hours, I transcribe the notes, shoulders hunched, hand cramping, brain disengaged. I don't process much beyond the necessity of copying. It is a physical exercise. When I get to the end of the first trial, I turn a page to find a sheaf of shorthand notes – the original court records. I get to the end of these and there's nothing more. I look and look again. There are no records from the second trial. It will be impossible to tell how the testimonies changed.

(Later, to be sure I hadn't missed anything, I employed a researcher with shorthand skills to go to the archive and translate the notes at the back of the file. She emailed me the findings and, as I suspected, they simply duplicated what I had. 'What a terrible thing,' she wrote in her note. 'My heart broke reading this. Who could do such a thing to children?'

I hadn't owned to the family connection and was mortified, by how unrespectable it all was, and to have put this nice lady through an ordeal. 'Yes,' I replied. 'It is awful, isn't it.')

After returning the ledger and packing up my things, I leave the reading room, cross the car park, and to the concern of the guards in the booth, say I am going for a walk. I turn left and blindly climb a hill, which it turns out leads to the parliament buildings. These are large, classical structures with a panoramic view over Pretoria. Opposite is a small garden, behind a chain-link fence. I step over the fence and sit on a bench, looking out over Pretoria in the direction of Johannesburg. There are large red flowers, which I think I recognise as protea; I've seen them illustrated on Joan's airmail letters. Flightless birds hop about on the lawn.

I am exhilarated. I have read the contents of the file and yet here I am, alive, sitting on a bench in the afternoon sun. I experience a surge of vindictive triumph and conduct a long exchange in my head with the dead man, whom I don't permit to speak. 'Right, you fucker, you can answer to me.' This is mine, all of this. I am driving it now. 'You have to own it' – one of those phrases in the therapeutic lexicon I have always despised, but it suddenly seems apt. I will own it so hard it breaks apart in my hands.

On the way back to the hotel I ask Paul to make a detour. From the court papers, I have addresses for the family going way back, including the place where my mother lived in Johannesburg at the time of the trial. It was here, during the course of one afternoon, that she resolved to carry on living.

'Do you know where Soper Road is?'

'Soper Road?' says Paul. He looks at me through the rear-view mirror.

'Yes.' He carries on staring, so I add, 'Someone I knew used to live there.'

We drive through the city in his air-conditioned BMW, around people pushing huge, baled loads, men selling cigar-ette lighters and smaller things from the depths of their palms, children running about in T-shirts that look as if the holes in them are holding up the fabric, like a viaduct. Paul hits the central-locking button with a flamboyance designed, I think, to enforce my sense of dependence on him.

At the corner of Wolmarans and Twist the names became familiar, not because I've been here before but because they borrow from London. The mansion blocks, great 1950s mon-strosities, bear faded signs that read 'The Hilton' and 'Park Lane' and 'The Devonshire' and then, incongruously, 'Grace-land'. Their windows are broken, stuffed with newspaper and front-loaded with balconies groaning under bits of trashed wicker furniture. It is as after a flood, when the water has drained, leaving tidemarks up the wall and the furniture stacked, teetering, in corners; the work of an angry pol-tergeist.

'What number?'

I peer through the window and count them down. The numbering is erratic. Either the place has been demolished or the street at some point renumbered. We park approximately where it should have been, and Paul glances nervously in his mirrors. I wait for something to happen, for my heart to re-spond to the moment or for my body at least to override the air conditioning and break into a sweat. 'I don't think you

should get out,' says Paul. I had thought that grief, like cat litter, had no secondary uses, but there it is. Blankness.

'OK. Let's go.'

When I get back to the hotel, I go straight to the business
centre. The name of the judge at the High Court seemed familiar. I feed his name into a search engine and stare at the
results. I feel sorry for all of us, then, shameful bit-players on
the periphery of history. Six years after acquitting my grandfather, this man had, briefly, become the most famous judge in
the world. In 1963, while the world watched, Justice Quartus
de Wet presided over the Rivonia treason trials at the High
Court in Johannesburg, at the end of which he sent a young
Nelson Mandela to Robben Island for twenty-seven years – a
piece of exceptional leniency, it was thought at the time, since
he was expected to be given the death penalty.

'Oh, love,' says my dad, when I ring him from the room. 'If
you want me to fly out, I'll come tomorrow.'

'No, it's OK. I'm OK.'

I type the afternoon's notes into my computer. I don't look
at them again for three years.

Hot and uncomfortable: my grandfather (back row far left) with his in-laws, my grandmother Sarah's family, including her niece, Gloria, in the bonnet.

7

A Very Interesting Group of People

My mother's father looks relatively normal in photos. There he is, sitting in a group surrounded by members of his new wife's family: her brother-in-law, Charlie, and her nieces and nephews. Jimmy looks young, slightly sheepish perhaps, or shy. They are sitting on a patch of dust in rough clothing, a few parched sprigs of vegetation behind them in what the back of the photo identifies as Zululand. They look hot and awkward, as if they have just stepped off the boat.

In fact, the DeKiewits, my grandfather's family, had been in the country since the turn of the twentieth century, when they emigrated from Holland. My grandmother's family had much deeper roots in South Africa. Their name was Doubell, which it pleased my mother to think of as French, although she must in her heart have known better. I'm not in South Africa long before I notice with a shock that Doubell, like other French-sounding names in those parts – Roux, Terreblanche, Joubert – is Afrikaans by association. My grandmother's ancestor might have come from France a hundred years earlier, but her mother was a Van Vuuren and her grandmother was an Oosthuizen, and whichever way you slice it, those are not French names.

My grandfather was born in Johannesburg to first-generation European immigrants, which put him higher up the social scale – a whiter shade of white – than his young wife, although in any other immigrant community, as the newer arrival, this would not have been so. His family were poor, resourceful, ambitious, multi-child-bearing, and given the nature of the country they had moved to from the security of Holland, deeply eccentric. By the time my mother was in her mid-twenties, the family name had become somewhat famous. She used to tell me about this with a mixture of pride and anxiety. Her father's first cousin, Cornelius, with whom her father had grown up and who bore the same surname, was in the newspapers a lot in the era. He was a historian with stout anti-apartheid views who after leaving South Africa for England had found tenure at a liberal arts college in the US.

Not long before my mother emigrated, he visited Johannesburg from his home in upstate New York to deliver a lecture under the auspices of the South African Institute of Race Relations. My mother read about him in the newspaper and felt encouraged; if she didn't go mad or shoot herself, she thought, there was a chance some day she might amount to something. She longed to meet him, her father's illustrious cousin. But she hesitated to get in touch. She had been in the newspapers, too.

It is a strange quirk of history that, while I know none of my closer relatives, I know Cornelius's granddaughter, Caroline. She is American; we became friends online and then met up when she was in London one time. It is thanks to Caroline I know anything at all about the world my grandfather grew up in: Cornelius wrote a short, unpublished memoir of his childhood, which she very kindly sent to me – and which, in spite of myself, I have raked through time and again, looking for clues; why, of the two boys who grew up next door to each other, did her grandfather became the successful academic and mine the murderer?

It doesn't get you anywhere, this kind of speculation, but there is a temptation to mine for small variables. Did one have an inspirational teacher, which the other didn't? Or suffer a bang to the head which, I discovered, during my brief obsession with serial killers as a teenager, got lots of violent men started?

There was the wider insanity of a country in which a white child was encouraged to believe that however badly he behaved, he was intrinsically more valuable than an entire race of people. As a pathology, it might have been designed to create psychopaths. But both boys were subject to that. The most there is in the memoir is a suggestion of favouritism. Cornelius, older than his cousin Jimmy by a few years, was a teacher's pet. He was good at Latin. The boys' grandfather, the dominant influence in their early lives, loved him very much and vested in him the hope of the family. Jimmy's father, Johannes, seems also to have been very fond of Cornelius. From much smaller things great resentments have prospered.

The family came to South Africa sometime in the 1890s. Gold had been discovered there in 1886 and the country started rapidly to modernise; there were good job opportunities for young men from Europe. Arie, Cornelius's father, had first considered going to Latin America, but there was the problem of the language, and so he settled on South Africa.

For a few years he made good money, working on construction of the railroad to Mozambique. When the Boer War broke out, his loyalty to the new place was so strong he fought for Paul Kruger against the British. He was captured and escaped at the same time as Winston Churchill was going through the same experience on the other side. After that, wrote Cornelius, his father looked on Churchill as a sort of inverted twin, fortune's favourite. He was very bitter about the divergent routes their lives took.

Arie's family was part of the problem, particularly his father, a notoriously difficult man. They lived on the island of Texel, off the coast of Holland and part of an archipelago extending all the way to Denmark. They had been fishermen historically and were now builders and labourers. When peace was declared at Vereeniging, Arie called on his family to join him, and the entire clan – his brother Johannes, his three sisters, their husbands and his parents – took the three-week voyage to Cape Town. Arie was an adventurer, but what the rest of the family thought they were doing, these Low Country people, transplanting themselves from Holland to a ramshackle frontier town in the southern hemisphere is anyone's guess. They were devout Lutherans, so perhaps there was a masochistic need to be tested. In the case of Arie's parents, the journey itself was a sign of election: these elderly people left home at a time when they had already exceeded the average life expectancy. (That Arie had failed to make his fortune in the new country doesn't seem to have deterred them. This is the root of all catastrophe in the family: no one ever knows when to call it a day.)

To read of Arie's parents is to travel warp-speed from modern times to medieval. His father, Cornelius and Jimmy's grandfather, believed that if you dug up a field, there was a chance you might dig a devil up with it. Like the Dutch who went to America two centuries earlier, the grandfather had a concept of 'freedom' which valued one freedom only: the freedom to be a religious maniac. He was a fanatic whose fanaticism cost him every job he'd ever held. When he tried to be a grocer, he would only serve those he had seen in church, dismissing all others with the words: 'You were not at the service in church yesterday. Today I cannot be of any service to you.'

When he was a carpenter and a builder, he was fired from every work site for arguing with the foreman.

'Having known Grandfather,' wrote Cornelius, 'I know that swearing only comes into its own in the Dutch language. Grandfather's swearing had grandeur; it had the quality of a thunderous sermon in a New England pulpit, blasting the congregation with its own sins. He swore indeed as he prayed, with the same intensity and earnestness.' (I looked up some Dutch swearing recently to see what kind of health it's in. Translations don't do it justice, I'm told, but 'prick-biscuit', 'buddy-fucker', 'get cholera', 'ass-beetle' and 'Your mother's ass has its own union' are all happy locutions in the Dutch language.)

Cornelius remembered his grandmother as a tiny, hunch-backed creature with an almost epic ability to endure. She was from a family called Haring – the Dutch for herring – and didn't want to emigrate, but her husband's will was greater. She had been a midwife who had seen twelve of her seventeen children die in infancy. She had a strong satirical streak, and long before her husband's death, took to wearing a black widow's cap around the house, to her children's delight. She shrank from her husband's fanaticism, a personality trait that long after his death would resurface repeatedly in his descendants.

Those three weeks at sea must have passed for the grandfather like an exercise in spiritual cleansing. What he took to be his soul thrilled to the open water with a force that in a different man might have been called lascivious. The only book he read was the Calvinist version of the Bible in high Dutch, and he sat on deck, taking it literally.

His wife sat elsewhere on the ship. She was at a serene stage in her endurance. She thought of her grandchildren and concocted scenarios in which her husband fell overboard and she returned to Holland, alone.

At some point, the grandfather opened his mouth to reassure her and for the briefest of moments saw something in his wife that frightened him, something that implied resources in this small woman that were not only withheld from him, but that were in some sly way actively pitched against him. He dismissed the thought instantly. The ship sailed on. In the rare moments he gave to considering her feelings, the grandfather rationalised that no matter how difficult the new country might be, it would at least dislodge the thing they didn't talk about – the twelve coffins borne one after the other to the cemetery. The babies' caskets were small enough for him to carry in his arms. The larger ones he balanced on a wheelbarrow.

The country they found on arrival was still smouldering amid the ruins of the Boer War. Arie met them on the dock at Cape Town and escorted them to the train, where they would take the three-day journey across country to the city in the east, one of the newest and highest cities in the world, 6,000 feet above sea level.

'Arie, my boy!' The grandfather clapped his younger son on the shoulder. 'And here we all are, together again!'

'Father.'

Arie suffered a moment's panic. On the platform beneath the blazing Cape sky, his hunched mother, his wan sisters and their husbands in their northern hemisphere clothes. His father's cheer did nothing to reassure him; the old man was at his most ebullient when facing down doubt.

Then he saw his elder brother in a brown suit and with a mild expression, and his spirit surged.

'Johannes!'

'Arie. Meet my wife.'

A woman stepped forward, and Arie laughed and put a hand to her belly. 'Congratulations! He'll be the first African child in the family!' (The grandfather took leave of barking at the porter to suffer his own, fleeting moment of panic.) Somehow they boarded the train.

This is how I imagine it went, although there is no eyewitness account. Cornelius was a baby and my grandfather not yet born – although he was the first in the family to be a native South African. What is known is that Johannes, his father, was a thoughtful, gentle man; my grandfather was not brutalised as a child. (The tyrant was his uncle, Arie, who, like some deranged emperor, banned his wife and children from referring to him as 'he' and, on dark winter nights, forbade them from lighting the oil lamps until he got home. They sat, recalled his son, shivering in the dark.)

Outside the house was a different matter. Gold-rush Johannesburg, like its American counterparts, was a place of casual violence and endemic alcoholism. In Holland they had been living in a painting by Whistler; now they were in a Hieronymus Bosch. The fires of the mine dumps burned day and night. The rhythmic shudder of the drilling sent dust up from the floor. They moved into a complex of wood-and-iron shacks to the north of the city, arranged around the focal point of the grandparents' two-room home, a corrugated-iron structure which the grandfather painted bright red, daubing the name of the family on the outside wall.

It was in these two rooms that communal family life took place. The floor was compacted earth, with a coal stove in the middle that burnt all day to keep off mosquitoes. The roof was galvanised iron, which made life inside hot. Water collected in a rain barrel outside in the yard.

Slowly a life came together. The grandfather wouldn't learn English on a point of principle and Afrikaans seemed to him an absurd invention, but he was forced to acquire some basic Zulu to deal with the human traffic at his gate. Despite his lofty religious principles, his position on the black man was that he was unthreatening but essentially useless. His wife's fear annoyed him. It undermined his illusion of government in the house.

As best she could, the grandmother eked out a routine, sweeping and going to the market, where she conversed in Dutch and never learnt a word of any of the languages of the country she now lived in. In the morning, she made Mazawattee tea. At noon, she switched to coffee. There was barley and brown sugar for breakfast, and brown beans and black molasses for lunch. Tapioca on Sunday. She made toffee out of condensed milk and unrefined black sugar. For birthdays there was coconut ice or flan.

Once a month she deposited a penny in a stocking behind the sugar tin; she was saving for her own funeral.

When her family congratulated her on the occasion of her fiftieth wedding anniversary, she said merely, 'It is long.' Her air, wrote Cornelius, was one of 'complete sadness'.

He did not feel this way about his childhood. It was poor, he wrote, but 'to be a child in a family of generations, where welcome is taken for granted, is the supreme advantage of poor people: they communicate elbow to elbow'. There was sadness there, too, however. Cornelius was conscious of living in a family of ghosts; when he looked around the table, he thought of his father's twelve dead siblings in the cemetery in Holland.

It was into this world that my grandfather Jimmy was born. His father worked as a blaster in the mines. Johannes always smelt faintly of dynamite, recalled his nephew, looking back on those scenes of his childhood some fifty years later, from the comfort of upstate New York.

When a boy in the family turned six, it was the tradition to give him an airgun. One day, a man came to the gate begging for work. He was bolder than most, and putting his hand on the gate, opened it and started to walk up the path. The grandfather, standing in the doorway, shouted, '*Voetsek!*' – a ruder version of 'Sod off' – and Cornelius shot the man in the backside. It was only an airgun pellet, but the man whipped round, stunned, and started back for the house. Cornelius ran and hid behind his grandfather, who at lunch that day gave a sermon about the sin of injuring one's neighbour. 'Lord, thou hast seen the act of a sinner.'

There was moral order in the house, but it was very confused. The grandfather's moralising did not stop him from endorsing the racial pecking order as it appeared in the country at large: white northern European, white Afrikaans, white southern European, black African and, at the bottom of the heap, the Chinese, who took the most dangerous jobs in the mines. At school, Afrikaans was despised and the African languages completely ignored, as was the history of the country prior to colonisation. In America, children might play Cowboys and Indians and consider it an honour to be the Indian. Not so here.

The children spoke Dutch at home and English at school. J. M. Coetzee has written about the terrors of South African schooling, and although his experiences were several decades later, nothing much seemed to have changed. Cornelius recalled two types of teachers: young women from England out looking for adventure or a husband, and sadistic ex-British army officers who continued to fight the Boer War in the classroom, dividing pupils into the conquered and the conquerors. When white South Africans were officially made subjects of the British Empire, Cornelius wrote in his diary, 'I am now a British object.' With delight, he recounted how one day the Afrikaner boys who filled the back row and were always being beaten by the teacher got up, en masse, and sauntered down the aisle. The teacher fled. They left the classroom and were never seen again. By the end of high school, not a single Afrikaner pupil remained.

Looking back, Cornelius put his success down to two things; one was, indeed, a sympathetic teacher, a gentle Welshman who encouraged him to go to university. Cornelius went first to Witwatersrand University, then to the University of London, and from there on to America and Cornell. The other pivotal moment in his young life was something he witnessed as a child. The children weren't allowed out after dark, when the streets were full of drunken miners, staggering from the pub to pass out in the road. One night, Cornelius watched through the window as a drunk white miner beat a black man almost to death. The thing that stayed with him wasn't the violence itself so much as the fact that the man didn't fight back. The next day, all that remained was a bloodstain in the dirt. His education, said Cornelius, began when he saw it.

The greatest influence, however, was unavoidably his and Jimmy's grandfather, the old tyrant who, when he fell ill, told his family, 'This is not a sick bed, it is a death bed and leave me alone.' He was taken to the hospital, where his loud and unstoppable orations from the Bible annoyed the staff so much they called his wife to come and collect him. She arrived just as they were pulling the sheet over his head. The grandmother returned to the shack and wept until she was blue in the face. Nothing her children said could console her. The old man's last act of spite had been to die first, forcing her to spend all she'd saved on his funeral. By way of estate, he left his family the cigars in his vest pocket, a pouch of tobacco, a copy of the Bible and a pamphlet entitled 'The Speedy Spaniard'. But Cornelius remembered him fondly. 'My boy, what have you done today?' he would ask his grandson every evening, and Cornelius, in fine detail, would tell him.

My grandfather Jimmy did not go to university. Perhaps the Welsh teacher had left by the time he came along five years later. My mother said he boasted of having been a medical student and dropping out, but who knows if this was true. In adulthood, he had little to do with his family. In the paperwork from his murder trial I noticed that his mother had testified as a character witness. And he had maintained vague contact with his sister, Cornelia, known as Nelly, who had the misfortune of thirteen children and a husband who gambled, and thanks to whom my mother had thirty-two first cousins. Beyond that, my mother knew nothing of her father's family, although she was, in a general way, proud of her Dutch origins. She thought the Dutch were, by and large, sensible people, her father being the exception.

I wouldn't have found out about any of this myself if, in the 1990s, I hadn't written a piece in the newspaper about ancestry software. It was when tracing your origins was all the rage and you could, I wrote, decide on any line of descent for yourself if you sifted the dirt skilfully enough. To illustrate the point, I fed my mother's maiden name into a family-tree database and within five minutes established we were descendants of Rousseau. After the piece came out, a man with my mother's maiden name emailed from America to say he was a distant cousin and did I know we had family in England? It was through him I met Caroline, Cornelius's granddaughter.

I thought my mother would be uninterested. Every few years or so, retired Canadians would pop up via email, asking if I could shed light on the mysterious branch of my mother's family that seemed to end with my grandfather. It made my mother and me laugh – the idea of going round the world *looking* for people you are related to. But when the piece came out, illustrated with photos of her mother as a young woman and her father as a young man, she took a copy next door to show off to the neighbours. She was furious about a spelling error in the picture caption. She was a proud person, but I had never seen this before: pride in where she had come from.

The relative in England was an elderly lady called Theodora, who turned out to be Cornelius's sister – a first cousin, then, of my grandfather's. She was living in the East Midlands, and my parents and I drove up to meet her. My mother was nervous and excited. Forty years earlier, she had got up the nerve to write to Cornelius, and he had replied kindly, owning to the connection and expressing a desire to meet her so he could tell her about 'a very interesting group of people' – her father's family. She kept the letter all her life. It was a source of great regret to her that they never managed to meet up.

And now here was Theodora, framed by her front door, built like a little bull and with her hair up in a bun. She looked at us with sharp blue eyes, and we followed her through to her living room.

She had grown up, she said, in a mining district in northern Johannesburg, a very rough and ready sort of place in those days. She had been very close to her older brother Cornelius, who had been her great champion and who, in the face of wider opposition, had campaigned for her right to apply to university – although he had disapproved of her chosen subject. Chemistry, he said, was too hard for girls. Nonetheless, Theodora had applied to university in England, and in 1930, won a scholarship to read chemistry at Oxford. She had stayed on to do postgraduate studies under the tutelage of her mentor, Sir Robert Robinson, who in 1947 won the Nobel Prize for discovering the molecular structure of morphine and penicillin.

My mother had almost to be physically restrained on receipt of this news. When I went to Oxford, a work colleague of my dad's had said unthinkingly to her, 'She must get it from her father.' Now here was this woman, elegant, articulate, sober, confirming my mother's lifelong fantasy that beyond the swampy genes and terrible scenes and hints at some public disgrace there was something else: scholarships to Oxford, houses filled with art, a woman with mettle equal to her own who had pulled herself out of the dust and the darkness. Finally – finally! – some external evidence of what it had been necessary for her to believe all this time: that it was not fluke but, as my mother always said, it was Who We Were.

It was an extraordinary scene; my motherless mother, no family, no history, whom I had never seen defer to anyone, bowing in an almost courtly fashion to this elder of the family. Theodora put on a green hat with a feather in it and we went out to lunch.

'No,' said my mother, on the way home in the car. Her eyes zipped this way and that. 'No, she is a very impressive woman. Not a barrel of laughs, but impressive.' Whatever internal dialogue was taking place my father and I let proceed uninterrupted; it didn't require our input. My mother wondered how different her life might have been if, in those early years in London, she'd known Theodora had been living a mere fifty miles away in Oxford. It made me think of that scene in *The African Queen* when Bogart and Hepburn, at the end of their tether and still stuck in the swamp, finally give up, whereupon the camera cranes upwards and with a jolt you see how close to open water and safety they were.

'But of course,' said my mother quickly, 'then I might not have made my own way.'

I saw Theodora again, for the last time, in that period between my mother's death and my trip to South Africa. She was in a nursing home by then and was well into her nineties. Still the same fierce look, but furious with frustration at her dependency. Something else had changed, too. Floating at the rim of the crocheted blanket was the broad face, bumpy nose and wide, penetrating eyes of the woman my mother became in the last two months of her life, when cancer accelerated her ageing. There was something almost Mongolian about the planes of that face. 'God, she looked like Mum,' said my dad, on the way home in the car.

Theodora hated the nursing home. 'They're all mad,' she said. She kept to her room and read texts on alternative medicine. When her eyesight went, she got what she could on audio tape from the mobile library. My dad went out for a walk and left us to talk. While her brother, in his memoir, had remembered his grandfather, it was the grandmother Theodora remembered. She would put duck eggs in her cleavage to hatch them, she said. Although she was illiterate, she was a great storyteller and would entertain her grandchildren with stories from European history; she was very good on the Napoleonic Wars. 'She was a clever woman,' said her granddaughter, 'not that she got any credit for it.'

Of the grandfather she recalled only meanness. There was an incident she had never forgotten. When Theodora was a very young child she had dropped a penny in the yard, and a chicken had eaten it. Giggling, she'd run into the shack to tell her grandfather, and without saying a word he had picked up a knife, raced out into the yard and without further ado slit the chicken down the middle to retrieve the penny. At almost ninety years' distance, Theodora looked horrified anew.

Did she remember Jimmy, I asked, her cousin, my grand-father? 'Yes,' she said. 'He was younger than us, and of course I was in England from my early twenties and rather lost touch with the wider family.' She looked at me curiously for a moment. 'There was some trouble there, I think?'

Theodora dissolved once more into the middle distance. 'I expect he was quite bright. We all were. But, of course, you never know which way a person will go.'

Nice eyebrows: my mother's first passport.

8

Friends Are Like Jewels

Joan flings open the door, Danny fighting for a look-in behind her. 'Oh, my darling!' she exclaims. 'Oh, so tall and so like Pauline!' She whips around to address her husband. 'Step back, old man, you're crowding me. I said STEP BACK. Oh, it's so good to see you!'

Joan is one of the most marvellous people I have ever met. She has bright-blue eye shadow, yellow hair and a turtleneck jumper the colour of fish paste. She has a way of talking in great bursts of energy that ground themselves, in crackling fashion, down the tall, thin figure of her husband. Although broadly South African, her inflection is just like my mother's, more so than my aunt's, in fact, and I think of how friends in their youth grow to sound like each other. Joan recently had a triple heart bypass – she is seventy-five – which means she limits her alcohol intake to neat whisky. She and Danny moved to this apartment as a retirement measure, but she still misses the house and fumes at her daughter, Jennifer, for letting them sell it. All this I get in the first three minutes while she shows me around. From the large, airy terrace there are views over a communal pool to the suburbs of Johannesburg and beyond. It is very striking. 'Ach,' says Joan, batting a hand, and I follow her back into the kitchen.

'Now,' she says, 'all I have to do is chop some parsley. It's only canned soup. Do you like soup? I don't have a milk jug any more – where's my milk jug? Ask Mrs Zinn, that's Jennifer. All sold in the move – so many things I've lost. My beautiful fridge-freezer. My dining-room table.' She throws her head round the corner. 'DANNY, DO YOU WANT COFFEE? He doesn't hear a word. I might as well talk to the wall. WALL, DO YOU WANT COFFEE? The old man irritates me now, I find him very irritating. If I had my time again, I'd hold out for someone more interesting. Never settle, Em, it isn't worth it.' Joan grips my hand and bursts into laughter. 'Oh! It's so good to see you!'

I could sit here all day, watching Joan fuss. I haul myself up onto the kitchen counter to get out of her way. She darts from cabinet to cabinet preparing the lunch.

I know very little of the history of her friendship with my mother. There was a photo of Joan with a soufflé of 1980s hair at her daughter Jennifer's wedding, on the back of which she had written 'Mother Dear'. I liked her for that. But while her letters, on green airmail paper decorated with pictures of flowers from the southern hemisphere, were eagerly received and lovingly replied to, to me they seemed strangely impersonal – certainly compared to the vivacity of the woman in front of me – full of details of child-rearing and home ownership, wry digs at married life, the odd reference to current events; and my mother's, on blue airmail paper stamped with the Queen's head, were just the same. They came of age in an era when 'letter-writing' was perhaps subject to more formal requirements than now.

And yet a friendship maintained by mail over that distance is a strange and touching thing. It requires a dogged faith in the strength of the original connection. In my mother's case, it also required a faith in the rightness of her decision to move, a conviction that her change of circumstance had been for the best. The pride of those letters!

I found a great cache of them after her death, the rough versions she kept stuffed in a drawer. Over the years, my mother documented for Joan my achievements at the tennis club, the swimming club, the exam hall. In 1997, in a fantastic bit of showmanship, she attributed my failure to secure a job at the *Wall Street Journal* to 'the state of the Asian economy'. I have no idea where she got that from. She described the garden, the wildlife, the cat, and the letters came back in kind, not just from Joan but from others, too. They contained an increasingly huge cast list of characters; pets, marriages, divorces, jobs, operations. 'Darling Joan,' read the letters. 'My darling Pauline', or, from Jennifer, 'Dearest Aunty Paul'.

Despite her best efforts, a note of regret occasionally crept into my mother's tone. 'And how is my old friend Danny?' she wrote to Joan once. I'd stopped short when I read this. 'Old friend' was a rare piece of sentiment. Danny, Joan's husband, was a young naval officer when they met. When she wrote, 'And how is my old friend Danny?' my mother hadn't seen him for forty years.

At some point the letters came in from adult children. 'Sorry to tell you . . .' 'Sorry to break the bad news . . .' 'Pauline, Mom was so very fond of you . . .' 'I still remember your working days with Mum and Lily Sachs, dear Gertie and Bubbles. Those were very happy days in Mum's life.' Whole lives conducted by letter.

'Well Paula I will say "*totsiens*" for now . . .'

'God bless you Paul and write again soon.'

'Well I suppose I must go now, hugs and kisses.'

'More and more as the years go by I see that friends are jewels . . .'

'And love, always, to you Paula.'

'God bless.'

It is my mother's lunch table. Cold things: ham, boiled eggs, mustard, tinned asparagus, sweetcorn heaped in a bowl. Joan shouts for Danny to come to the table. She pours herself a whisky. 'We like a drinky-poos, don't we, Roxy?' she says to the dog. We sit down to eat.

'Mayonnaise, Em? Mustard, Em? Pepper? More ham? Would you like a German biscuit?'

'WHAT ARE YOU DOING?' she shouts at Danny, who winks at me. His wife has caught him in the act of slipping food into his pocket.

'He keeps it in his bedside drawer for a snack,' says Joan. 'Sis, man. One day, I'm going to put a rat trap in there for him.'

After lunch, we repair to the lounge. Danny, shuffling papers, indicates he wants to show me something. Joan says, 'He's become very boring about that. HAVEN'T YOU, OLD MAN? Very boring.' Danny gracefully ignores her and points a finger at the page. It's some kind of legal document. Sotto voce his wife explains that he was assaulted in the street some time ago and has assembled a dossier on the assailant, a man called Strydom. 'Dutchy,' spits Danny and falls promptly asleep, his hearing aid whistling.

Joan and my mother were barely out of their teens when they met at the offices of Pilot Radio, formerly I. A. Abrahamson, an electronics company in central Johannesburg. They were both office juniors. That was the era when they would stay out all night drinking Pernod at somewhere called the 100 Club, going into work the next day with wet hair. They had afternoon tea at a place called the Florian, and somewhere else called the Flying Saucer. After a few years of commuting from their respective family homes, they took the plunge and rented a flat together in town, on Clarendon Circle.

With Danny still snoozing, Joan reaches down behind the coffee table and drags out a heavy wicker basket, stuffed with mementoes. 'If only you'd come earlier,' she says. 'I lost so much in the move. But let's see what we have here.' She starts rifling through papers, shifting about in her chair and talking excitedly.

'She had a very sharp tongue,' says Joan, 'I'm sure I don't need to tell you that.' She is still smarting from the time she walked into the flat, hair tightly curled having come from the hairdresser, and my mother, looking up, grinned at her friend and made the motion of a judge passing sentence, lowering his gavel. 'Oh, I was cross,' says Joan, and bursts out laughing. 'I suppose it did look like a wig.'

I laugh. Danny sleeps on.

I ask: was she ever a communist? Joan looks embarrassed and sips her whisky. 'Oh no, I don't think she'd have been involved in anything like that.'

'I thought, when she worked at the law firm . . .'

Although she gave politics as her reason for leaving, I never got much of a sense from my mother of the country's broader political life. For the first half of her childhood, they lived out in the sticks, and later, I suppose, they were wrapped up in their own drama. It was at the law firm that she first encountered white people, mainly Jewish immigrants from the Russian Caucasus, who sought actively to undermine the system. She was very drawn to it, she said, to the people and the cause. I remember how furious she was when Ian Botham and the England cricket team broke sanctions in the 1980s ('that English scum' were, I think, her exact words), but there were occasional cracks in her attitude. I have a vague memory of her dithering in the vegetable section of the supermarket, where as far as I recall we didn't boycott Cape apples. There was, I think, a lingering sense that, however awful it was, it was disloyal to bad-mouth her country behind its back; that it equated in some way with shame of the self. My mother wouldn't permit that.

Joan smiles at me. It was a big deal to my mother when she got the job at the law firm, she says. 'There was someone she admired very much there, I think?'

'Sima Sosnovik.'

'That's it.'

Joan roots around in the basket and pulls out a photo of my mother in Penelope Pitstop-style glasses, standing in front of a signpost for Land's End. In those early years in London, she went on a coach holiday to the West Country. She'd told me about it; it had been rather lonely, she'd said.

Joan digs in again and pulls out a Christmas card, which to my amazement is signed 'Marjorie', my mother's stepmother.

'Yes,' says Joan. She raises her eyebrows. 'She and I got along quite well. We stayed in touch for a while.'

There is a pause. I can't believe the mythical Marjorie is someone Joan actually knew. She tells me she met her when visiting my mother at home. There were children everywhere. Marjorie was polite. 'Have you seen any of them yet?' asks Joan.

'Tomorrow.'

Joan sighs. 'It was all very difficult. I understood that.' She looks away. I'm reluctant to push her, but I want her to say more. We sit in silence for a moment.

She ignites at a memory. 'Pauline only had one shirt. An absolute scandal. Every time she stayed overnight at our house she was up at dawn, scrubbing in the sink. It breaks my heart to think of it. I blamed Marjorie for that.'

I croak, 'Were you there when the trial collapsed?'

'I was.'

She shuts down. An angry pause. 'She had a nervous breakdown.' I have done the wrong thing. Joan looks straight ahead, still outraged on her friend's behalf and protective of her privacy, even in front of me. I want to know what she means by nervous breakdown; I want to know how my mother pieced herself together again, what she said to Joan and what Joan said to her. I want to know how she managed to assemble herself every morning before work, with all this in the background. But Joan is so livid I'm afraid to ask more.

We are quiet for a moment, and in the quiet I think Joan senses my need for her to come up with something momentous, some jewel-like word or gesture that will make sense of it all. 'I had a panic attack once,' says Joan finally, wearily. 'I rang Pauline in her flat. She had moved to her own bedsit by then. It wasn't much, but she was so proud of it. She took the morning off work and came straight round to see me.' Rather than consoling her friend, my mother gripped Joan by the elbow and frog-marched her to her office. The panic subsided and Joan did a day's work. 'She was the only one who knew what to do.' That's it? That's it.

She sighs. 'It's not for sissies, this life.'

Danny shakes awake, disrupting the dog and scaring the shit out of us. He gets up and disappears into the bedroom. 'What's the old fool up to now?' snaps Joan, and the tension evaporates. I get up to leave. At the door, Danny comes back and presses something into my palm: a gold and onyx signet ring. I give him a big hug and a kiss; Joan gives him a prod in the lower back. I think, 'And how is my old friend Danny?'

Joan remembered that visit to our house in the 1980s, when she was travelling around England with the friend she brought to lunch. Twenty years later, she grabs my hand in the doorway and with real anguish cries, 'Oh, why didn't I tell that silly woman to find something else to do with the day? We couldn't talk. After all that time and we couldn't talk!'

That night in the hotel I think, 'She should never have left.' This was her home, she should never have left. She made good friends in London, but there was no one like Joan, who knew her before the walls went up. Joan was someone from whom she had nothing to hide. She had a good job, her own flat and great friends. Why, when she'd worked so hard to establish herself, would she leave to start all over again?

It is only later that something occurs to me. This is after I have flown to the Cape to meet Denise, her other great friend from that era. In their early twenties, she and Denise lived a few miles apart and along the same bus route, about an hour south of the city. They travelled in to work together. There was some rivalry between Denise and Joan which, it amuses me to note, doesn't seem to have subsided much fifty years on. 'When Paula came back to visit us the first time,' Joan had said that afternoon, 'I took two days off work, whereas she had to fit in around Denise.' She sniffed. 'Paula always said that was the difference between us.'

Denise is softer than Joan. Her large blue eyes well up with tears several times. They used to go on holiday together, she says; once, they drove to the coast and laughed all the way there. Denise's mother was very fond of my mother; 'my other daughter', she called her, and once invited her to spend Christmas with them. On the way home from work, Denise got off the bus first and my mother travelled on to the more remote outpost where her family lived. 'It was a long walk in the dark from the bus stop to her home,' says Denise, 'and I used to worry for her. But, gee whiskers, she was always so cheerful.' I don't have the heart to interfere with this image; to ask Denise a lot of horrible questions about horrible events, although it's clear she knows there was something else going on. 'Spot of bother in Pauline's home, wasn't there?' Reg had said to his wife when they picked me up from the airport. 'That's right,' said Denise, looking pained, while jump jets in my brain fired up for take-off.

'Nasty business,' said Reg.

There was a suggestion that my mother had been interested in Denise's brother, a doctor, and despite being the 'other daughter', I sensed from a throwaway remark that the interest had been discouraged. In any case, when they were all in their mid-twenties, Joan married Danny and Denise married Reg. My mother didn't marry for another fifteen years. Her emigration, I had always thought, was a mixture of ambition and flight from disaster, but it seemed to me now there were other reasons, too. Sitting in her living room in Cape Town, Denise recalls my mother congratulating her on the engagement and saying sadly, 'Everything is going to change.'

'And I said to her, "No!"' says Denise, tears spilling down her cheeks. 'We'll be friends like we've always been. But we moved out of town and had the boys, and it never was the same. She was right.'

It was Denise who wrote to my mother, 'More and more as the years go by I see that friends are jewels . . .'

There was, I think, an element of pride in my mother's defection from her peer group. Her disinclination to marry must have felt like a failing. If she left, she could buy herself time. She could slip her generational bindings. She could do as she pleased and, win or lose, write home insisting she was having the best time in the world.

Figuring out how to be: Mum in England in the 1960s.

9

Gold Jewellery

She came to London knowing no one, clutching a single letter of introduction and a sheaf of references going back to her first job at sixteen. I found them after her death, stashed in the secret drawer. There was something terribly poignant about those papers. My mother had told the story of going to see *Dracula* at the cinema in Johannesburg and being so scared that, when she got home, she put bulbs of garlic around her bed before going to sleep that night. Hanging onto those references for forty years struck me as a similar gesture.

Unterhalter's Mattress Works had found her 'well above average' and expressed regret that their merger with the Edblo Bed Group had forced them to let her go. The *South African Mining Journal* recorded her cheerfulness and failure to take a single day's sick leave in a year's service. Wolpert and Abrahams went so far as to say that as well as being neat and conscientious, she had 'a very pleasant personality'.

The letter of introduction was from the head of the law firm. Mr Natie Werksman, of Werksman, Hyman, Barnett and Partners, wrote to his friend, Mr John Craven Esq. of the Anglo-African Shipping Company Ltd, sending his kindest regards to Mary and alerting his friend to the arrival on his shores of his strongest bookkeeper, whom he would consider it a favour if Mr Craven would assist. Two months later, Mr Craven sent a telegram from his office on Mincing Lane, London, to a temporary address at the Overseas Visitors Club. He thanked the young lady for her letter of 12 December. He sympathised with her predicament, but regretted he could offer no solution beyond suggesting she share a flat with a friend, as so many young people seemed to be doing these days. 'It is', he added, 'very thoughtful of you to let me know how you are getting on.'

The company that was so important to my mother was founded in 1917 by Natie Werksman, and by the time my mother joined in 1956 it was a booming practice on Johannesburg's Commissioner Street. Most of the staff were Jewish and, until she corrected them, assumed my mother had anglicised – or, rather, Dutchified – her name to DeKiewit from Dekowitz; it stuck as a nickname and she carried it with her to London and beyond. When my dad teasingly used it, it had always made her smile. These days, like most blue-chip firms in Johannesburg, Werksmans has moved out of the city centre to the suburbs. The old colleague of my mother's I had emailed from England had met me in the foyer there a day or so earlier and we had gone for lunch. As advertised, Alick was charming and energetic, with a friendly moustache and twinkly eyes. He was a little bemused by the meeting, but game and tremendously cheerful.

'I was a lowly clerk!' he said, as we ate shrimp and drank fizzy water in the sun. 'And a clerk in those days was like a salt miner! We were nobodies! I remember Pauline was always very generous. We couldn't believe she actually talked to us!'

He was the political one. He once visited Bram Fischer, the great anti-apartheid lawyer and activist who died in jail, and the day after got a call from the security forces, warning him off. He waitered at a function for eminent lawyers, where Joe Slovo stood up and addressed the room. Slovo was a familiar name in our house, the head of the South African Communist Party and, eventually, the only white man in Nelson Mandela's cabinet. He was a great hero of my mother's, as was Ruth First, his wife. 'Jews,' said Slovo, 'I'm disappointed in you. Compassion is one of the staples of our religion and you've put making money first.' Everyone laughed and shouted, 'Show us your red socks, Jo!' When Alick nervously poured him some wine, the great man said kindly, 'You must be a clerk, bloody useless at everything.'

I asked Alick if he remembered a Sima Sosnovik. 'Yes! Sima. In accounts. Very formidable.'

'My mother looked up to her a great deal.'

'Your mother was formidable, too,' he said.

I poured more water and picked at my shrimp. 'Were you aware of her being involved in any trouble at all?'

'What kind of trouble?'

'She was involved in a court case.'

'No.' Alick lifted his eyebrows. 'I don't remember anything of that nature.' There was an uncomfortable pause. 'What was it about?'

I hesitated. 'Domestic trouble.' I couldn't believe myself. I sounded like a bad public-information broadcast.

'No,' said Alick, and as with Joan, I sensed a subtle but distinct closing of generational ranks.

'The prosecutor's name was Britz.'

'Afrikaans,' he said. He didn't know a Britz but suggested I check with the Department of Justice.

There was a pause. Alick looked at me expectantly.

'I went to the national archive in Pretoria to find the transcript,' I said, 'but there was only stuff for the first trial. Nothing for the second.'

'Was the verdict at the High Court not guilty?' says Alick.

'Yes.'

'Well, that's why.'

I can't imagine how lonely that first year must have been, or what internal reckoning went on as my mother tried to rebuild herself. I imagine her a little like the Enigma machine, ticking over for months and years, trying every possible mathematical combination until she cracked a way to live. When I finally came to interview her friends from that era, they depicted her as someone who was very obviously crushed – 'Compressed,' said one, 'but not *de*pressed' – but managing. Typically, her own summary of herself in that period was: 'I was shy and it was holding me back so one day I decided not to be.'

After the week's accommodation in the hostel expired, she and some Australian nurses she'd befriended on the boat moved into a suite of bedsits. My mother's was on the top floor. When she became ill with flu that winter, they took turns, after their shifts, to run up and down the stairs with soup and oranges.

She moved again, this time to a rooming house in west London, where she met Bob, who would become a great friend and provide her with one of her favourite stories from that era. A few years later, my mother was at a dinner party at Bob and his partner Nick's flat, carrying plates through a narrow corridor from the dining room to the kitchen when she tripped on the step, smashing the plates and cutting her own throat. They rushed her round the corner to the Charing Cross Hospital, where she was stitched up – the surgeon told her she had missed her jugular by a hair's breadth – and she returned to the flat, where she insisted that everyone finish the dinner party.

She found a job on reception at a private members' club in Berkeley Square, then in a doctor's surgery, and then at the law offices where she met my dad. When I was a few years old, she decided to go back to work part-time, and found a job two towns over as a bookkeeper in a jewellery store.

It was a slightly larger town than our own, and I liked to go there with her in the school holidays, to walk around the shops, buy pens from the stationer's and look in at the pet store. She would give me a pound, and I would go to the bakery and buy a sausage roll for lunch. Sometimes, after she finished work, we got our hair cut at a place called Antoine's.

The jewellery store was in a row of shops next to a florist's and a dress-maker's. My mother's desk was at the back, in a windowless cubbyhole one step up from the open-plan room where the other bookkeeper worked. While she hammered at the adding machine, I sat on a three-legged stool by her side and tried to make words on the calculator.

It was a point of pride for my mother never to go on the shop floor; she entered through the garage and via a side door – the stage door, as she probably thought of it – and during tea breaks came out from the cubbyhole to socialise with colleagues.

There was Jackie, the sales assistant, who dyed her hair a

deep shade of red, which my mother called burgundy and disapproved of. There was Only Eileen ('Hello, dear, it's only Eileen,' said Only Eileen to her husband, Arthur, whom everyone knew to be unemployed and available during the day for pointless phone calls. Her titter would carry through the partition and make my mother pause at the adding machine.) And there was Ron, who owned the shop. He could usually be found at his desk, head bent over a dismantled watch, knees grazing the improvised weapon he kept under his desk. In thirty years in the jewellery trade he had never had the opportunity to use it. When Ron said, 'We've never had an intruder,' I couldn't help feeling the wistfulness in his tone.

I loved hanging out there. I loved going onto the shop floor – specifically, I loved the transition from the back of the store to the front. My mother told me not to make a nuisance of myself and to limit my trips to a couple per shift. I tried to make them last. While everything out back was grey and held together by staples, out front it was hot and red and gold, like a royal box at the theatre. It sizzled with light. I loved looking at the heavy chain-link necklaces nestling on red velvet; plump ring trays with diamond rings and semi-precious birthstones; antique silver, turning black from the base up like a creeping blush. Ron's wife, Connie, would tell me to choose something to take home from a revolving glass carousel. I chose a solid-silver squirrel, about three inches high. As I passed Ron, he winked and said to me, 'Terrible woman, my wife.'

It was a large part of my mother's life, this work, and she enjoyed it. She enjoyed her skirmishes with Ron, who, she said, needed taking down a peg or two. He had a friend, Bill, a mechanic who timed his daily appearances to coincide with the tea break, and my mother fought with him, too. 'I like a good ding-dong,' she said. My mother had no time for Bill, but she didn't like the way Ron treated him; it struck her as bullying. 'He is obeast,' said Ron nastily of his friend one day.

'Yes,' she said, 'he certainly is *obeast*, it must be terrible to be *obeast* like that. People who are *obeast* must have the most difficult time. Aren't you glad you're not *obeast*, Ron?'

It was clear to Ron my mother was labouring a point of some kind. The following day, he observed casually, 'Terrible thing, to be obese.'

Ron was an enthusiastic supporter of Mrs Thatcher, who, he said, was 'keeping Britain for the British'.

'Ronald, you are a total fascist,' said my mother, and they both looked delighted.

When my mother related these exchanges to my father, he said irritably, 'Why don't you leave? You don't have to work.'

'I suppose the job suits me,' she said. 'I am the only one who stands up to him!'

She had an idea of herself, in relation to Ron and the others, as outré, someone who could bandy about the word 'fascist', as well as 'transvestite' and 'egomaniac', and have a large as well as a small sense of what they meant; someone for whom it was weird to the point of parody to be working among these kooks in a dark cubbyhole in the sticks. That's why Jackie's burgundy hair annoyed her, I think; it was a rival critique.

It was true what she said to my father: the job did suit her. She loved the balanced account book, the neat row of columns. Ron was in awe of her perfectionism. He might, if he'd been the type to introspect, have been surprised that anyone should take such pains over the work they did for him. Now and then they went on valuations together, to big country houses where the valuables were laid out on the dining-room table for Ron to examine. These had the tenor of day trips, and my mother always returned from them in high spirits. Ron was impressive, then; focused, looking through his eyeglass at the hallmark on an egg cup, revealing as fake what was thought to be priceless. At these times she felt proud to be part of it, proud of his expertise. She said Ron could have been an engineer if he'd put his mind to it and hadn't been such an awkward customer.

Over the years, my mother collected a lot of nice pieces from the shop, 'my jewels', as she called them. She was particularly fond of gold – of old gold. It is a widely held view among jewellers that the only good gold is old gold. (There is a commensurate view, that all old gold is stolen gold, but that's another matter.) New gold has a blank, childish look to it and is too yellow, like cheap margarine. Old gold is greenish. The gold in our house was taken seriously, insured with typed-up valuations, elaborately hidden from burglars in those improvised safes, along with her other jewels. Garlic round the bed comes in many different forms.

She ended up working there for nineteen years. When she retired from the shop, Ron made a clock for her, with the twelve letters of her name where the numerals 1–12 should be. He had noticed a while back that they numbered the same. 'I'm terribly fond of him,' she said, 'in spite of everything.'

After she stopped working, my mother's energy levels seemed to droop. She tried to learn bridge, but it didn't take. She switched from yoga in the village hall to Pilates. She talked with great enthusiasm about the teacher, whom she sponsored to run the London marathon. She sat for hours by the window, looking out at the trees, drinking cider or ginger wine and shining ever so slightly, the way people do when they're a bit off-kilter, a few drinks in or at that point of exhaustion when, just before the final collapse, their back-up generator kicks in and for a short while they shine, so it seems, at a cellular level.

When the condolence letters came in, I hadn't thought of Ron for years. Writing wasn't his medium; my mother always mocked his poor spelling. He wrote, 'Paula was such a strong woman in body and mind – she was, I always thought, indestructible. Everything she ever did for us was always just so and it used to give her great satisfaction to find an error of one penny!! We had many laughs together and some very interesting conversations about British colonial policy. After Paula retired I continued to use the office but it was miserable without her and I soon ceased to use it.' Of all the letters we received, Ron's was the one that made me burst into tears. It struck me as the truest dedication, a tribute to her strength and humour, but also to her idea of a job well done: precision, order, a stand against the chaos.

By the sea, early eighties: Mum, me and my cousin Victoria (with pig tails).

10

Everything That Matters

My cousin pulls up outside the hotel in an off-white truck. 'Sorry I'm late,' she says, jumping down. 'I never come to this part of town.' She is in khaki shorts and shirt and Timberland-type boots. She looks at my feet. 'Are those the only shoes you have?'

We are going dog training, Victoria and I, en route to her house, where Fay, her mother, is waiting. My cousin runs the course and breeds and shows dogs with her husband, Tony, with whom she owns a successful veterinary practice. After her visit to England, she and I kept up a fitful correspondence through our teens and early twenties, friendly but fundamentally misaligned letters. All her news turned on rugged outdoor activities and animal husbandry; mine was bookish and indoors-based, and then glib and in the city. You could almost hear the wrinkle of dismay that each of our letters provoked in the other. Even when Victoria married and had children, it amused my mother to note that most of her niece's communications favoured the goings-on of the dogs and the horses. She thought her a fine, sensible girl. 'I thoroughly approve of Victoria,' she said. There was no higher praise.

I look at my cousin as we drive through the northern suburbs on our way out of town. Her hair is shorter and darker than it was twelve years ago, and what I took then for shyness now manifests as a kind of no-nonsense economy. I think with panic about the present I have in my bag for her. Pink champagne is probably an even worse crime than white footwear.

'Is it fun being a vet?' I ask.

She is so stern and substantial, I wonder what of our history Victoria knows. I have never thought about this before – what, if anything, the six of my mother's siblings who have children passed on to them. After all these years of avoidance and doubt, it is hard to believe there are people in the world who might have the same hang-ups I do.

I have had glancing contact with only one other cousin: Mike's son, Grant, for whom my mother had a soft spot. In the photos I have seen, he was the spitting image of his father, very South African-looking, with a wide face and bumpy nose – attractive and grinning. When I was thirteen, I had found a strange letter from him addressed to my mother. It was stuffed in a folder in the kitchen with all the supermarket coupons and clothing catalogues. In large schoolboy handwriting, my cousin detailed how hard he had been practising his cricket to get provincial colours, that he was learning the guitar and that he had passed a home-economics exam in which he cooked sago pudding with meringue topping and an egg custard. I couldn't see why Grant had written to her, nor why she had kept it from me. Then, at the bottom of the letter: 'Thank you Aunty Paula for sending me the Marlboro.'

I read this again and looked at the date; he was fifteen. My mother was buying cigarettes and sending them to my fifteen-year-old cousin who was still at school. His mother had added a note at the bottom: 'Paula you spoil that child, he was so excited to receive the cigs – no charges as it was 1kg.

He has sold a few boxes to his friends.' If anyone had offered me a cigarette, she would have killed them and burnt their body on the village green. If I had accepted and sold them on at a profit, there would have been a playground massacre. It was like stumbling on evidence of a life prior to witness protection, where the rules were completely different. I put the letter back where I'd found it and didn't mention it when my mother got home from work.

The dog place is in a field about an hour outside of town. My cousin gets out of the car, throws a whistle round her neck and calls to order a group of dog-owners milling around in the sun. She begins to put them through their paces. 'You should stay up here,' she says, turning to me and indicating the short, mown grass of the children's play area. She gives me a mildly satirical look, then plunges down the hill after the dogs and their owners, forcing me to run with her as a matter of pride. The dogs yelp with delight as the owners thrash their way through the shimmering grassland.

It ends, thank God. We climb back up to the top of the hill, where a small blonde child runs over and throws her arms round my cousin. Her daughter is a cheerful eight-year-old who has been dropped off by another mother. I have watched her grow up in photos sent by my cousin, most of them taken at dog trials, with the little girl clutching a rosette for her winning dog or with her arms wrapped round the animal's head. Now she takes a leash from the back of the truck and snaps it expertly onto a young, black Labrador. She is every bit as capable as her mother. The three of us get in the truck and start the drive home.

We had a lot of photos of Fay's three children in the house, two blonde-haired, one red. My mother approved of red-haired children; it was an *Anne of Green Gables* thing, I think, and the fact that before her own hair darkened it had, she insisted, been on the red side of blonde. In one of the photos, Fay's children were dressed in matching outfits. In another, the blond-haired boy was holding out a banana to feed a monkey in their garden. Fay's redhead was the sweetest-looking boy you ever saw, grinning in his school photo, and later, as a young man, standing haloed in sunlight. He grew up, got married and had children, and when he was killed in a car crash in the early 1990s, Fay rang my mother. I remember hovering in the hallway, alarmed by my mother's unnaturally quiet voice and the firm, soothing urgency of her tone. It was the parental voodoo that gets done in the face of a genuine emergency. When she got off the phone, she told me the news and, looking at me across a distance of several million miles, said brokenly, 'Fay's baby is dead. She needed her mother.'

After driving further out, we stop at a house set back from the road, surrounded on all sides by open country. I walk up the path behind my cousin. On the porch, a woman in brick-red culottes and a white shirt is sitting in a garden chair. My cousin greets her and disappears through the front door. My aunt stands up, visibly shaking, and takes two steps towards me. We hug and separate. A second passes as we rake each other's face for the missing third party. 'You don't look like Paula,' she says. She is half my mother's size, smaller, slighter, but otherwise similar. It is impossible to conflate her with the things I have read. We laugh nervously and go in.

My cousin is brisk and hospitable. She relieves me of the champagne and brings a tray of soft drinks into the lounge. Tony, her husband, is a large, attractive, affable man. He regards me with bemusement.

'So, your mom was Faith's sister?'

'Yes.'

'And' – he looks at his wife – 'you went to visit them in England?'

'Yes,' she says. 'Twice.'

My cousin is apologetic. 'I don't have much to do with the family,' she says, and it sounds like a coded directive to bugger off and find whatever it is I'm looking for elsewhere. The last time she saw any of her mother's siblings was when Doreen, our mothers' sister, visited five or so years earlier. Her hair was unkempt and streaming and she kept trying to pick up the toddler, who screamed. 'I didn't like it,' says my cousin, frowning. 'I didn't like it at all.'

Tony asks politely where I live. I tell him I have a flat in north London. This provokes a look of almost aggressive indifference. Most London flats, I add, are so small that when you throw a party in them it's like hanging out on a Tube train at rush hour. My cousin laughs – 'It sounds awful' – and we are suddenly on a friendlier footing.

Being a vet in these parts is not, I gather, a question of prescribing antidepressants to toy dogs or nursing pampered cats through cancer scares, but more one of keeping working animals maintained. From the way my cousin and her husband talk about it, it's a tough profession, more akin to farming. We go outside, and they give me a tour of the grounds. It is the first patch of earth I have seen that bears any resemblance to my mother's descriptions of this country: blazing sun on red soil; khaki foliage wavering behind a heat haze in the distance.

There is a peacock wandering around and dog pens for the breeding programme. The children skitter on the grass, fearless around the family's animals, particularly the Great Dane, a huge, dopey-looking creature, jogging around the garden like a miniature horse. My cousin's youngest is a little boy with almond-shaped eyes and long, fibrous lashes who comes up to the dog's chin. 'That child,' says my aunt, looking at her grandson in wonder. 'That child.'

I have brought the blue and yellow Arsenal away strip for him, and he puts it on and runs around in the sunshine squealing in delight. We spend the rest of the afternoon by the pool, watching the little girl do star jumps into the water.

As I leave, I pick her up and give her a hug. My cousin looks surprised. 'She doesn't normally let people do that,' she says. We regard each other with friendly amusement and, I think, a certain amount of respect. 'You can take your pink wine from the fridge. We won't drink it,' she says, but not unkindly. As she waves Fay and me off, I can guess what she's thinking: that whatever is going on between her mother and me, it's our business and she's glad to be out of it. I can't say I blame her.

My aunt's demeanour changes the second the car door slams. It is as if my cousin had been the adult, and in her absence, we become giddy as children. My aunt falls into a state of feverish reminiscence. 'Your mom –' she says, and we're off.

We are driving to my aunt's neighbourhood in the south of Johannesburg. It's a place I haven't heard of and can't even pronounce because, like a lot of Afrikaans, when pronounced correctly it sounds as if while saying it you are suppressing a powerful urge to vomit. It is early evening, the light a deep, burnt yellow and the road almost empty. While she drives, my aunt tells me a story from my mother's first trip back here, in 1967. My mother went to the store to buy beer, and when she got back to Fay's house, recounted how every car on the road had beeped its horn and waved at her. 'I'd forgotten how friendly South Africans are compared to the English,' she said, to which her sister, looking out of the window, replied drily, 'It might have something to do with the six-pack you left on your roof.'

'She told me that story, too!' I say. In my family-starved state, the sense of shared interest comes on like a head rush.

The house is in the U-bend of a cul-de-sac, in a quiet sub-urb made up mostly of bungalows. It is almost dark by the time we get there. My aunt presses a button and the electronic gates open and close behind us. She parks the car under a car-port alongside the house and we walk up the path. Through the gloom, I see a giant bird-feeder on the lawn.

Fay was characterised by my mother as the sensible one. She is the one who holds down a job and owns her own home. She has sensible children. She talks in a low, even, sensible voice and doesn't get ruffled. Which isn't to say she'll be put upon. She is tenacious like all of them, and when she gets go-ing on a grievance, she's like a dog with a bone. I have the same sense of her as one might have of a celebrity, long talked about and unnerving, finally, to meet. At the same time, I feel instinctively protective towards her. Unthinkingly, I have ab-sorbed my mother's position towards each of her siblings.

Fay shows me along a corridor to my room, where I dump

my bags, and we return to the lounge. I sit on a sofa in front of what looks like my aunt's version of The Shrine: endless framed photos of her children and grandchildren on a sideboard where a TV might be expected to stand. She disappears into the kitchen and comes back with a three-litre carton of white wine and two glasses.

There was a glaring omission in my mother's paperwork: no letters from Fay. I don't recall seeing a single one. There were plenty from her sister Doreen, several from her brother Steven, even a couple from her brother Tony, but none from her favourite sister. Now, after Fay hands me a full glass and settles on the sofa, she pulls out some keepsakes, and there's a letter my mother sent in 1976. 'The baby has all my faults,' I read, and I laugh. It's a backhanded compliment: my mother thought her faults a great deal more valuable than most people's virtues. Further down in the letter she complains of being without family support: 'I have no one to leave her with.' It was a refrain of my childhood, but I'm surprised to see it written here. There is no archness in the tone. Instead, there is something I never once heard in her: the ring of fresh vulnerability.

'She talked a lot about the wildlife, and weather,' I say. 'And all the jokes you used to play on each other.'

My aunts starts giggling. 'There was a maid called Flora.'

'Yes! I know about Flora!' I do not, as it turns out, know about Flora.

'She was mad,' says my aunt. 'She'd climb that peach tree in the yard and sit up there knitting. Poor Tony at the bottom. Her husband had run off and left her.' There was another chapter to the Flora story that my mother failed to mention and which my aunt now relates. Flora's insanity extended to waking the younger children in the middle of the night and ordering them out into the yard to 'harvest coffee beans' – acorns she'd buried in the dirt that afternoon. 'We went back into the kitchen and she brewed them up and tried to make us drink them,' says my aunt, 'before Mom woke up and took us back to bed.' She laughs. 'Totally mad!'

Attracting staff who weren't mad was difficult, she says, what with there being no money and the way her brothers would creep up behind them in the kitchen and drape a snake over their shoulders. Several already disturbed women had been dispatched, screaming, into the maize fields this way.

Fay digs around in the file of keepsakes and pulls out a photo to hand me. It's of a teenage girl in a uniform, leaning against a wall and looking cross.

'My sister Doreen,' she says.

'What's she wearing?'

'That was the uniform at the children's home.'

'What?'

Fay blinks at me, surprised.

'Where we were put, afterwards.'

I'm so taken aback I miss the cue. The conversation moves on.

My mother's portraits of her siblings stand up well against Fay's second opinion. Mike was the worst, with his practical jokes. One night, says my aunt, he burst into the girls' room, woke them up, put them in their school clothes and dragged them outside so they weren't late for school. While they stood in the dark, catching their breath, he broke it to them that it was eleven o'clock at night, lead them back into the house and gave them chocolate to say sorry. They all spent the night on the loo; it was a laxative.

Tony was a terror for different reasons, drinking and fighting and getting into trouble.

'My mother was fond of him,' I say.

Fay shakes her head and repeats what she said to me earlier. 'He means well. It just doesn't always come out right.'

Doreen and Fay are next to each other in age. They have been through phases of being close and phases of not speaking to each other. A few years earlier, when Doreen found herself between addresses, she moved into Fay's spare room, where she lay around smoking and sulking and running up a huge phone bill until, after a blazing row, Fay asked her to leave. For a while, she lived back in Hillbrow, an inner-city area where my mother too had once lived. The neighbourhood had changed since then. Doreen sent my mother a clipping from the local newspaper, illustrated with a photo taken during a shoot-out on her block in which a policeman crouched by a wall, gun raised, with arrows in red pen to indicate Doreen's door. Soon after that, she moved to the coast to be near Jason, her only son. She and Fay had made up and occasionally spoke on the phone.

'My mum said she was terrific fun, but you had to keep an eye on her,' I say.

'Ha,' snorts my aunt. 'That's an understatement.' Her sister is in her late fifties, as Fay is. She had been a model in her twenties and fancied herself as a femme fatale. She flirted with everyone – men, women, teenagers, geriatrics. Doreen once encouraged a teetotaller called Joyce to drink an entire bottle of sweet sherry, until Joyce vomited so copiously she threw up her own dentures, and having no money to replace them, had to work her shift as a cashier at a cinema toothless.

'Poor woman,' says Fay, and starts giggling. You were to lock up your spouse, if Doreen ever came round.

My aunt sobers. 'I sometimes wonder how much of Jimmy there is in her.'

And there it is; the taboo is broken. I don't miss it this time. 'What –?'

'I've never talked about it.'

'What, never?'

'Never. Not once.' My aunt says this proudly. She is trying to impress me, I think, which is to say, to impress my mother.

'And Victoria . . .?'

'Doesn't know anything.'

There is a long pause. My aunt looks at me. There is only one possible thing to say in the circumstances. I reach for her glass. 'Refill?'

The rest of what happens that night has had to be pieced together from notes I make a full two days later, when I can grip a pen again. The conversation circles around possible entry points. My aunt says her memory of events is very sketchy. She has a complete blank where the trial should have been.

'Nothing?'

'Nothing.'

The word she uses is 'psychopath'. 'He was a psychopath.' There are two memories on either side of the darkness. The first is of a knife at her throat; the second is of a scene from the children's home afterwards. Nothing in between.

It was her father holding the knife. The room was full

of children. It was somebody's birthday party, she can't remember whose. Her father burst into the room, found his daughter, and while mayhem ensued, threw her against the wall and put a knife to her throat. He threatened to kill her if she said anything against him.

'After that, I don't remember anything.'

I am too frightened and ashamed to tell her I have read the court papers. It feels like an obscenity – to know what she said in the witness stand when she herself can't remember.

'I . . . do you remember any of the . . .?'

My aunt's face shuts down. 'I don't remember it at all.'

I look at my aunt and see the brave, articulate twelve-year-old who described incident after incident of abuse to the court and then fended off her own father's questioning. Remembering on that occasion got her nowhere. She has every right to remember nothing.

My mother must have been devastated, I say, when the trial failed. I let my voice wobble, and alongside my aunt's perfect calm it sounds self-indulgent. She shrugs. 'Your mom tried. But he was cleverer.'

He left their sister Doreen alone, says Fay. I've never heard this before.

'Yes,' she says. And then she says, 'I think she was jealous.'

'What?'

'Yes.'

At the time I put this down to sibling warfare so vicious no insult is taboo. Later, I speak to a therapist, who tells me that molestation is often presented by the molester as a gift. In households that are violent it is usually the only affection on offer, and the child is made to believe it is a form, if not of love, then at least of selection. As we talk on, I find myself wondering where the eldest of my mother's brothers were, why they didn't do something, and then recant the thought guiltily. What could they do? They were children, too.

Instead, I say, 'It nearly killed my mother when she got news of Mike. It seemed so unfair.'

'What?'

'That he should die of a heart attack when he was so fit and healthy.'

Fay looks at me strangely. 'Who told you that? Mike drank himself to death.'

Fay was fifteen when my mother left. I had never thought about her departure from the perspective of the other side. Her claims to have led a central role in the lives of these people didn't square with their absence. Except that it did, I see now. There are people whom you can't be in a room with because their pain is your own. 'I was devastated when she left,' says Fay. 'But I understood why.'

I say something tactless then: that my mother didn't come back to visit for seven years because she 'didn't want to get sucked in'. This hangs in the air.

'I would never have left this country for personal reasons,' snaps my aunt. But she relents a minute later. There is a memory she has of her older sister from when they were living in De Deur, a town in the sticks to the south of Johannesburg. It's where my mother caught the bus every day with Denise. Their house was in the middle of nowhere, down a track and surrounded by grassland. On my mother's twenty-first birthday, the children clubbed together to buy her a present, a pair of pink silk pyjamas. She was so delighted, says Fay, she stripped off then and there, and putting them on, walked clean out of the house, the children running behind her, screaming with delight.

My aunt smiles. 'Everything that matters came from her.'

Here is my aunt's second memory, fading in from the black. It is of their father. After the trial, he came to visit Fay and her sisters at the children's home, as was his right. He had charmed the staff so thoroughly, she recalls, that they read his letters aloud to each other. Incredibly, Fay and her sisters were made to keep a photo of him by their beds.

Fay remembers so little, but she remembers this: her father walking towards her in the home, carrying a suitcase of clothes for her. She told him she didn't want them. He persisted, and again she said no. In a temper he slammed down the suitcase and left. It was the last time she ever saw him.

When I wake up the next morning, it's in a single bed beneath the window in my aunt's spare room. I lie there for as long as I can and then, bent double, shuffle to the bathroom. I look down at the sink and at my own hands, which, through the prism of my hangover, look utterly foreign to me. Still bent double, I walk down the hall, past the photo display and into the kitchen, where I look around in vain for something to heal me. The counters are fanatically orderly, everything put away in cupboards or Tupperware boxes. There is even a padlock on the washing machine, to stop the maid from using it.

Through the window I see my aunt pegging out washing. I step outside and feel the sun strike me like a skewer, inserted into my brain via the ear. The grass is as coarse as a doormat. I make it to the centre of the lawn, and kneeing Fay's dog away from my crotch, lie on the ground. My aunt pauses in her duties to peer down at me. The expression on her face makes the hair on my neck stand up: serene, detached, sympathetic to my mortal status in contrast to her god-like invincibility. One of my mother's textbook looks. Of course. I put my head on the lawn and prepare to die.

'Aren't you feeling rough?' I groan.

'No,' she says, as if to be hung-over is the most bizarre outcome of a night of heavy drinking. Fay laughs. 'I don't feel a thing.'

In all those hours of talk, we had not talked of Marjorie. Of everything, it feels like the most taboo subject. Fay might understandably feel vestiges of loyalty to her. 'Did your mother betray you?' is not a question I have the nerve or the heart to ask. She is the blank in the story. And yet she wasn't always a villain. I think of her listing in my mother's address book, under 'Mum'.

I am too frozen on Sunday to have much of a reaction to what my aunt told me beyond a sense of relief – that we are on the other side of something and have both survived – and gratitude for her generosity. I am almost embarrassed by the lurid nature of the memories. It's an inadequate response, but at some level all there can be is incredulity: who bursts into a kids' party and, in front of everyone, threatens to kill his own daughter with a knife? I mean, who *does* that? All those exaggerated looks of my mother's suddenly seem less theatrical than entirely proportionate.

That Sunday morning, I slowly recover and we have breakfast at the round dining-room table. My aunt is brisk and cheerful. 'Sit,' she says, and brings out coffee and yoghurt. When the phone rings, Fay picks up and, eyebrows shooting into her hairline, says, 'Yes, a very long time. Yes, she is. Hold on.' She holds out the phone and says, 'It's my brother Tony.'

On the way back from Joan's, I had asked the driver to take a detour to Tony's last known address, a house way out east where no one answered the door. I had torn a page from my notebook and scribbled a note saying I was Paula's daughter and he could catch me at Fay's over the weekend, and shoved it through the door. He had moved out, but one of his sons still lived there. On the phone now my uncle sounds hesitant and a little stunned – both that I have managed to find him and, even more amazingly, that despite being the Most Chaotic Member of the Family, he has managed to call me back. The distance covered in this one act is so vast that if he had been patched through from Mars, the surprise on both sides couldn't have been greater.

You'd think Tony's reputation for going off the rails would be meaningless in the context. But he went for it in such cinematic style it was almost conventional, an adherent to type that could unite everyone in their dismay. From what Fay has told me, the family's overriding image of Tony as a teenager is one of him completely drunk, driving a car across a maize field, but my mother remembered him as a little boy she felt guilty about. When he traipsed after her and Mike, they whipped around and told him to bugger off home. 'Shame, Tony,' she always said.

My uncle says the credits on his phone are low, but we can talk until they run out. 'It's strange to hear your voice,' I say. 'My mum was very fond of you.'

'I didn't think she noticed me,' says my uncle, gruffly.

'That's not true. She spoke of you often. She kept all your letters.'

By all, I mean two. The first was dated October 1960. I found it in the secret drawer, after her death, on two bits of paper torn from an exercise book. 'To dearest Pauline,' wrote the nineteen-year-old tearaway to his departing sister:

I want to take this last chance to wish you a pleasant journey and all the success of the future and I wish to thank you very clearly for all that you did and sacrificed for our sakes, whilst times were hard. Those are things of the past, but we will always remember and appreciate all that you did for us, the same way a child will come to its senses at some time, and start being thankful for all its mother has done. This has been a dream of yours for a long time and I'm so glad for your sake that it is actually coming true. We all hope you have a wonderful time. God bless you, Paul,

Tony.

The second arrived in the last year of my mother's life. 'I've had a letter from my brother Tony,' she said when I walked in the door. It was open on the kitchen table. I picked it up and turned it over. 'Where does it start?'

'It just starts.' She giggled. 'It's very peculiar. Read it to me.'

Finding a suitably ridiculous voice I began reading: 'And

God commanded the sun to rise and it sent out its searching rays . . .' I looked up.

'I told you,' said my mother.

I continued. '. . . And lo, the daylight revealed a pathetic conglomerate of rabble sheltering under a lone thorn tree.' My mother giggled again.

'Is that you, the pathetic conglomerate?'

'Who knows. It's very peculiar. He seems to have found the Lord.'

I read on. 'From the midst of them stood up a young maiden, tall and beautiful, she stretched and yawned, dusting herself off after a troublesome night. But nought' – I snorted – 'but nought could daunt the courage of this young maiden. She turned smiling at our mother and said –' I paused.

'Go on.'

'And said, "We may be poor but we sure see life."'

My mother grinned rather fixedly.

I continued: 'Though life dealt you many challenges and injustices not once did I detect any malice or selfishness. You remind me of the Bible's Ruth.'

Now she snorted, softly.

'My dearest sister,' I read. 'Thank you for not deserting us all when we were little. You are –'

In alarm I scanned quickly down the letter.

'Go on.'

'You are an old iron horse, a strong tower to which we could run and hide. Be not afraid, my sister. We shall not die but at the sound of the last trumpet soon the dead in Christ will rise. Be vigorous and be courageous. "You are precious to me says the Lord, I have called you by name and you are mine." Do not underestimate the power of God or for a single moment think that he does not know or care. "I know," says the Lord, "I know." And we love you too. Tony.'

Standing in our atheists' kitchen, I started to cry. My mother looked off into space. 'Shame, Tony,' she said. 'He always was full of nonsense.'

'I'm divorced from Liz, you know that?' says my uncle down the phone.

'I know.'

'She left me for a better man.'

Tony is now the oldest. I wonder if it is strange for him, but before we can talk any more, we are cut off as his phone credit expires.

'He's so sweet,' I say to his sister.

'Sweet? He's a devil. He put Liz through hell.'

'When did you last see him?'

'Oh, nineteen years ago.' I must look stunned because she bursts out laughing. The house where I dropped off the note was four miles away.

My mother's sister, Doreen.

11

Hearsay

It is a kind of joke within the family that Doreen, the Last White Woman of Hillbrow and second racketiest of the siblings after Tony, should be living in the genteelest part of the country, a resort on the Garden Route, that great magnet for the English and their impersonators. Doreen certainly found it funny. Not long after moving, she sent my mother a postcard of a fancy hotel on a cliff overlooking a magnificent stretch of coastline, where tea and a sandwich cost a day's wages.

'It's ever so posh,' she wrote. 'Everyone so proper and civilised. On entering I thought of you immediately, Paula, and how you would fit in so well there. I ordered a single G+T (the Queen Mum and her daughter Lizzie consume copious amounts of G+T, do they not?). All the staff are British.'

My mother rolled her eyes but she enjoyed these communications from her sister Doreen, filled as they were with a sense of their own consequence, going against the English style of concealing one's efforts. Doreen's letters came in, fourteen, fifteen, sixteen pages long, written entirely in capitals. 'Read it to me,' said my mother, and I would.

'HE LOVES ME HE SAYS, HE WILL POST MY RING TO ME HE SAYS, THERE IS NO OTHER HE SAYS. PAULA, AM I A BLOODY OLD FOOL?'

'AFTER MUCH DELIBERATION, I TOLD FAY WHAT I AM GOING TO TELL YOU, SOMETHING BARBARA TOLD ME . . .'

'I'M SORRY TO HAVE TO TELL YOU ALL THIS PAULA, BUT I FEEL YOU HAVE A RIGHT TO KNOW . . .'

'SHE DOES TELL GREAT AND DESTRUCTIVE LIES, IT'S A SICKENESS . . .'

'I DID TELL YOU WE WERE DIVORCED DIDN'T I?'

'I'VE GONE BLONDE PAULA. LIKE DOLLY PARTON SAYS IT TAKES A LOT OF MONEY TO LOOK THIS CHEAP.'

In the 1980s, Doreen went on a diet which involved eating only red foods and wrote to my mother to ask if she could source some red light bulbs for her in London; she thought the ambience might help and she couldn't find them in Johannesburg. In the mid-1990s, she joined the charismatic church. 'She probably fancies the pastor,' said my mother. Doreen even went through a phase of writing to me. I think she was Beatrice then. (One day out of the blue she changed her name to Beatrice, which she told everyone was to be pronounced the Italian way. For the benefit of her correspondents, she spelt it out phonetically: BE-A-TREECH-AY. Then one day, without comment, she reverted to Doreen.) For a while her letters had JESUS IS LORD scrawled all over the envelope.

To my mother she wrote: 'HOW I WOULD LOVE TO SEE YOU AGAIN. SO PAULA THINK ABOUT IT PLEASE.' My mother gave the appearance of thinking about it.

Before leaving Johannesburg for the coast, Doreen had fallen in love with the vet who had put her cat down. On an impulse one evening, she scraped together the airfare and flew from George to Jo'burg to have dinner with him. He was rather surprised, wrote my aunt to my mother, when she turned up unannounced at the clinic.

The town of George is in the western Cape, 600 miles south-west of Johannesburg and a two-hour flight over the heart of the country. After landing, I spend a pleasant hour on a bench in the sun, before a blue van pulls up and a man with long wavy hair and startling blue eyes gets out; then a woman with bleached-blonde hair, dark roots and incongruously black eyebrows.

She and I greet each other, while Jason, her son, stands, arms folded, regarding the scene with apparent amusement. Doreen had always been advertised as the great beauty of the family, alongside tough competition, and although she is small where my mother was tall, her face is a variation on the same theme: round chin, high cheekbones, dark eyes sizing me up. A woman who dislikes other women, I think, and dismiss the thought instantly. We hug and get in the van for the two-hour drive east.

While we drive, Jason tells me that he lives in a kind of hippy enclave halfway up a mountain, where he works as a freelance designer and artist. Doreen is an artist, too. I have one of her paintings at home. It's good, a portrait in oil of a black woman with a blue headdress, staring with a kind of cat-like superiority out of the canvas.

She is only living with her son while she sorts herself out, she says. She was a receptionist for years but is tired of working and, after getting a psychiatrist to sign off on her nervous breakdown, is now living on sickness benefit. Doreen summarises her life history in cycles of belief and disillusionment. She has been through Scientology, numerology, cosmology. She used to swear by Linda Goodman's *Sun Signs*. 'Oh, we had that in the house!' I say. It was a big yellow paperback of my mother's, well-thumbed. But when Linda Goodman fell into a diabetic coma, Doreen lost faith in her. 'So in tune with the spirits, but she didn't see it coming. I was disappointed.'

She sighs. She fell out with the charismatic church, too, where Pastor Harold proved a disappointment.

'Everyone does in the end,' says Doreen, and smiles.

An hour into the journey we pull over for my aunt and cousin to smoke. As we walk back to the van, she stops suddenly, letting Jason get ahead of us. My aunt turns to face me and, with proprietorial fierceness, says, 'How are you doing?' No one else on the trip has asked me so far, not for want of care, I think, but out of deference to something aloof in my attitude. I will not be consoled. My mother's sister, shorter than me by several inches, eyes straining to the point of bulbousness, throws her cigarette on the ground and continues to look at me.

'OK,' I say. 'It's a bit . . .'

She gives me a hug. In spite of all the warnings, I fall for her instantly.

An hour or so later, we pull off the road and drive down a track towards the beach. The bar is rustic, with wooden tables and benches, ill-fitting windows flung open to the salty, humid air. Outside, vegetation crawls through the sand in thick, arthritic tendrils.

'It's expensive,' says my aunt, glancing down at the cocktail menu.

'I'll pay,' I say instantly, and feel like an idiot. 'Since you're having me to stay.'

'No, you won't,' says my aunt.

'Yes, she will,' says Jason, and grins. 'Mom, it's ten rand to the pound.'

'Don't you bully my niece,' says Doreen, and exchanges looks with her son that I can't decipher.

We order blue cocktails with pineapple wedges on the rim and thick, cream-based drinks in tall glasses. We order rum and cokes and tequila chasers. Abruptly, my aunt gets up and goes to the loo. My cousin leans across the table over the litter of our drinking binge. 'Is it true your mom shot him?' he says.

'What?'

'I heard your mom shot him, the old man.'

I am so surprised I smile. 'No, I don't think – I haven't heard that.' But my mind flashes back to a memory: my mother standing in the garage getting something from the freezer, then turning to me and saying, 'I thought I might have to shoot my father.' When I didn't say anything, she laughed sheepishly and said, 'I shouldn't joke about these things to you. It isn't fair.'

My cousin leans back in his chair and grins lazily. 'That's what I heard.'

His mother, weaving slightly, returns from the bathroom and sits down heavily on the bench next to me. She looks from one of us to the other.

'How are you children getting on?' she says.

I have no idea what time we leave the bar. My cousin gets behind the wheel and we drive along the highway in the dark. My aunt wheedles and cajoles for him to stop at a shebeen to buy more drinks. 'No,' he says.

'I should have put you in an orphanage,' she snaps.

'Mom, you're not having any more. You know how hectic you get when you drink.'

Changing tactics, she says, in silky tones, 'Jay, my babes, come on, just one.' When he refuses her, she lapses into a sulky silence. After forty minutes, we pull off the road onto a badly surfaced track, climbing up a hill to the village. We seem to be going very fast, or else it's the effect of the darkness and alcohol and the way the van swerves this way and that to avoid potholes.

The house is isolated, a cabin with no immediate neighbours. We walk in, and my cousin introduces me to Snoopy, his dog, and gives me a duvet; I collapse onto the sofa and fall into a deep sleep.

When I wake the next morning, Snoopy is on my legs. I am conscious of my aunt moving around heavily in the kitchen. In the corner of my eye I see her white nightgown and blue leggings. The air is sour. I cough. Nothing. I make some more noise and eventually get up, walk to the kitchen and stand directly in her path. 'Hello.'

'Oh, hello,' she says vaguely. I put on my most obsequious face and ask if she slept well.

'Mmm-hmm.' She moves around me to make tea. There is no fridge. The milk and butter are kept on the counter and, thanks to my cousin's artisanal methods, don't spoil. There is a large bunch of bananas on the countertop too, unripe, rock-hard. 'You could kill someone with them,' I say without thinking, and my aunt looks at me sharply.

'Yes,' she says. She laughs suddenly. 'I thought that, too.'

We take our tea out onto the terrace, where the light is pearly, with magnificent views over the valley. At one end there is a defunct bath filled with plants; next to it, bongo drums. My aunt smokes a roll-up, sticks out her legs and flexes her feet inside giant woolly socks. It is tepid outside at this altitude in the morning.

I sense in my aunt a combination of affection and wariness and something like pride. She is thirteen years my mother's junior, a year younger than Fay. Despite her voraciousness, she has not been terribly lucky in love. My mother always said her sister's first marriage was tempestuous. She married again thirty years later, but it didn't last. Her most recent boyfriend, she tells me, was Czech. She used to steam open his mail to see if he was cheating on her.

Doreen asks about my life. I find myself deliberately editing things to match her bravado, pulling out my worst traits, boasting of my nastiest episodes. We get into a competitive exchange of horrible stories. I tell her how I once kicked a date out of my flat at 2 a.m. on the coldest night of the year. She tells me how she used to play people off against each other. I tell her how I love my friends but don't ever want someone clogging my life up at home. She says she would never seriously put herself out for the man in her life. We are competing, I understand, for the approval of a dead woman.

She tells me about her second husband, Roger, whom she met in a rough bar in Johannesburg. She sent us photos of him. He looked raddled and insane. My mother said, 'She's really done it this time.' The night of the wedding, says Doreen, he hit her so hard her head bounced off the wall.

'That was a mistake,' says my aunt.

We are both silenced for a moment by the unexpected honesty.

'And the vet?'

My aunt laughs. The family rumour is that the vet is gay, but before I can get there she says, 'I knew he was gay, of course I did.' She tosses her head. 'I was just doing it for the drama.'

She asks after Fay.

'She's good. We got horribly drunk. Or at least I did.'

My aunt says when she first moved to the coast, she and Fay used to have three-, four-, five-hour telephone conversations, intermittently telling each other to hold while they got up to refill their glasses. Eventually, Doreen moved to a place where there was only a payphone, to stop the 'addiction'.

'You know she saved me from drowning once?' she says.

'No?'

'Yes. When we were children. Shame, Fifi. Silly woman.'

My cousin ambles out onto the terrace in baggy pants and a T-shirt, scratching his head and sipping his tea. He looks at us with affable condescension. I feel my aunt's mood sour again.

'It's beautiful here,' I say to my cousin.

'Isn't it?'

'It's too far from town,' says his mother.

'Ma, it's the bush.'

'*Ja*, and you're bush pigs.'

To Doreen's amazement – 'He doesn't usually put himself out for people' – my cousin has organised a tourist itinerary for me. I hope she'll come too, but she seems to sink a little lower after lunch and says she is tired and wants to stay at home. We have a nice afternoon. My cousin is charming, good fun. We go dolphin-watching. He takes me hiking, on a trail that opens out with a spectacular view of the ocean. On the path back down, I jump ten feet in the air at a stick jutting out from the undergrowth.

'What did you see, Emma?' he says, grinning.

On the road back, we stop the van for a family of monkeys to cross.

My cousin has seen his share of the world: he's travelled in the US and Europe, worked in bars, lived abroad. Like his mother, he has the louche frankness of someone confident in his ability to charm. As we near home, he lightly, naturally brings up the family history.

'When did you find out?' I say.

'I don't know,' says my cousin, and is thoughtful. 'My mom must have told me when I was really young.' He shrugs. 'I seem always to have known.' For reasons of pride, I can't ask him to elaborate on the shooting. I can't have this kid (he is not a kid; he is thirty-eight, ten years older than me, but like his mother, seems essentially teenaged) tell me something like that about my own mother. I will have to find a grown-up to ask.

'Our grandfather sounded like quite a character,' he says.

'Yes.'

He looks at me slyly. 'You know Victoria doesn't know anything?'

Fay said this too, but it strikes me as absurd. There's more than one way of knowing a thing.

'Of course she does,' I say. 'Why do you think she doesn't let the family anywhere near her children?'

The house is dark when we get in. I call out a tentative hello. My aunt is in her room, sprawled on a coverless mattress, smoking. 'Hello!' I say again cheerfully, and she murmurs an acknowledgement.

I retreat down the corridor. In the lounge, I check the trap I set, an arrangement of the phone cord over my suitcase. Fay had warned me it wouldn't strike her sister as outrageous to go through my luggage. The trap is unsprung.

'Night!' I call guiltily. My aunt's bedroom door shuts.

But the next morning she is cheerful. After lunch with my cousin, my aunt and I lie out in the garden on a blanket in the sun. It is the most relaxed we've been together since my arrival.

'Isn't this cosy?' taunts Jason, when he walks past.

That evening, we get in the van and drive down the hill to see my mother and Doreen's brother, Steven, who lives and works in a craft centre on the outskirts of town. By a quirk of geography he and Doreen are the only two siblings now in regular contact. He is an artist, too, the second youngest of the siblings and the only one to have been to university. He has a degree in psychology, or, as Doreen puts it, 'is full of bullshit'. Before leaving the house, she said to me, 'I feel I must warn you about my brother's bullshit' – just as Fay had warned me about Doreen in advance.

In the van, my aunt suggests we stop in town to buy wine for the visit, and Jason yells at her. 'Mom, what's wrong with you? You know he struggles with that.'

I have brought a couple of Steven artefacts along with me in my bag: a photo of him aged twelve looking doubtfully into the camera in his scout uniform; and a letter he wrote to my mother in England, five or so years later, when he was doing his national service. The return address was a town called

Wonderboom. It's such a singular name, like a word invented to capture a contradictory state; horrifically beautiful, savagely great.

The angelic twelve-year-old is now a man in his mid-fifties, lean and rangy with a scraggly beard, smoke from his roll-up curling into the air as he sits in the craft centre's garden. At his feet are two enormous dogs, an Alsatian and a Rottweiler, whom he introduces as Jesse and Jezebel. Doreen greets him sardonically; Jason gives him a bear hug. My uncle looks at me intently for a long time. I look back at him. My mother would be amazed at her baby, I think.

In that boyhood letter, Steve told his sister he was enjoying reading a short story by Somerset Maugham, 'although it was somewhat difficult in places', and thanked her for sending the book to him. He wrote of how disappointed his mother was in the failure of Doreen and Fay's marriages – both of them under twenty-five at that stage.

'Every night,' he wrote, 'I watch the sun setting behind the hills which are part of the Magaliesberg mountain range. The crimson sunset makes the black silhouetted hills seem like erupting and somehow this indescribable beauty always makes me think of you.'

He wrote of how he wished his mother would come to life; it was painful to see her going on like this, 'day after day'. He said how nice it had been to see my mother on her recent trip back, but that he got the sense she had been disappointed in them all. He hoped this wasn't the case. It was signed, in boyish script, 'STEVE XXX'. Of all my mother's letters from that era, this was the most worn.

Doreen and Jason don't stay long. 'Look after her,' says my

aunt, as she bids her brother goodbye and gives him another of her indecipherable looks. I watch them leave with a pang, and my uncle and I adjourn to his hut by the water.

To people who have lived in genuinely wild places, this place, I'm sure, would be laughably tame. My mother told me that her brother had spent time, drifter-like, on a beach in Mozambique; that he had lived in thatched-roof houses where he leaned from the window and picked over-ripe fruit from the trees outside. She admired this wildness in him; it appealed to romantic ideas she had about free spirits, which is a bit unfair on Doreen, I think, since when she did the free-spirit thing everyone accused her of being a sponge and a layabout.

To Steven, this is practically an urban environment. To me, it's the incarnation of my mother's Deadly Wildlife of My Youth, a nightmare come to life. The toilet is down an overgrown path where snails crunch underfoot. The stoop of my uncle's hut opens onto a body of stagnant water, thick with plant life and where things click and slither in the gathering gloom. The mattress where I'll sleep is on the floor of a half-enclosed porch. My uncle says he will leave one of the dogs out with me overnight. He smiles. 'Jezebel has never let a snake get past her yet.'

Steve was the only sibling my mother said she thought would visit. 'I really thought he would,' she said. 'He had no ties.' She was very proud of him. While still practising as a psychologist, he had pioneered something called Wilderness Therapy, which involved taking teens who'd been traumatised by violence in the townships out into the bush. It was the subject of a TV documentary part-funded by Irish television. He sent my mother the newspaper clippings. She made me sit and read them. But it was as a baby she liked to remember him, with 'a soft little head that moved in and out when he breathed'.

We sit on the stoop, our backs against the wooden frame of the hut. My uncle smokes in the darkness.

'How are you bearing up?' he says.

'Fine!' I say.

I take out the letter he wrote to my mother from Wonderboom and hold it out, thinking he will be charmed and delighted, but my uncle waves it away. 'Ach,' he says. I stuff it back in my bag. I suppose even in the best of circumstances, no one wants to be greeted by the ghost of their own past.

'How much did your mom tell you?' he says.

'Some.'

'Did you talk to Fay and Doreen?'

'Fay yes, Doreen no. There wasn't time.'

Doreen is flippant, he says, Fay is in denial. Steve talks with a low, quiet intensity, which I imagine his sisters, when they're minded to, regard as self-importance. He never married, he says, because after seeing the way his elder brothers treated their families, he couldn't be sure he wouldn't go down the same road.

Sitting here in the muggy darkness, looking out at the water, it is easy to talk about difficult things – at least easier than it was in Fay's brightly lit lounge. There was something he used to dream about, says Steven. He supposes it is his worst memory. He was four years old and standing in a doorway, seeing his mother on the floor and his father kicking her. He dreamt about this scene over and over until, one night, he entered the scene as an adult, intervened and put a halt to the violence. The next day, says my uncle, 'I felt the most amazing sense of grace.'

He remembers a copper jug. It was hurled across the room by his mother and met its target, his father, with a satisfying crack, whereupon all hell broke loose, and when the law turned up, it was to a scene of such mystifying chaos that, forty years on, it is still the young policeman my uncle feels sorry for: his mother screaming, 'Arrest him!'; his father with blood pouring down his face; the children going berserk.

He lets out a sarcastic chuckle.

When his father couldn't get regular alcohol, he says, he drank methylated spirits strained through bread; when he was really desperate, he drank Old Spice. He injected morphine into his legs and between his toes. Sometimes, he sent one of the children out to the chemist's to buy 'carbon tetrachloride'. If the chemist asked why they needed it, he told them to say it was for polishing their shoes.

'You'd come home from school,' he says, 'never knowing who'd be alive or dead.'

In the midst of all this was family life. There was kindness there, too. He remembers his brother Mike, eleven years his senior, telling him if he planted a feather in the ground, an egg would grow out of it. Every day for a week, Steve planted feathers in the ground and, after he'd gone to bed, Mike crept out into the yard and buried an egg for his little brother to find the next day.

When Jimmy wasn't drunk, he says, he could be quite creative. He made a Christmas light show for them once, with coloured polythene. He wrote thousands of poems and did line drawings, which he kept in a map drawer. He lectured Steve once for saying something racist and told him the system was evil. But, as in all things, his position was unstable. My mother had told me once that when she was a teenager a black man had asked her out, and when her father got wind of it, he had gone out, found the man and beaten him half to death.

Steven remembers an ice-cream cake. It was one of his sisters' birthdays, and they were opening their presents – all the kids used to get presents if one of them had a birthday, he says. There was the cake, there were the children and there was his father bursting in. This is how he remembers it. His father charged across the room, grabbed his sister Fay by the hair, pinned her to the wall and put a knife to her throat. Then he left.

I am sitting very still. 'Can you hear more?' says my uncle.

'Yes.' I am grateful he has even asked this question; that someone, somewhere in all of this, has broken with my mother's hard line to allow for the possibility that these things are difficult to hear. That one is allowed to be hurt without betraying their strength.

My uncle remembers a trip to an air show. It was a family day out, with his father and two of his sisters. Halfway through the afternoon, his father disappeared with Fay, leaving Steve and his younger sister alone, shivering in their swimming costumes. They thought he had left them there for good and started panicking. Fay had been in her bathing suit, too; her clothes were in a heap on the floor. I had read about this in the trial papers. Of all the incidents in Fay's testimony, this one was the most shocking, taking place as it had on a family day out and in the midst of so many other families. Eventually, he and Fay reappeared, and when they got home, Fay went and told her mother, as she had on many previous occasions, but this time Marjorie fetched her children and ran from the house.

I have read about this in detail, and yet I realise I am desperate to hear someone say it out loud. No one ever says it out loud. Fay and I managed to spend seven hours talking without saying a single word to describe what was actually going on.

'What was happening?' I ask in a small voice.

My uncle looks at me incredulously. 'He was off assaulting her somewhere, in the bushes.'

This isn't good enough, this language. Steve seems to read my thoughts. He tells me a story about being in a library when he was young and seeing a book on the shelf with the word 'incest' in the title. A jolt went right through him. He wanted to take it out but was too embarrassed. It took him a very long time to be able to say it, he says.

Later, when he went to university and studied psychology, he read textbooks in which they called it seduction, not rape, because of the way in which the abuser managed to con the abused into feeling complicit; that they had 'allowed' it to happen.

He says, 'I would walk around the township and I could point them out, which girls had been abused. You could see it in them. There's a luminosity to incest. The taboo is so strong and the damage so great. Luminosity – do you understand? It travels across oceans and down generations. They shine with it.'

It is late now. My uncle lights the bug lamps. The dogs twitch and slumber. Beyond the edge of the stoop the world is in darkness.

My uncle asks if I know about the shooting.

'Not really,' I hedge. 'Jason mentioned something.'

My uncle rolls another cigarette. It happened in a mining community out west of Johannesburg, where they lived when Steve was very young. He thinks my mother and Marjorie planned it together – 'probably over a few drinks', he chuckles – to shoot Jimmy when he came in from work. My mother shut the children in one of the bedrooms and told them to stay put. When their father came home, Steven heard the gun fire six times. She was a terrible shot. One of the bullets penetrated the bedroom wall. Wherever the other five went, it wasn't where she intended. Their father was there the next day, and the day after that. He didn't go to the police.

I struggle to imagine this scene as anything but comic. We both laugh.

I ask if he knows anything about his father's conviction for murder. He turns to look at me in amazement.

'No?'

I tell him what I found in the archive; that he served part of a life sentence for killing an old man in the course of a robbery, a few years before my mother was born. He shakes his head. 'Shabby. If he'd robbed a bank, fair enough. Something ambitious. But this? An old man? It makes me sad.'

He remembers nothing very much of his father's later trials. Steve was too young to testify. I experience a strange shift in perspective: a realisation that the court case was not even remarkable, just another in the litany of failed attempts to get help.

Steve asks if I'm OK again, and after I reassure him that I am, we say goodnight and he retreats to his room at the back of the hut. I lie on my mattress at the front. For a good hour, the bug-killing candle crackles with dying insects. Jezebel sleeps on the floor by my side, and eventually I fall asleep, too, tense and exhausted.

I'm not sure what wakes me – the sound of her snarling or the sensation of something falling through the open window onto my feet. Instantly, the dog is up on her front legs, tail in the air, snarling in the direction of my lower legs in the sleeping bag.

It is too dark to see, but whatever it is, it is soft and pulpy and is making slow progress up my legs. I'm too scared to look. It stops at my knees. What's it doing? Checking its watch? When I am seconds away from having a heart attack, the weight suddenly shifts. Something plops onto the floor and I see a dark, hunchbacked shape which the dog nudges expertly, tenderly towards the door. It is a frog, that's all, flopping out onto the stoop and away into the night. I go back to sleep.

The next morning, my uncle drives me to the bus station. On the way, he tells me about something that happened in the street recently that struck him with the force of an exorcism. A 'demonic drunk guy' was staggering around, waving a knife and scaring the pedestrians. Steve, passing by, told him to stop it. The man lunged at Jezebel, and without hesitating, Steve knocked him out cold with the home-made Zulu fighting stick he happened to be carrying. It had the same effect as his action in the dream, when he stood between his mother and father.

We have forty minutes to kill, so we go into a diner by the bus bay. The waitress looks strained as she serves us, and by the time she brings out our food there are tears flowing down her cheeks. My uncle asks what's wrong, and with weird honesty she says her brother was found hanging that morning.

'I can't believe she came into work,' I say uselessly. When we leave, he gives her a big tip.

There is something my uncle would have liked to have shown me: a box of papers that were in his car that was recently stolen. It was memorabilia that included a lot of his father's line drawings and poems. They were very fine, he says, and I wish in that moment I could see them, too. Then, on the bus to Cape Town, I wonder why. Does it make my grandfather less monstrous that he drew a nice picture or was 'sensitive' to poetry?

We drive along the Garden Route through dusty Dutch towns and neon-green valleys. I think of my mother getting up from her chair and saying blithely every time, 'I will arise and go now / And go to Innisfree.' She always quoted that line from Yeats. 'Nine bean rows will I have there, a hive for the honey bee / And live alone in the bee-loud glade.' She was so tone deaf she even quoted poetry flat, and I would howl at her for killing it. We had the poem at her funeral. I think about it now in relation to her brother. She would be happy, I think, that Steve had found some kind of peace here, if that's what it was, sitting and smoking and looking out from the stoop. Then I think of the waitress at the diner, tears flowing down her cheeks. This fucking country.

I have another letter from Steve. He sent it to my mother after I left home, but before she was ill. She rang to tell me about it and, not having the patience to wait for me to come home, read it to me over the phone, her voice rising and falling with the same flat cadences she used to recite poetry. It was the only time, apart from after Mike's death, I heard her fighting to keep back tears.

My Beloved Sister, in a couple of months I will be a qualified psychotherapist and will set up my own practice next year – I have had a couple of dramatic years pioneering wilderness therapy and working with severely disturbed young people from the Katlehong township and squatter camps. All this is not to boast over my unexpected glory but to let you know that I have not been malingering here in Africa! In some strange alchemical fashion I have managed to wrestle something valuable out of my existence – I was discussing it recently with my therapy supervisor and she asked me how I accounted for it. Without hesitating I responded that it came from the magic of being a child at your beloved feet my sister. The therapist informed me that I had an obligation to let you know it – it isn't an obligation, but a supreme joy to thank you for those little veins of gold that finally wove their way into everything sacred in my life – Steven.

'Better than Manhattan's': the Johannesburg skyline.

12

Eloff Street on a Saturday Morning

'What does she do all day up there?' says Fay on the phone when I get back to Johannesburg.

'Smokes,' I say. 'Looks out of the window. She seems happy enough.'

'She thinks the world owes her a living. And Jason?'

'I liked him.'

'He charmed you.'

'I feel sorry for her,' says Fay.

'I feel sorry for her,' says Doreen airily, when I ring her to say I got home safely and have spoken to Fay. 'And Steven?'

'I liked him.'

'You were taken in by his bullshit.'

'I'll come back next time for longer.'

'Yes. Well.' She is suddenly distant. 'I must be going now. Give my regards to your father.'

My dad has found a buyer for the house, and I am going back to help with the last of the packing. After he picks me up from the airport, we drive through the suburbs of south London, and all the things I might tell him seem absurd to the point of embarrassing. I had a good flight, and by the way, did Mum ever mention to you she shot her dad?

These stories don't travel. Over the phone, I had told my dad some of what I had seen and heard, and he had said lots of sensible things that reassured me immensely. Being able to talk to him like this only emphasised the extraordinary nature of my mother's self-sufficiency: no parental safe harbour and all the experiences I found painful just hearing about, hers first-hand.

Still, there are limits to what can be said when you are accustomed to not saying things; when saying things has always been construed as a weakness.

'How is it going?' says my dad as we drive from the airport. London seems small and grey and wonderfully familiar.

'They're a pretty wacky bunch,' I say, and I laugh.

I am glad to be home, although it is not quite home any more. Something has happened to the house. While my mother was alive, it had looked like a complicated but more or less explicable system – not the crazy-person hoarding of newspapers. There was an architecture to it all, invisible to the naked eye, which with *noblesse oblige* my dad had been permitted to slot into for thirty years. Now, everything looked bizarre – fragments of a civilisation once infused with importance whose meaning had, somewhere along the line, become obscure.

My dad and I move through each room, bin bags in hand. By the door in the kitchen, an entire closet filled from floor to ceiling with plastic bags. In the drawer beneath the sink, hundreds of rubber bands she picked up in the street where the postman had dropped them. In the cupboards, endless margarine tubs, washed and neatly stacked for – what? A container crisis that never came?

My mother would have been brilliant in the war or in Mao's Great Leap Forward. She could've fulfilled scrap quotas for entire villages. Long before it was fashionable, she took up recycling and had a waste-disposal system in place that would, typically, find her fishing through the rubbish to pull out a pear core wrongly categorised by my father or me and which she would hold aloft between thumb and forefinger, to cry, 'Are you TRYING to starve my birds?' (vegetable matter went under the feeder, to supplement the seed ration).

'Don't interfere with my system!' she said, if you had the temerity to suggest throwing something away. The Smartie lids or ice-cream tubs; the iron-on patches and old bottles of sun cream. Shoe horns, hair clips, unidentified grey liquid. Langdale's scarlet food colouring. Askey's handy-pack wafers. A lifetime's supply of used envelopes. In a drinks cupboard in the living room we found a disturbing mandarin suspended in syrup like a foetus. Pipe cleaners; packets of sugar from Iberia, the national airline of Spain. Beads in a tin. Fucidin H cream 'for external use only'. Insect repellent, Cupradox dental sticks. Algipan balm, shower caps, cork mats, belts belts belts. An army sewing kit. A tiny bib, liberated from a pair of child's dungarees; cat collars, double-sided sticky pads, loose pyjama cords. Empty boxes of mint thins, still breathing the ghostly air of peppermint. Sacks of birdseed; something called bloodworms for the fish.

'Why are you writing it down?' says my dad, and I can't say. It looks like a life's work. He has been struggling alone with it for weeks and is at the slash-and-burn stage, but I am still dithering over every last item. My front pockets are stuffed with name tags she used to sew into my PE kit, even though she hated sewing. In my back pocket is a horrible porcelain magnet in the shape of a cat that my mother bought at a Christmas fair and stuck to the inside metal frame of the window in the kitchen. These things will end up in a storage unit in London, and for years I will pay through the nose to keep them there, in misguided observance of my mother's core principle: that there is nothing in life that can't be made use of.

In the kitchen, I reach up to a drawer above the stove and heave out a glass jar of desiccated coconut. My dad smiles. It would be taken out twice yearly when my mother made curry, hefted onto the table with a groan and her favourite catch-phrase: 'You could kill someone with that.' (People notwith-standing, she approved of things that exceeded their proper proportions.)

'How old is that stuff?' I would say.

'Old enough to be your mother.'

'I'm not eating it.'

'Nonsense.' From the back of the cupboard, poppadoms, which she transferred to the plate with a magician's sleight of hand.

'Let me see the packet.'

'Sit down.'

'I'm not eating till I see the packet.'

'For goodness' sake.'

'Excuse me' – this was the era when all my sentences began with 'excuse me' – 'best-before dates do exist for a reason, you know.'

'There's nothing wrong with it,' said my mother. When she said 'There's nothing wrong with it' before you'd even started eating, you knew you were in trouble. I made a dash for the cupboard.

'You're going to get such a slap in a minute.'

Next to a box of ice-cream wafers with an outdated typeface, the poppadom packet. 'For God's sake. Best before April 1976.' Something like that – I remember they predated our move to the house. She smiled in triumph.

'You wouldn't last five minutes in Africa.'

I hold it aloft, my dad opens the bin bag.

Most of the emotion generated by seeing the house go is used up by the sheer hard labour of dismantling it, hauling sacks of refuse into the car and out again at the municipal dump. We drive back and forth three times a day. For some reason, the more trivial the item, the harder it is to part with. The margarine tubs look particularly pitiful at the bottom of the skip. Discarding them feels like an assault on her dignity. After the last of it, the removal vans come to take what's left into storage, and with an overloaded car we drive into London. My dad is staying with a friend until the paperwork on the new house is finalised. After almost thirty years away, he is moving back to west London, where he and my mother started out together.

I see some of my friends in those weeks I am back. To those who ask, I talk about the trip in general terms. I talk about the weather and the price of the sushi. There are certain people I instinctively avoid, those who after my mother's death wanted nothing more than to stroke my arm and console me; who urged me to call them in the middle of the night. (I am not against this offer per se, only when it's used by those whose need to be confided in outweighs all other considerations.)

'I feel like I'm not hearing something?' says an intuitive friend at lunch, after I have fobbed him off with trivia about my trip. I hesitate. I don't want to embarrass him. The story makes too great a demand on the listener. I can't stand it, the look of embarrassment and panic on a person's face as they cast around for an appropriate response. Suddenly, I understand my mother's glibness, her insane giggle when she said, 'I thought I might have to shoot my father.' What *is* the right tone for that kind of statement?

With a lurch, I realise how afraid she must have been, that these things in her past would put her beyond reach of common understanding; that they would make her alien, even to me. I give a brief outline, and although he responds with measured incredulity, is sympathetic without being prurient or arm-stroking, afterwards I'm convinced it was cover for his real response: gut revulsion – towards my family and me for what happened in the first place, and towards me exclusively for the vulgarity of passing it on.

Something happens around then that, although I'm not willing to see it, drives home just how gripped I still am by my mother's orthodoxies. I interview an eminent movie star for my newspaper who, during the course of the interview, unexpectedly tells me that later in life she discovered that her mother, who had killed herself decades earlier, had been sexually abused as a child. 'They say you inherit the guilt,' said the actor, 'but what you really inherit is the silence.' I am so horrified that instead of following it up, I panic and change the subject. Although this aspect of her background hasn't been reported on before, I do not include the line in the piece.

On a rainy March evening, my dad drives me once again to the airport. After the odd, transitory weeks in London, I find I am excited to be going back, to have something known to go back to. Now I have an outline of the story, I want to colour it in.

'Be careful,' says my dad.

'I will.'

'If you want me to come out there, you'll let me know.'

'I will.'

'Mum wouldn't want this to take over your life.'

'It isn't. Honestly.'

'Bye, baby.'

'Bye.'

It is different this time. I land in bright sunshine. Instead of going to a hotel, a car takes me to a house in a street of other houses, with a pavement you can walk down to a strip of bars and restaurants. Until I find somewhere more permanent to live, I am staying in a guesthouse, known to me through the informal network of journalists that in my previously dingy state I hadn't felt fit to exploit. (Journalists will, generally speaking, help each other out, if it doesn't compromise their own interests too much and if the help can be administered over drinks in the bar.)

The first night back, there is a drinks party in the garden of the guesthouse. In the balmy twilight air, I sit and drink white wine and feel my shoulders relax. The company is familiar, re-assuring and fairly representative of the neighbourhood: two

Australian medics on their electives; two British journalists who live in Johannesburg and drop in every night for a drink; and an American called Alan, who holds out his hand to introduce himself.

'I work in disaster relief,' he says. One of the journalists catches my eye and swiftly drops it. 'That's my day job. But really I'm an unfunctioning artist. Notice how I say unfunctioning, not dysfunctional.' He raises his eyebrows, and I must look blank because he gives a small laugh and says, 'Don't make the mistake of taking me seriously. I have a certain humour not everybody gets.'

Alan is staying in the guesthouse, too. The night before, he says, he went to the bathroom in the middle of the night and, yanking what he thought was the cord for the light switch, summoned an armed-response unit to the door. It is the second time he has done this in a week. I ask what he is in Johannesburg for, and he says he is here on his own time, to investigate the 'frontiers of post-racist society'.

The Australians stare.

'Yes,' says Alan. 'When I lived in San Francisco, I got up in PR disguise sometimes, to see what it was like. You know, to be targeted by racists.'

'Why would racists target you for being in public relations?' asks one of the journalists politely.

Alan closes his eyes. 'PR as in Puerto Rican,' he says. 'Another oppressed people.'

In the days that follow, I do all the things I didn't do last time, things that will ground me, I think, as I travel deeper into my mother's history. I buy a local mobile phone. I figure out where to buy groceries. I walk around the neighbourhood, the sun on my back like a hand, pushing. Up the hill, past the bead shop, past the paper shop selling weird vegetables in a box by the door, under the covered walkway, where hawkers sell beaded wire animals and other knick-knacks laid out on bright fabric. In the street, men in neon vests mill about keeping an eye on the cars. They are paid by local businesses to deter thieves, but after a couple of days of waving madly at them each time I pass, I suspect their deeper purpose is to relieve Western visitors of an urgent need to be nice to a black South African. One of them, Joseph, spends most of the day asleep under a newspaper on a derelict porch, knocked out by the sheer force of foreign goodwill.

A man standing in front of the second-hand bookshop sees me coming and retreats, slightly, into the shade of the door. I had gone there on my first morning, and after buying an ancient, liver-spotted copy of Rilke – 'Lord, it is time / The summer was so great' – held out my hand across the counter.

'Hello!' I said. The man was white, with thick milk-bottle glasses and a lime-green shirt. He took the full force of all the pent-up condescension left over from my exchange with the car guards. Reluctantly, he shook my hand and introduced himself as Mervyn. Mervyn, I decided, was quirky and fun.

Past the sushi restaurant, the gallery with the piece of driftwood arranged artfully in the window, the brunch place that serves two types of tapenade. At the end of the street is a shopping arcade, laid out in a horseshoe around a car park. There is a telecoms provider, a supermarket, a travel agent and a place on the corner where chickens turn, bumper to bumper, on a slowly revolving spit. The whole complex could be in a regional English town were it not for the foliage – army-surplus brown – and the heat, rising from the parked cars in broad, muscular waves. Walking through it is like pushing your face into a substance which, for a split second, continues to hold its impression.

It is a truism of South Africa that you are more likely to be killed in a car than by a murderer (although if you are murdered, it is most likely to be by someone you know. Johannesburg is dangerous, but it's not immune to the law of averages). I hire a car and start tentatively to explore the quiet roads around the neighbourhood. Studying the map, there are street names that strike me at the level of myth come to life. After forty years in England, my mother's references were still Johannesburg-based, so that in a crowded street, while you might say, 'It's like Piccadilly Circus,' or 'It's like Grand Central Station,' my mother would say, 'It's like Eloff Street on a Saturday morning.' There it was, in the grid of downtown Johannesburg: Eloff, between Joubert and von Brandis, as famous in our house as Oxford Street.

From the court papers, I have a list of my mother's old addresses, where she and the family lived during her teens and early twenties. Most of them are within a couple of hours' drive from the city, at the outer edges of metropolitan Johannesburg and in the rural communities beyond. I have an idea that, when I've acclimatised to the roads, I will drive to these places. This seems important, although I have no idea what I'll do when I get there. But I have to do something, and what else is there to do?

One of the first major drives I undertake is to Fay's house, five miles south-east down a six-lane motorway, taxi minivans weaving in and out with terrifying speed and imprecision. Past the South African Broadcasting Company, a black tower not entirely stripped of its sinister apartheid-era associations. Past the mine dumps that stand along the southern edge of the freeway, flecks of gold in them catching the sun. I hear they are being re-mined; it turns out too much of value was thrown away. Past the turn-off for Orlando East and Baragwanath hospital, the biggest hospital in the southern hemisphere. There is a sense of the air opening up and the sky expanding and getting lighter, fading to the shimmering white of real heat and the crushing weight of boundless space. Past Soweto on the right and east for two miles along Columbine. At the side of the road the grass is knee-high and waving. The buildings thin out, the pools disappear, the edges of things waver as the heat roars in. Another country begins.

My aunt is standing at the gate, waiting for me, a slim figure in the shade of a tree. 'Hello, my darling,' she says. Hello. Hello.

Although it is only two miles away, Fay has never been to Soweto – 'I can't believe it, it seems ridiculous' – and I am keen to see it. One morning, we are met at her house by an elderly black man called Opa, or rather, a man trading under the name of Opa, the Dutch word for 'grandpa' and the most unthreatening name possible for a black man's professional dealings with white people. Opa will be our tour guide for the day. We get in his car for the fifteen-minute journey.

Soweto is the subject of endless chirpy editorials in the local press about the rise of the black middle class, epitomised by a new shopping centre and red-brick homes with cars parked out front. This is not what tourists come to see. We drive through the fancier area quickly, Opa pausing to point out Winnie Mandela's house, which has a guard out front and satellite equipment on the roof, before speeding up again to reach the top of the hill. From here, the majority of the township can be viewed: an expanse of shanties in every direction as far as the eye can see. On the map it appears as a blank space.

'When the – how can I put this? – white people came to South Africa,' says Opa, 'they encountered the – how can I put this? – black people.' As delicately as he can, he condenses the last hundred years of South African history as if it involved no human agency whatsoever but was merely a series of ahistorical forces bearing down on the country like weather. We pull in at some gift shops opposite the Baragwanath hospital, where the minivans terminate, throwing up dust and conking out at wild angles to each other. I buy some beads. My aunt seems pleased. Opa explains that lots of people mistakenly think the word 'Baragwanath' comes from the Zulu, but in fact it's English. Many of the early immigrants who came to work in the mines were from Cornwall, he says; Baragwanath was one of them. For lunch, Opa takes us to a dark, busy restaurant in Soweto called Wandies. We have green beans and chicken, and while Opa lingers over the buffet, my aunt and I sit opposite each other and talk about our day.

'This has been just so good,' she says. 'So interesting. Opa is wonderful.'

'Yes,' I say. I am happy to be here with her.

Over the next few weeks, we go on many more excursions. We see England play South Africa at cricket. I collect her in the car and bring her back to my neighbourhood for dinner at a Thai restaurant. We go to see a show, a *Lion King* derivative called *African Footprint*. My aunt is a bookkeeper at a large company, and I go into work with her. She introduces me to her colleagues, and we spend a pleasant morning hanging out in her office. One evening, after spending the day together, she asks me to give Maria, her maid, a lift to the bus station in town. I have chatted quite a bit to Maria at my aunt's house. She has told me about her teenage son. When Maria laughs, she holds up a hand to cover her mouth. By the time we get into the city, it is dusk. The bus station is in a very dark street, crowds of people moving about in the shadows, and I am nervous. 'Will you be OK?' I ask as Maria gets out. She looks at me severely, tightening the belt on her jacket. 'Of course,' she says, and I see it in her face: 'Oh, you people have no idea.'

At lunch one weekend in a shopping mall in Meyersdaal, I pull out some papers and slide them across the table. We are eating fish from the Klip River and drinking white wine. In the background, motor racing whines on the TV. Like Steven, Fay hadn't known anything about her father's murder conviction. I tell her about it now. My aunt doesn't react immediately.

'I'm glad,' she says finally.

I'm puzzled. 'I don't understand?' I say.

'I'm glad he went to prison somewhere along the line.'

I turn over the top sheet of the paperwork. She glances down. 'Yes,' she says. 'That's his signature.' She reads on, through the judge's remarks to the sentencing. 'Hard labour,' she says. 'Good.'

The towns of my mother's youth sound harsh to the ear and are no less severe in reality. One day, I drive two hours south on the motorway and pull off onto a small, dusty regional road. I am looking for the faintest hairline on the map, a track that runs through open country and which, according to an address I have from the court papers, leads to the house where my mother walked out into the fields one morning in a pair of pink silk pyjamas. After missing it several times, I turn onto an unsurfaced road that runs through grassland as high as the roof of the car. In a ghost story, after the engine died down I would see a flash of pink silk in the tall yellow grass and a second later hear laughter. But there are only the red roofs of a few mean scattered houses, with faded yellow walls and grilles on the windows. There are small purple and white flowers in the grass. I return to the main road and pull into the settlement's only sign of life, a liquor store, where men hang around the door in oil-stained dungarees. On the horizon is a line of trees, leaves streaming, sunlight gauzy behind them. It could be northern France, I think, and then one of the men shambles over to start a conversation, and I get in the car and leave.

Vereeniging is full of funeral parlours and pawn shops. Outside the art-deco station an old steam engine stands, of the kind, I suppose, that my grandfather once drove. I stand on the bridge, looking down the tracks towards Johannesburg, the heat rising from the concrete like flood water. Witpoortjie, in the district of Roodepoort, where the family lived at the time my grandfather was arrested, is gaudy and chaotic, people spilling out into the street from the pavement. Meyerton, Zwartkoppies – all flat, sullen, rebuked. I don't always get out of the car. In a quiet street in a town fifteen miles west of Johannesburg I find the magistrates' court where the first hearing took place, a squat municipal building behind razor wire. I stand there and wonder what I'm supposed to do next. I have always thought that by fixing things exactly, one widens their possibility; or, in this case, lessens their power to torment. But driving to these places and just standing and looking seems woefully inadequate. I reach for some other ritual – laying flowers? Saying prayers? – and find nothing. At the end of all those, hot, tiring afternoons, I wonder what the point has been. Perhaps it is this: that as long as there are places to visit and things to find out, my mother and I still exist in the present; are engaged, still, in conversation. And then I think of the places I can't go.

'Paula never talked about those years,' Fay had said over lunch at Meyersdaal, meaning the years after my grandmother's death and before Jimmy remarried, when my mother lived alone with him. 'I should have . . .' Her expression was beseeching. I smiled. It always comes back to this, I think, one way or another. I should have asked about the past. The cowardice was mine. It reminds me of that bit in *Superman* when the dad keels over in the dust in the barn and dies, and the Superchild looks up at the sky in the direction of his Kryptonic mother and howls, 'With all my powers I couldn't save him.' With all my powers of education, all my competence and good taste; with my life-saving certificate and my grade-five piano; with my equity and insurance; with all that *perspective*, through which almost anything can be rationalised away or excused; with the invincibility that comes, simply, from having been loved, I couldn't ask a simple question, because I was frightened the answer would destroy me. My aunt said, 'When I think of those years and what she –' Ha. Well. We both had to smile then, since we knew from long experience that such imaginings are impossible. The airbag inflates. There is no seeing around it.

Most of the people I meet in those early days are either journalists or aid workers, people who come to South Africa determined to do their own laundry and within a week submit to the logic that having domestic staff helps the local economy.

Dora does my laundry.

The journalists look down on the aid workers for their worthiness. The aid workers look down on the journalists for their loucheness. The domestic staff look down on all of us, I imagine, as we cringe and dither in the face of their duties, and in one of eleven official languages think: pricks.

A new friend, a South African journalist, is going to Canada for a few months and offers to let me house-sit in her absence; a vacant property is vulnerable to invasion. It's a beautiful two-storey house, with a deck overlooking a lush garden running down to a pool. *Architectural Digest* are always bugging her to let them feature it, she says, and she always declines on the assumption it just serves as an advertisement to burglars. I won't be wholly alone there. For a while, the upstairs bedroom is rented out to a photographer for the Agence France-Presse, who is away most of the time covering atrocities in Zimbabwe. And while the high, wide garden wall is being rebuilt, a man called Albert will stay in the pool house at night.

Over the next few weeks, a pattern establishes itself. In the mornings, I sit in the pool house rearranging chapter headings for the book I'm supposed to be writing. There is a chair, a desk and a large purple exercise ball. When I'm not rearranging chapter headings or staring out at the pool, I'm wondering whether or not to use the exercise ball.

Mid-morning, I run up the path to make tea. The path is rough underfoot. Ferns brush my legs with what feels like a retractable groping action. Lizards scatter on the low garden wall. My mother used to say that if you dropped a stone on a lizard's tail, it would fall off and grow another. We once spent an entire week on vacation in Majorca chasing them to try to put this to the test, but they were always too fast for us.

In the kitchen the floor is tiled and cool. The tea is clear and red with a picture of a tree on the packet, bent-limbed like a broken umbrella, like a symbol of the broken heart of Africa, like . . . Dora comes in just then.

'Did you work this morning?' she says. She flicks the mop at my feet. That woman sees straight through me.

For lunch, I go to a place called Ant's, which used to be a weapons and ammo store and is now a coffee shop serving cappuccino and the two types of tapenade. Ant himself is a bearded Afrikaner, very dyslexic, who is hoping to collaborate with someone on his memoirs and who once threatened to extinguish a rival snack outlet for what he said was their plagiarism of his meat platter. I find a municipal tennis club and twice a week have coaching with Therese, 'South Africa's number three', who makes me run back and forth in ninety-degree heat as retribution for the Boer War.

When I walk back to the house, I pass Siya, one of a group of itinerant men who seem to live in a park at the end of my street. Siya is young and agile, with dreadlocks and a big, coloured beanie. He is the most friendly and sometimes falls into step with me. We walk in dappled sunlight down the middle of the street, partly from pleasure, partly from habit; you are advised not to walk too close to the edge of the park where Siya and his friends disappear to at night.

He tells me he has come from the Transkei to make his fortune. He says this with an ironic smile that acknowledges the fact he is living in a park. He owns a guitar and has started song-writing. He asks me to let him know if I hear of any jobs or empty garages going.

'I could be your nightwatchman,' he says. I tell him about Albert. Siya nods thoughtfully.

I offer him part of the Chelsea bun I am eating, and Siya takes it and looks around as if wanting to return the gesture. He points to a house with a sign on its gate that reads, 'Beware: this property is protected by live snakes'.

'See that house?' he says.

'Yes.'

'There are no snakes in that house.'

We are at my front door. 'See ya, Siya,' I say, and he wheels around grinning and heads back to the park.

In the evening there are drinks in the garden of the guesthouse, or else I drive to the cinema in one of the malls. Compared to London, the city is easy to get around, nowhere more than forty-five minutes from anywhere else and the roads wide and straight. The malls are American in style and full of affluent teenagers. Nobody who doesn't have to drives through the old city centre at night.

I go to see Joan and Danny again. 'Man, you've hardly eaten,' she says. 'Pickled onion, Em? Avocado, Em? Shame, the man said they'd be ripe today, they're not ripe. Piece of Christmas cake, Em? Old Pa, what do you want?'

One night, I am invited to a party at the house of an English baroness. The baroness isn't in residence but has lent her house to an English friend for the summer. A journalist pal drives me there, to a neighbourhood forty minutes away, in the north of the city. 'Howzit, baba,' he says to the guard in the guard hut – showing off, I think – and the man waves us through.

When they colonise the moon, the developments will look like this, a series of units within the silent acres, devoid of life as if the air was unbreathable. The party is just getting under way as we arrive. In the back garden by the pool there is a barbecue presided over by South African men holding beer cans; a little way off, English men regard them with a mixture of superiority and envy. There is no denying it: South Africans have a natural authority with a pair of meat tongs.

A man asks me why I am in South Africa. 'Escaping the English winter,' I say. He points to a man in a black V-neck sweater standing alone in the corner and mouths, 'CIA.'

I don't know it then, that everyone on this circuit suspects everyone else of being a spy; that people who are not spies pretend to be spies; that one is to be alert at all times for suspicious behaviour, to store away and thrill oneself with in duller times to come.

Later on that evening, with pitch-perfect post-colonial

condescension, the spy explains to me that while in global terms South Africa is not terribly influential, it has 'strategic importance within the region'. I nod vigorously.

There are a lot of aid workers here, mainly Scandinavian and British women in firm sports bras who dash around town alleviating suffering as you or I might wipe down a table.

I am introduced to an Australian journalist called Michelle, who hands me a business card featuring an underwater photo of a shark and the words, 'Michelle Bovine, journalist, General News, Foreign Affairs, Marine Science'. She is a minor celebrity at the party by virtue of having moved into a house where the Vaulting Wanker had last been sighted. This, it is explained to me, is a neighbourhood streaker whose routine it is to run across people's gardens, masturbate in the general direction of their house and then vault over the fence into the night. One of his early victims had been the daughter of a prominent anti-apartheid campaigner murdered by the security police. When news of the Vaulting Wanker reached the papers, the man who murdered her father read about it and, wanting to atone, got a message to her from his prison cell that he would have his people look into it and, if she wished, make sure the Vaulting Wanker was quietly eliminated. She declined his kind offer. I sometimes think this story contains everything you need to know about South Africa.

Michelle, who had not seen the Wanker herself but had at least gazed upon the ground where he had wanked, offers to give me a lift home. A large, drunk man grabs us as we leave and reminds us to run through all the traffic lights. 'Will they be all right?' he says to no one in particular and crumples into the wall.

In the car, Michelle tells me she has come to South Africa to make her name as a war reporter.

'Which war?' I say.

She frowns. 'Well, in any case, what I really want is to get into television.'

I am going about this perversely, I know. I am here for a maximum of six months, and yet insist on this charade of spending the first five hours of every day at my desk in the pool house. Fay thinks I am crazy. She asks if I want to go on safari with her, but I can't face the 4 a.m. start. I can't face anything much beyond the pool house each morning. I tell my aunt I have work to do. I tell myself the same thing. I call the Department of Justice and have them fax me a list of prosecutors called Britz, past and present. Half are dead; the rest, when I call, turn out not to be relevant. From the court papers I have the name of the arresting officer: a Sergeant Nel. You may as well look for a Smith in the South African phone book, but I ring a dozen or so Nels, to no avail.

I have, I realise, become blasé about risk. It seems to me statistically improbable that anything will happen to me in this country, where everything bad that can happen in a family has pretty much happened. At night, I lie in my ground-floor room and look up at the narrow window beneath the ceiling, wondering, if push came to shove, whether I could fit through it. It is unclear what Albert's duties are in relation to me. It's also impossible to tell how old he is. He could be anything between forty and seventy-five. Albert arrives at dusk with a portable stove and refuses my offer of tea. While I sit on the terrace in the evening, I see the light from his stove dancing in the corner of my eye. In the morning he is gone.

At least once a week either Albert or I trigger the network of alarms I set and which criss-cross the garden invisibly. Sometimes they trigger themselves when I am out during the day and I get home to find a pink slip under the door – like the one you get from the postman when you've missed him, only what you've missed in this case is a fat man in a uniform limply waving a gun at the undergrowth and looking for signs of an intruder. I get the feeling I am one false alarm away from him saving us all the trouble and shooting me himself.

One morning, when I go into the kitchen, Dora tells me that a friend of mine's car, parked under my bedroom window overnight, has been broken into. She stands poker straight between the work surfaces, drinking her tea with her back to the door. I lean against the counter.

I ask what Albert said, and Dora waves a hand, either to signal the irrelevance of this or the irrelevance of Albert.

'What time did he leave this morning?'

'Seven.' Dora comes in on the first bus and leaves mid-afternoon. I tell her about Siya's offer of night security. Siya is young and strong, I mean, stoned, but I might feel happier –

'Who?' says Dora.

I mime the shape of a large hat on my head. 'Siya with the braids from the end of the street.' Dora has to cough suddenly and excusing herself, leaps through the back door to throw her tea dregs into the flower bed. Who, she says, re-entering the kitchen, do I imagine broke into the car?

'Absolutely not,' I say. 'Siya wouldn't do that. He's my friend, he knows I live here.'

Dora looks at me. 'He's bad, those boys are bad.' They robbed the bakery earlier that month, she says.

When I walk out for lunch that day, Siya is in his usual post at the end of the street. He holds up a hand in greeting. When I frown at him, he winks. I huff on to the shops.

As a liberal foreigner, you are discouraged from going on about crime in South Africa; it's seen to be rather poor form when there is so much else of cultural interest to talk about. I am on my mobile one night, walking the block from my house to the guesthouse for drinks, talking to my friend Merope in London. She is complaining that Foxtons have overvalued her flat; now it'll stick around on the market for ever. As I round the corner, I walk straight into two large men who with a swiftness approaching grace grab my wrist, twist it up my back and, in what feels like a weird country-dance move, wrench it upwards until my hand instinctively releases. 'OK, OK, take it,' I say, in what I think later was an oddly petulant tone. Barely breaking their stride, they continue up the street while staring at the phone and trying to work out how to hang up the call. Merope's voice issues mosquito-like out of the earpiece.

I walk into the guesthouse, shaking. 'I got mugged,' I say to the room full of people, and despite my fright, try to pull off a complicated manoeuvre of getting maximum sympathy for the mugging and maximum kudos for appearing not to care about it. The English in the room started flapping gratifyingly. The South Africans, once it had been established no gun was involved, assume a total lack of interest. I turn to the host. 'I need to make a call,' I say. 'The person I was speaking to will think I've been murdered.'

I am shaking so much it takes a few goes before I can remember the dialling code.

'When are you going to learn how to use your fucking phone?' says Merope.

'I was MUGGED.'

'Oh. Shit. I thought you hung up by mistake like you always do. Are you all right?'

'Yes. They just took my phone.'

'Sorry. I thought you were being a div.'

'It's OK. They couldn't work out how to switch it off. I think you killed them with that really boring story about your flat.'

I don't want to worry my dad about it, but the next morning I feel I haven't had enough sympathy for the mugging and, against my better judgement, ring Fay.

'I was mugged,' I say pitifully.

'Oh,' she says. There is a short silence. 'Are you OK?'

Her tone is neutral, not unsympathetic exactly, but not encouraging either, and I imagine she is thinking, 'Really? You're coming to me of all people with this trivial nonsense?'

I laugh. 'It was quite funny, actually,' I say, and we are back on safe ground.

In all those afternoon drives I've been taking there is somewhere I haven't felt inclined to visit. It is one outrage too many, an event I decline to take on as mine. And then my friend Adam, a British journalist, has an interview come up four hours or so south of Johannesburg and halfway to Durban. He suggests a road trip; we will stay overnight at his contact's house and drive on to the coast for a day or two. When I look at the map, I gulp; his contact lives five miles or so from where, six years before my mother was born, my grandfather committed the murder.

There is no exact address for Adam's contact, whom I will call Z; just instructions to drive south for three hours on the motorway, look out for a biltong shack at the side of the road, turn left and drive for another twenty minutes up an unlaid track. When we get to the crest of the hill, says Z, we're to call him. The path to his house is impassable; he will come and collect us in his Land Rover.

He is, from what Adam says, the type of man I naively thought didn't exist any more: a former British army officer involved in what might delicately be called risk assessment, a job which requires him to spend long periods of time in countries that don't issue tourist visas. Unlike the people posing as spies on the Johannesburg barbecue circuit, these men are older, wider, redder in the face and not inclined to wear cashmere. Adam is writing a book about the mercenaries of southern Africa and has been spending a lot of time in the company of these men, by far the most entertaining of whom is Z.

We follow his instructions to the letter – left at the shack, along the unlaid road – but take a wrong turn somewhere and end up at a dead end, a grassy clearing outside an abandoned-looking barn. 'Is there someone we can ask?' I say. We look around at the desolate scene and burst into laughter. Z doesn't answer his phone.

For a while, the excitement of plans gone awry keeps us going. There is no real urgency. We have potato snacks. We get out of the car and, like children after a long journey, unfurl and lean into the thick humid air. Then it is dusk. Adam backs the car up the track and we retrace our steps until we find the crest of the hill. A jagged path leads sharply down, around a bend where, just visible, is the roof of a building with a number of large satellite dishes on it.

We imagine Z has been called out. That he is attending to an emergency at a neighbouring property. That he can't get reception on his mobile, although we are sure he must have a satellite phone. We imagine They have found him, whoever They are, and he is lying in a pool of his own blood with a knife through his chest. Adam opens the door and gets out.

'I'll stay with the car,' I say. 'It's not because you're the man. It's because you're the one who knows him. It would be rude for me to turn up at the door.'

'Right.'

There is a moment's pause and then, in a burst of determined energy, Adam heaves himself up and starts off down the hill.

I decide to give him twenty minutes before heading back to the main road to call the police. The sound of a vehicle climbing the track makes my heart soar, then plunge. What if it isn't them? What if it's Them? Roaring over the crest of the hill is a Land Rover with a red-faced man at the wheel. 'Sorry about that!' he booms. 'I got separated from my phone!' From the passenger seat, Adam gives me a wan smile.

Twenty minutes later, we are installed in Z's country-style kitchen. The inside of the house is like a Swiss chalet, with warm, exposed beams and thoughtful furnishings in a variety of pastel colours. 'Pink gin?' says Z. He pours generous measures, while reminiscing about his days on the intelligence circuit in Cape Town. 'Of course,' he says, 'Mr Bong was very obviously Chinese intelligence. And I said to our new ambassador, "You're very lucky, the head of French intelligence is over there, I should go and introduce myself if I were you."'

His specialist subject is African coups, many of which have been centred, at recruitment stage, in South Africa's second city. 'You know who was behind it all, don't you? The Nigerian–Lebanese axis. Bloody Lebos. And of course everybody knew about it before it happened. Even the bloody Canadians knew. Six knew and decided not to tell the Foreign Office, in their wisdom.' Z looks off into the distance, as if at a parallel and infinitely better universe where people listened to their spies. More pink gin. 'I mean, for goodness' sake, you don't debrief at that level in-country!'

'No, no,' I murmur. After a few more pink gins and the welcoming arm of the sofa I doze off. I wake up as Z is saying, 'Tim's brother disappeared in Tongo. One rather assumes he was done in.'

The country is parched and rocky around here, sparsely populated and tricky to cultivate. It's an area known for its large number of Scottish immigrants; the farms on three sides of the property where the murder took place were called Braemar, Clydesdale and Abergeldy. Johan Hendrik Potgeiter, an Afrikaner in their midst, had called his farm Kromellenboog – Afrikaans for Crooked Elbow, which described the shape of the stream that ran through it.

On Christmas Eve 1925, three men set out from Ladysmith, heading in the direction of the remote rural community. They travelled by motorbike, and if they had been trying to accrue witnesses as part of an elaborate hoax on the system, they couldn't have been seen by more people. A Madwendwe Kubeka saw them ride past his school in the direction of the farm. A Mr Venter saw them standing beside the bike at the side of the road. They even stopped to ask a woman where they could find water. Her name was Ntombikazulu Mazibuku. She turned up among the state's forty-four witnesses.

The farmstead was at the end of a long track, concealed from the road. It had been reconnoitred in advance by the men, and Potgeiter, an elderly man, identified as an easy victim. During the course of the robbery, he was assaulted and died. The three men were seen by several people leaving the farm, heading in the direction of Brakwaal station, where they abandoned the bike and boarded the train. Mr du Plooy, the station foreman, remembered them clearly.

A few days later, they were arrested in Ladysmith, where they were found to be in possession of twenty-five one-pound notes, a pistol, some electric cord and a set of silver hairbrushes. They had stolen a total of £300 from the old man and were charged with culpable homicide and robbery; they pleaded guilty to the latter.

At sentencing, Judge Tatham, while acknowledging that the victim's death was not their sole purpose, had no desire to be lenient. It was, he said, 'an act of almost incredible meanness'. He referred to a similar case recently prosecuted in the Transvaal, for which two men had been sentenced to death. 'Psychologists', he said, in a modish reference for the time, 'tell us that there is no power so strong as the power of suggestion.'

In his rather long-winded summation he wished to make a broader point. 'In a population such as this,' he said, consisting as it does largely of coloured people, white men who engage in transactions of this character must receive no more mercy than natives. They ought to know better. They ought to know the effect of their example. It is essential that the suggestion to commit a dreadful, cowardly and mean crime such as this should be accompanied by the suggestion that if it is committed, it will meet with the most severe punishment. It is impossible for me, having regard to the brutality of your conduct, having regard to its deliberation, and having regard to the importance of making an example of you to prevent others from committing a crime of this sort, to sentence you to a less term of imprisonment than that of 10 years with hard labour.

He had considered ordering them to be flogged as well, but decided against it, and so, on behalf of George V, by the Grace of God of the United Kingdom of Great Britain and Ireland and of the British Dominions beyond the Seas, King, Defender of the Faith and Emperor of India, sentenced them to what was considered at the time a life sentence. There are, he said, 'two classes of crime for which one is disinclined to show mercy. The first is offences against little children, who are unable to protect themselves, and the second is that of robbing old people, who are equally helpless.'

The next day is Sunday. Z, delighted to have guests, has invited a family from a neighbouring property for lunch. The children, red-haired and freckled, flee outside and bound on the rocks like Irish setters. 'Will they be all right?' I say. The youngest is about four. Their mother waves a hand; they are as familiar with this environment as the rocks themselves, she says. She has the air of a woman used to dominating a landscape.

'Now then,' says Z, pushing studs of garlic into a raw leg of lamb and turning to me. He wipes his hands on his pinny. 'What's all this about a murder?'

I go upstairs to retrieve the papers. The map accompanying the trial notes looks like a child's treasure hunt, with the word 'Murder' written at the top, in a round, slightly babyish hand, underlined and with a symbol to show where the body was found. I give a brief presentation of the facts.

'Who was the judge?' says the woman.

'Someone called Tatham.'

'Yes,' she says. 'He was my great-uncle.'

From the kitchen a loud snort.

'Where did it happen?'

'A farm called Kromellenboog.'

'It's over there somewhere. Named for the shape of the creek; it's Afrikaans for crooked elbow, you know. And who did he kill?'

'An old farmer called Potgeiter.'

She pauses for a moment and gives me a shrewd look. 'His grandson still lives in the district.'

Z looks up with renewed interest. 'Well, there's one for the local paper. Truth and reconciliation and all that. My grand-father killed your grandfather. Worth a photo at least! Come on, let's call him!'

My good humour evaporates.

'No,' I say.

Z has the diplomacy to drop it. When we leave, hours later, amidst promises to meet up for drinks when Z's next in the city, Adam asks if I want to make a detour to the spot on the map. I hesitate.

'Come on,' he says. 'We're right here. We might as well.'

It is harder to find than anticipated. The map is approximate and all the dirt tracks look the same. We pull off the highway and climb yet another unlaid road, cross a stream and, on a slight rise set back from the path, pull up in front of a mean-looking farmhouse, surrounded by scrub. There is no signage, save for one discouraging trespassers. 'Is this it? I think this is it.' We sit in the car and stare. Adam waits patiently, out of respect for whatever private moment I might be having. I'm not having anything. I feel ghoulish and silly. Whatever internal process these expeditions are serving, this place falls outside of it. I can just hear my mother's impatient response: 'Stop looking for nonsense.'

'Come on,' I say. 'There's nothing here. Let's go.'

Mum and three of her brothers: Tony on the left, Michael on the right and Steven on the floor.

13

Tony

You had to work hard to get sympathy for being disadvant-
aged and white in South Africa, a country where 90 per cent
of the population was born into a disadvantage so intractably
worse than yours that however bad your lot, you had only to
look over the horizon to Soweto and – poof! – there went
your alibi. To seriously contend, you had to be a fuck-up of
such unholy proportions that it attracted a kind of wolf
whistle across the spectrum. 'Jeez, man. Look at that guy. He's
really going for it.'

My uncle Tony is living in a garage behind a shop in the
east of Johannesburg. He is eight years my mother's junior.
I remember his ex-wife, my aunty Liz, passing through England when I was young. She and my mother shut themselves
in the kitchen, whereupon my dad and I, without conferring,
instinctively posted ourselves to distant corners of the house,
as far from the epicentre as possible, where in low tones some
kind of country-and-western song was being performed, the
it's-hard-to-be-a-woman back and forth centring on the terrible behaviour of my mother's brother towards his wife and
children. My mother threatened to kill fictional characters
who beat up children on TV, and yet of her brother said only,
'Shame, Tony.' To her, he was always the little boy she should
have been kinder to.

It takes an hour to get there, after many wrong turns and

reversals. I drive into an abandoned warehouse complex and do a U-turn fast enough for the gravel to fly. People I have drinks with every night boast of going to parties in the townships, but these parts of town are deprived in an unfashionable way and by unfashionable people. There are no automatic gates in front of the houses, nor signs threatening burglars with an armed response. Most of the properties are protected only by an ankle-high chain-link fence and the likelihood that anyone breaking in will be confronted by a drunk, angry white guy cradling an unlicensed shotgun.

Tony has instructed me to park in front of a corner shop called Sandy's and to go in and ask for him. It is the only business open in a row of boarded-up premises across the street from a boarded-up gas station, where a few grey figures of indeterminate race lie slumped against the wall. They look like lagged boilers with legs.

'You're here for Tony,' says the woman behind the counter, taking one look at me.

'Yes.'

She jerks her head. 'Back out and around the corner.' I can feel her eyes on the back of my head as I leave.

Behind the shop is a small, concrete yard where an Alsatian strains on a leash, and next to it a garage with the door open. A man stands in the middle of the open doorway, surrounded by car engines and old batteries, tools hanging from the walls, oil-stained rags on the floor. He is wearing a white shirt and grey suit. As he jack-knifes forward to greet me, I recognise his face from the photos and in that moment realise why Fay can't be in a room with him. He looks just like his father.

This living arrangement is only temporary, says my uncle, while he sorts himself out. Sandy and her husband Mike let him stay here in return for light security duties: he keeps an eye on the shop. 'I'm cheaper than the dog, eh?' says my uncle, and smiles. He pulls over a gas canister and urges me to sit. Then he jumps up and urges me to follow him on a tour of the garage. He shows me the cubbyhole off to one side where he sleeps, with a shower cubicle in the corner. There is a mattress on the floor, a pot plant on the windowsill and some old school photos of his now grown-up sons taped to the walls. One of them, my cousin Kevin, was killed in an accident while doing his national service. 'You know Kevin died?' he says, pointing to a photo.

'Yes, I'm so sorry.'

My uncle rubs his forehead. Absent from the gallery is a photo Fay showed me, plucked from her box of memorabilia and handed to me slyly, without comment, like a test. It was a school photo of one of Tony's sons, ten or eleven years old, staring rather dolefully at the camera with a cut lip and the beginnings of a shiner. 'Jesus, Fay,' I said. 'Where were the authorities?' My aunt had looked at me as if to say, 'Come, come. I think we both know better than that.'

My uncle pulls out a book from the pile on the windowsill and hands it to me. It is called *The Cure for HIV and AIDs* and is by someone called Hulda Regehr Clark Ph.D. He has been studying her work, he explains.

'Have you heard of her?'

'Er. No.'

She's an American scientist, he says, who ran into trouble with the FDA and had to flee to Mexico. She was working on a medical invention, which Tony, using her research as a basis, has developed. He squats down and, rummaging in a box on the floor, pulls out a contraption to hand to me: two bits of copper piping attached by crocodile clip to a battery pack. You hold a length of piping in each hand, says my uncle, attach the battery to your waist, then switch it on for seven minutes and off for thirty. This influences something called the 'human intestinal fluke'.

'Oh, right.'

'Everything has its own frequency,' says my uncle. 'Even the human body.' He pauses. 'You look just like Paula.'

We return to the garage, and I perch on the edge of the gas canister. Tony continues: 'You get cancer from the alcohol in cosmetics and shampoo. The benzene goes straight to the thymus and the parasite breeds in there. This electrocutes them.' He holds up the piping.

'Did you meet Sandy in the shop?' he says.

'Yes. She seemed very nice.'

'Huh.' My uncle grins. 'People call Sandy a suicide bomber because she walks around with this battery pack on. She had ovarian cancer, now she is OK. I wish I had known this in time for your mom. I fixed Mike's gall-bladder problem, too. It has a 100 per cent success rate.'

'How many have people tried it?

'Sandy and Mike,' says Tony.

At that moment, one of the grey bundles from the gas station throws her head round the door.

'I need lend of ten rand,' she says.

'What for?' booms my uncle.

'Food.'

'You won't spend it on wine?'

She shakes her head. I gather this is a well-oiled routine. Tony fishes in his suit jacket and hands her a note. She shuffles out. 'I'd like to beat her up and kick her butt,' sighs my uncle. 'But the Lord said thou shalt provide for those who have not.'

He asks what I have been up to, and I tell him about my travels through the towns of his childhood. I tell him about stopping in De Deur outside the liquor store. My uncle grunts. 'I remember that place. I hope you didn't go in. I bet the old man's tab is still outstanding.'

We can't hang out in the garage all afternoon, and since there are no cafes around here, my uncle suggests we get in my car and drive somewhere. 'Do you object to casinos?' he says.

My uncle leans out of the passenger-side window and hands over a card to the man in the tollbooth, who runs it through a scanner and hands it back to him. I gather he's been here before. Tony turns to look at me tenderly. 'If I ever catch you in here, I'll beat you up,' he says. In the following order, I think: 'If you do, you'll be talking to my lawyer.' Then, 'I don't have a lawyer.' Then, 'My dad's a lawyer!' Then (I'm not proud of this), 'Thank fuck I'm middle-class.' Finally, with astonishment, I think: 'He was only trying to be nice.'

Like all casinos, there are no windows, no natural daylight, no clocks, nothing to pull the gamblers away from feeding their children's lunch money into the slot machines. It's not uncommon for men to shoot themselves in the parking lot after losing everything, says my uncle. We settle at a round, chrome table at a cafe in a strip mall away from the main gaming room, where the ceiling is painted to look like the night sky and Celine Dion plays in the background.

There has been no formal request on my part for information, but the reason for my being here must be so nakedly apparent that Tony clears his throat and asks if I'm ready.

'Yes,' I say. I ask if it's OK to take notes, and he nods. I have wondered in advance about the state of Tony's memory. He is the oldest now, with potentially the oldest memories, but he is also the most hampered by addiction. His filters are burnt out, and as such, I imagine, he is long past the point of trying to cover anything up. My uncle sits there, straight-backed at the table, and with the formality of a man bearing official witness, starts to talk.

They were always moving house, says Tony. But the house he remembers best from his childhood is the one an hour south of Johannesburg, where my mother turned twenty-one; where they gave her the pyjamas. There was no electricity, only candles. If they wanted to cook, they'd chop down a blue gum and throw it in the stove. They bathed in the water tank outside the house, first pushing aside dead birds and other debris. In lieu of running water, a man would come round with the water cart, pulled by a donkey, and they would buy forty-four gallons of water for two and six. My uncle has an extraordinary memory for numerical detail.

One day, they bought the donkey, too, for two shillings. 'We had a little Box Brownie, and Ma put my brother John on the back of the donkey and stood back to take a photo. When she looked through the viewfinder, he wasn't there. The donkey had died right under him, legs out. Two shillings down the drain.' He tuts at the waste.

For a while, Tony ran a thriving business catching snakes and selling them to other boys at school. They were rinkhals – a type of spitting cobra – and he would grasp them around the throat, snap off their fangs with pliers, shove them down his shirt and take them to school, where the teacher would say, 'Anthony, sit still,' all morning. He was still bitter about the way things turned out. One day, he sold a snake to Brian Whitson for two shillings, and after taking it home, Brian let it escape through a hole in his skirting board. Brian's mother made them move house rather than live with the uncertainty of when and where it might resurface. 'That damaged business,' sighs my uncle.

'We called Paula beanpole. Mike called her that. Throwing rotten tomatoes, that's family life, see.' His eyes zig-zag, remembering. 'We had a dog called Caesar. The police exhumed him and he'd been poisoned. We used to throw him scraps and he'd jump up, and the third time we'd throw him soap and down it'd go.'

His mother was always pregnant. With each new pregnancy, he says, his father would disappear into the bush looking for herbs and leaves to terminate the pregnancy. 'But they always hung on.' I see my mother's face shutting down as she says, 'My stepmother was pregnant with twins, once.' My uncle grinds on, eyes flicking this way and that as he scrolls through the past.

Boys slept on one mattress, girls on another. 'A coir mattress – that's like coconut stuff – bed bugs and no insecticides. Light from a tin with a wick in it; oil he brought from the mines. Foul-smelling stuff.' The toilet was a drop shaft, down a path outside. 'You'd take a candle with you, and halfway there it would blow out and you'd scream.'

Every now and then a plague of fleas would sweep through the house, and the cat would be blamed. 'One day, the old man grabbed our cat and dropped it down the long drop. Mom sent John and me to get it out. We took the axe and cut down a tree with a long branch. We lowered the branch down and the cat shot up it, scattering shit, and it never came back.' He chuckles. 'John was covered in it.'

Their father was talented, he says. He could make anything with his hands. 'When Paula turned twenty-one, Jimmy built her a cupboard with mirrors, and a light that came on when you opened it. It took him six months to build.'

He also fancied himself as an intellectual. My mother had said something about this – that her father always boasted of having started medical school at Wits, before dropping out. I had rung their admissions department, and after some per-suading, they had gone away and looked him up but found nothing; although if he hadn't graduated, they said, one wouldn't expect to.

'He believed in all this metaphysics, mental telepathy,' says my uncle. 'Every time he got drunk he'd get out these letters from doctors who'd thanked him for something or other. He would start his drink-sodden lectures with "The basic fundamentals of life . . ." They went on and on. Big Jim liked an audience, he liked to lecture. And we weren't prepared to listen to that crap. That drink-sodden mono-logue. Mom tried to shut him up, and that's when war broke out. Then Mom would provoke him. We heard her scream-ing, "You got fired?! And ten mouths to feed!" I thought, "Fired? Did he get burned? Or shot?" But he lost his job because he drove the train into a mule when he was pissed at the wheel.

'We thought he would kill her. She'd run like hell, and everyone would scatter. She was the slowest runner, so she'd climb out the window and I'd put myself in front of the old man so she had time to get away. He never ran further than the front door. He was lazy, and it was cold and dark outside. Besides, once he'd chased us out, he had the house to himself.

'Big Jim would be standing at the front door, looking for who he wanted to kill. He's full of ink. He picked up this steel grate, once, which we had by the door and threw it at me and Mom. We were crouching in the shadows. It went over our heads. It would've killed us. She would run to my room – my room was always the emergency escape, at the end of the house. She shot up the passage to my room. I'd see Mom fly past, then Faith, Doreen, Steven, your mom, John, out of the window, over the barbed-wire fence, over the next fence into the veldt and under a thorn tree. We'd wake with frost on the grass, shit between our toes. Faith was taking the grips out of Doreen's hair. Your mom got up and dusted herself off. "We may be poor," she said, "but we sure see life." "Yes," I said, "that just about catches it. We've got a house but we sleep outside in the veldt!"' He laughs lustily.

'He was a powerful man. They met in the passageway. I heard what I thought were blows landing, bang, bang, bang, five or six times. John said, "That's a gun." It was Paula's gun. I said, "Sheesh, Paula has a gun?" Quite a woman. Next thing, he's standing paralysed in the passage. She put two bullets in the wall, two in the ceiling and there were two we couldn't account for. Knowing our dad, he would have taken a bullet and been too proud to say anything. He'd have slunk away and got it out with a penknife afterwards. From then on, we said, "The old man is carrying lead."

'He had a sister, Nelly. She didn't disown us, but everyone else did. They said, "You're Jimmy's boys," and that was it. People have asked me about my dad. I say, "I didn't know him, I didn't see him, and when I did, he was drunk."

'You go to school, you haven't got sandwiches. I stole raw potatoes and ate them. When you've been at that level, you understand many things. It's not the Russians, not the communists. Your biggest enemy is your own family. You expect love, help. Instead, you find someone who wants to slit your throat.

'We would be woken at two in the morning by a hell of a racket. We'd look outside, and there'd be Mom with a spade and Paula with a torch, and the old man would be screaming at them to dig up his pots, but don't break them. If you don't find the drink, he'll kill you. If you do, he'll drink it and kill you. There were bottles of brandy in the cistern and under the hen. He'd send me to get them, and the hen would peck at me thinking I wanted her eggs. You see what you miss?

'At the bus stop in the morning, the other kids would say, "Why is your mom wearing dark glasses? Why is she wearing a jumper when it's eighty degrees?" You are embarrassed, ashamed. They would say, "Jeez, man, what happened at your house last night? We heard screaming." You are supposed to be proud of your mother and father, but I felt shame. My dad, fired first from one job then another. We never stayed in one place for long. He was run out of town. We changed schools so often.

'The railway ran by the house, and the old man would stop the train and spin the wheels for us. Round and round they'd go. He was drunk as a coot. There was a donkey man who came to clear rubbish from the house. At lunchtime, this man, with his mule and buckets, was crossing the railway line and the whistle blew for lunch at the mine. The mule wouldn't move. My dad ran straight over it. And he hit a car on the crossing, too. I don't know if they died. He was fired. My mom said, "If you hadn't been drunk, you wouldn't have hit that car and been fired." You see, you have these little pieces that you try to put together. "Fired?" I thought that meant he'd been shot. "Fired and ten mouths to feed." The stress and the drinking.'

There were lighter moments. 'One day, we said, "What's cooking, what's happening to Paula?" She'd painted on a beauty spot and wore lipstick and pink nylon. She walked back from the station when it was raining and there was a black streak down her face, and we fell about and said, "Is that beauty spot washable?"'

When Tony was sixteen, he got a job at the mines. It was against regulations to leave mid-shift. One day, the foreman fetched him and said there was an urgent phone call for him in the office. 'It was Mom. She said, "Come quick, the old man's got a knife at Fay's throat." We were afraid to call the police. He ruled us with too much fear.

'At the mines he drove the winding engine, which lifted and lowered the cage into the earth. One day, he invited us to go down into the mine. Paula took us, herded us all into the cage. We had little helmets on. The old man let the cage drop in free fall. Metres from the bottom he put the brake on. He thought it was funny. We thought we were going to die. We were so afraid. Paula led the way out.

'God put Paula there. She carried such a burden. Mom wouldn't have coped without her. Why I loved her? She didn't abandon us. She didn't desert us. Mike did that. I was fourteen, he was sixteen, and he went to Welkom, to the mines. He wasn't prepared to help. She endured hardship, poverty. At sixteen she earned her own money, she could have left. But she stayed. Without her help I don't know what would have happened. It's not long after that he had his knife at Fay's throat. The little ones, the little chicks, given to a home. After the trial he used to come to visit the children every two weeks. Paula said to my mom, "How dare you let him back in?" That was the end for them.

'He wasn't all bad or always bad. He would do people a kindness. Thing is, when he made crap, he made really big crap. We needed a mediator, but there is only one mediator between God and man, and that is Jesus.'

A while after my mother's twenty-first birthday, her father got drunk, says my uncle, dragged the vanity unit he had made her into the yard and destroyed it with an axe.

I am crouched over the table, scribbling in my notebook. My uncle's memories are coming so fast he can't control the order they come in. When Tony was a teenager, he moved out and into lodgings offered by the woman who ran the local dry-cleaner's. He started to date her daughter, Liz, and the two married. Liz's father was a tyrant, says Tony. My uncle wouldn't touch his own father, but 'I put Liz's father in hospital twice in one afternoon. The ambulance hadn't left after dropping him off the first time when he said something about my mother, and I whacked him a second time. We went out and told the ambulance to take him back.

'You see . . .' He pauses. 'Mike would beat me up, my own brother. We didn't go to hospital. The hurts were mental and emotional. Living in fear. There's no outward evidence of it. I would be dozing off and Miss Wells, in class, would hit me. I'd spent all night awake in the veldt, running with my brothers and sisters, sleeping in the foul hop, no books, no breakfast, no shoes, chicken shit between your feet and straw in your hair. And the teacher would hit me. She would use me as an example. If someone did something wrong in class, she'd say, "If you're not careful, you'll become someone like Anthony." I so wanted to tell someone. But the hurts were deep. You get people who write far-fetched crap; people don't believe things like that exist.

'I would have liked to have done many things in life. The foundation' – he pushes his palms down, as if counteracting a strong upward force – 'flattened. A child needs to sleep at night. We were despised, rejected. I was hated by my own family. That is why I love Jesus. Jesus says, "Pick up your cross daily and follow me."

'I drank like hell. They even gave me shock treatment. I was on Antabuse. They put you to sleep for four days, so you sleep through the DTs. I was seeing things. The doctor said, "You're going to die." It's like playing with a dangerous snake. Solomon must have been a drunkard because he describes it so well in the Bible. I heard thousands of people screaming and raging.

'"Be still and know that I am God" – September 1974. I

read it in *Reader's Digest*. God lowered the boom. What a psychiatrist couldn't do, what shock therapy couldn't do, God got it in one. I went to the doctor and said, "Burn these appointment cards, I'm going!" He said, "You don't know how sick you are. You can't cross a road without someone holding your hand." But I was cured.'

'Mind over matter,' I mumble.

My uncle looks outraged. 'No. You are robbing God of his glory.' He sighs. 'Your mother was a difficult woman.'

I try again. 'His mind over your matter.'

'Yes. That's it. Let me quote Jesus: "The fear of God is the beginning of understanding."'

He sighs again. 'When James was away, everyone was happy. Paula and Mom would giggle like schoolgirls. Then he'd come back, and we'd be on tiptoe. He'd materialise one day in the bed; you never saw him come through the door.'

With cramp in my hand and the table edge digging into my chest, I feel an overwhelming need to say something bland and reassuring.

'But you've all done so well,' I say. 'You're such good people.'

My uncle gives me a bald, hard look. 'I'm basically quite a rotten person,' he says. 'I'm violent and a drunkard.'

He sighs again and softens. 'We grew up in a hell of a problem situation, but there was love. You can endure so much – violence, poverty – if there is love. Paula loved us.'

I have been in the casino for ever. I am never getting out. I have been here for ever, I am never getting out, Celine Dion is never, ever going to stop singing. I excuse myself to go the bathroom. It is dim in there, the ceiling the same midnight blue with the sparkly motif. I put the lid down and sit. How strange to be in a casino toilet, absorbing this information. The weight of detail in my uncle's recollections is so crushing I can hardly breathe, but in the midst of my exhaustion I feel some measure of relief. Tony has corroborated that aspect of my mother's story I always found it hardest to believe: not that there was abuse, but that there was, in spite of it, such tenderness. I flex my cramped writing hand and go back to my uncle.

Tony has arrived at a point in his testimony that requires him to sit even more poker-straight, his eyes fixed forward. He clears his throat. With the severity of a painful and long-withheld duty that can, at last, be dispensed, he tells me that in the days of his recovery from alcoholism, he went to see a psychiatrist. The man put him on sodium valproate and made him talk about his childhood.

'Something terrible happened,' the psychiatrist suggested.

'Yes,' said my uncle. 'My father raped my sister.'

He pauses in the retelling. 'It took me twenty years to say it.'

What else is there to say? 'Life is not a bed of roses,' says Tony.

It is dark when we leave the casino. We cross the car park and get in the car. As I start the engine, my uncle fishes in his suit jacket and pulls out a pamphlet entitled 'God's Simple Plan of Salvation. A Matter of Life and Death.' He hands it to me, and I thank him. As we pull out of the parking lot, he sighs, and indicating the surroundings, says, 'I have no money. Half of what I have I give to the Lord, the other half I give to the casino.'

As we fly down the highway at eighty miles an hour, I sense in my uncle some final agitation. It is easier, sometimes, to say difficult things in a dark car while driving; no one is required to make eye contact. My uncle clears his throat.

'Your mother was molested, too,' he says.

'I know, Tony.'

'Sorry. It's left here.'

I drop my uncle off and drive home.

When I get in, I sit on the porch drinking tea for a while. Albert's light is a point in the darkness. I am moved by how seriously my uncle has taken this duty and by the fact he has not tried to protect me with euphemisms. Above all, I am moved that it should have been Tony, the train wreck, the overlooked child, who has done this thing and spoken to me with such force and candour. My mother would be proud of him, I think.

Shouts drift over the wall from the men who live in the park. I think back over the stories my mother told me; of the jokes they used to play on each other, of the animals and weather. I think of how one reality can sit inside another, like a Russian doll.

The next morning, I ring Fay. I give her a precis of the afternoon. I describe the garage and the casino, the inventions and Jesus. At the end of the conversation there is a long, stunned silence. Finally, Fay says, 'Tony has a *suit?*'

A few days later, my uncle rings. He has been thinking about it, he says, and there is something else he has remembered. When his father was in jail at Krugersdorp, awaiting trial, Tony had gone to visit him and had taken cigarettes. During the visit, Jimmy told him that he was sharing a cell with a corrupt lawyer who was giving him tips on how to defend himself.

'I thought it might help,' says my uncle, shyly.

'It does. Thanks so much, Tony. I'm really grateful.'

A father is a complicated thing. It isn't until many years later that it occurs to me to wonder what on earth he was doing visiting him in the first place.

My grandmother on her wedding day, flanked by Johanna, her sister, and her brother-in-law, Charlie. My grandfather is behind the camera. They are on their way to the courthouse at Babanango.

14

Babanango

I give up the pretence of doing any work. I take long, tepid, afternoon baths. I walk aimlessly around the neighbourhood, enjoying the bleaching effect of the heat and the light.

At night, I sit on the deck and drink tea. I read Antjie (pronounced 'Ankie') Krog's account of the Truth and Reconciliation Commission hearings, in which those willing to confess publicly to crimes they had committed during the apartheid era were granted amnesty. As a gesture, it was powerful, optimistic. As a healing process, it was practical. Under the stewardship of Desmond Tutu, a new definition of justice evolved: truth as a form of punishment. No one could read those accounts dry-eyed, but Krog, a well-known Afrikaner journalist, cried so much that she had been jokingly referred to by other journalists during the hearings as 'Pass the hankie, Antjie.'

For the first time, I have a dream of my family in which my mother is absent. It is just me and my dad, shopping in Oxford Street. That's the whole dream. We aren't trying to get somewhere to save her; I haven't put her somewhere and forgotten where. In the worst of these recovery dreams, my mother had been sitting in a hotel room, somewhere in a Dickensianscape London, and while talking to her I'd had a sudden, horrific realisation. 'You're dead,' I said. 'You're already dead and you don't even realise it.' She had looked at me so sadly.

'Don't say that,' she said and I ran from the room, through a series of alleyways until I wound up in a branch of Boots in Holborn. When I tried to find my way back to the hotel, the street had gone.

One morning, I shake off sleep, wash my hair and put on a dress. The opportunity has arisen to do something everyone who goes to South Africa has a small, fluttering hope of doing: to be in a room with Nelson Mandela. It is a press conference at his charitable institute in the northern suburbs, convened to honour the life of his late friend, the journalist Anthony Sampson. There has been a recent Mandela health scare, and most of the journalists in the air-conditioned room have spent the previous week scrambling to update their obituaries of the former president. As a result, the atmosphere is febrile and weepy, and when he walks into the room, stately on the arm of his personal assistant, every world-weary hack, every bombed-out old lag and war correspondent gets to his feet and applauds. People mop their eyes. Mr Mandela sits down and, scanning the room, shows off his ability to summarise all human wisdom in a single utterance. 'Good friends,' he says, smiling, 'and doubtful friends.'

My good friend is coming to stay for two weeks, and I drive to the airport to meet her. I have made a sign to hold up at the arrivals hall: 'POOLY POOLY POOLY!' She rockets through customs dragging a pink, shelled suitcase, whereupon much screaming: 'Pooly Pooly Pooly!' Everyone turns to stare at us, the tall skinny white woman and her shorter black friend. 'Welcome back to the motherland,' I say.

'Oh God, they're doing my head in already. When I got off

the plane, the man wouldn't stop going on about my afro.'

The plan is to do tourism – regular tourism, not the twisted tourism I have been doing. We are going to look at places where great historical events occurred and drive to areas of natural beauty and feel uplifted by things that are bigger than we are. Since Pooly spent her teens and early twenties demonstrating against apartheid outside Manchester town hall with a Socialist Worker placard, this should be fun.

Back at the house, she unpacks the care package she has brought me from home: a packet of Wotsits, a packet of wasabi peas, a Fry's chocolate cream bar and a cutting from the *Evening Standard* about a man we both hate being named one of Britain's thirty most brilliant people under thirty. We scream and repair to the Mozambican bar on the corner, where the barman sends over free drinks; mixed-race parties, even British ones, look good for business in this part of town.

The next day, we go on a bus tour of Soweto and take photos of each other giving the thumbs-up outside Nelson Mandela's old house, specifically his bins, which to our delight still have 'MANDELA' daubed across them. We drive to the outskirts of town to the Apartheid Museum, a stark, brilliantly designed building reminiscent of the Holocaust memorial in Berlin. At the entrance each visitor is given a ticket categorising them as white or black and they are made to enter the building through different doors, a gimmick which, while we giggle on drawing tickets that invert our races, has the effect of being kicked in the mouth. It is only 4 p.m. when we leave, but we drive straight to the bar and don't leave until the early hours, so slammed on banana liqueur that I wake up the next morning horrified at the fact I drove two blocks home. In the garage, the car is parked at an angle and the wing mirror is cracked from my drunken reversing. We tell ourselves it was a necessity, that walking home in that state would have been more dangerous than driving, but the shameful truth of it is, there is simply less of a taboo about rule-breaking here. You might get murdered but you almost certainly won't get a parking ticket.

The day before we leave for a road trip to the south, we go for lunch with my two aunts, Fay and my aunty Liz, Tony's ex-wife. I have seen her once since arriving in South Africa, for lunch at Fay's house. She had brought a date, an Afrikaner who looked like a cross between W. H. Auden and Plug from the Bash Street Kids. Fay and I joked afterwards that he could lend his face to a fantasy clothing label we came up with called Hill-Billy Inc. Liz has amused, cobalt-blue eyes, bright blonde hair and a breadth of shoulder that could knock down a door. I think she is superb.

We are having lunch at a country club in the east of the city, where Liz lives not far from her ex-husband's garage. I pick up Fay on the way. British people think themselves worldly on the subject of alcohol, journalists in particular, but today we are out of our league. It is a nice restaurant and we eat outside on the terrace, overlooking the green, but halfway through the meal there is a sense of eagerness from the two aunts to get back home and down to the real business of drinking. After a few gin and tonics, Liz starts to address Pooly as 'mamma', an endearment white South Africans use for their staff that makes us both giggle into our drinks.

After lunch, we get in my car and drive to Liz's house. My aunt asks me to pull in at a liquor store, one of those depressed-looking outfits with a grille over the window that open on the corners of rough estates. I buy bright pink wine, the most festive, non-industrial-looking bottle they have, and we proceed to the house, a bungalow with a pretty garden out front. When we walk in, a man stands silhouetted in the dimly lit corridor. Liz introduces him as Johannes, her boyfriend. He takes one look at the group, steps back without speaking and retreats down the hall. A door slams. Liz rolls her eyes, says something disparaging and exchanges looks with Fay. As we adjourn to the living room, the first bottle disappears almost before we sit down, and with Johannes locked in his room, as we imagine it, loading his gun, Pooly and I exchange looks of our own, hug the aunts, and leaving them to it, return to the car.

'Hey, mamma,' I say, 'which way?'

Because I cannot let it go, we have devised a road trip that runs through one of the country's main tourist attractions – the Zulu battlefields at Isandlwana, which also happens to be near Babanango, the place where my grandparents were married. Sentimentally, I think, 'It is where they were happy,' although I have no evidence for this. It is merely where they were young and, in at least one photo, smiling. I will settle for that.

I haven't given much thought to the route beyond trying to memorise the quickest way there. It hasn't occurred to me, for example, to note how after leaving the motorway the roads become minor, and then less than minor, petering out on the map into faint spidery lines in oceans of white. After a few hours on the road, Johannesburg's talk radio bleeds into Afrikaans Bible rock and then slowly dissolves into static. It gets noticeably hotter. The sky is lightning white. The road runs between fields of sugar cane, too high to see over. Eventually, our mobile phones, balanced in the cup-holders, peter out, too, and it is here, at this place so entirely beyond the reach of help, that I decide to tempt the universe.

'It'd be funny if we broke down,' I say.

A few minutes later, we pass a giant lizard in the road. It is huge, with a punk-like crest, giant scaly haunches and slow-swivelling black eyes, lumbering across the road with the indifference of a bad waiter. 'Stop the car!' screams Pooly. I pull over, and she jumps out.

'Come and look!' she says, crouching over it.

'I can see it from here. It's disgusting.'

I sit in the car with the window down, listening to the white noise of a thousand smaller noises: the clicks and shakes and chirrups from the cane fields.

Pooly returns to the car, looking at the screen of her digital camera. The lizard continues to sit placidly at the side of the road.

'Freakin' Godzilla.'

I turn the key in the engine. It makes a sound like gravel being shaken in a tin. I do it again. And again.

'Stop it.'

'I'm not joking.'

'Stop it.'

'I swear to you.'

We sit for a moment in silence. We look at our phones. We

try to remember how far back it was the radio signal died. Eddies of dust. A flash of being in the car overnight and the things that live in the fields crawling out in the dark to seek the cool, flat surface of the road and, perhaps, the car.

When we first hear it, it comes as a layer of noise on top of the crickets, like a distant lawnmower, building steadily. 'What's that?'

Pooly gives a small, incredulous laugh. 'You know what it sounds like?' I look at her. 'Motorbikes.' The only thing less preferable to being out here alone.

Within seconds it is like a scene from *Mad Max*. Bikes start to fly by, with that glottal-stop key change as each one passes the car, a slam of noise and air. The lizard's tail is still jutting out slightly into the road.

No one stops, and the high climb to panic just as swiftly drops to a rush of relief. We would have only the mild discomfort of a hot wait for a regular car to pass. I am flooded with such hysterical optimism that I say, 'In any case, bikers often have hearts of gold – what's that Cher film with the deformed son, and they're all bikers?'

'*Moonstruck*,' says Pooly.

'No, the other one –'

A tonal variation makes us turn; two bikes have slowed down and are pulling up between us and the lizard.

My elbow is hanging out of the window, and I instinctively pull it in. The two men are large, hairy and in full leathers, with black shades and bandanas around their heads. One starts to get off his bike, and as he turns, prominent on the arm of his leather jacket are two patches: one is a swastika; the other is the apartheid-era South African flag.

'They can't do anything to us,' I say quickly. 'We're British citizens. It would cause a diplomatic incident.'

Pooly has less faith in the state than I do and scoffs. South Africa doesn't give a stuff what Britain thinks of it, she says, and vice versa. Something stirs in the depths of my brain. 'You're wrong,' I say. 'It has strategic importance within the region.'

I throw my head out of the window, and operating on the principle that people will rise or descend to the expectations you have of them, put on a simpering English voice which I hope implies confidence in this man's mechanical skills and his general politeness to women in distress, but which I realise afterwards is the same moronic tone I use on Mervyn in the bookshop.

'HELLO!'

The man holds up a black-gloved hand to silence me. He turns his back and starts to walk away from the car, while the other guy dismounts.

'What the –?'

The first biker crouches down over the reptile, and gripping it under its throat and tail, heaves it up into his arms and starts to walk towards the scrubby edge of the cane field. This is menacing in a way I can't describe. Looking back, the obvious interpretation is that he was doing the creature a service, but to us it does not look like that. It looks like he is removing the only witness. That he has touched the lizard at all seems to break a powerful taboo, his kindness to a reptile indicative of his cold-bloodedness to humans.

'Oh God.'

The other man approaches my open window. He has a patch on his jacket, too. It reads, 'Can I see the front of your bottom?' Pooly's elbow is so far into my rib cage at this point I can hardly keep the mad smile on my face. She gives the biker a little wave, waggling her fingers in a cooee-type motion as if spotting him over the garden fence.

'Hello!' I say. 'We're from England. I can't get the car to start.'

The man's eyes flick from one to the other of us. I am wearing a pink, Jackie O-style 1960s dress over jeans, with white trainers. Pooly's afro is scraping the interior of the car's roof. The man turns to his friend, shouts something in Afrikaans, and they both stare at us for a moment. Finally, in a clotted voice, as if English is barbed wire in his mouth, he says, 'Is it a hire car?' The smile on my face is so broad it is hurting.

'Sort of. I'm hiring it from a friend.' This seems to displease him.

'Something's burning,' he says. He makes an impatient motion for me to open the bonnet, and then he and his friend disappear out of view. A few moments pass.

'Fascists under our bonnet,' I say to Pooly.

'Yeah,' she says. 'Be grateful you're not the black one.'

By the time a third biker pulls over, we are so numb to the situation that when he takes his helmet off and turns out to be a woman, with long, blonde hair and a weather-beaten face, the relief hardly registers. She approaches the two men and says something urgent to them in Afrikaans. I hear the name Piet and the word for 'English'. She shoots us a concerned look, and it is clear, suddenly, that she has stopped to make sure her friends are OK. Abruptly, she holds out her hand, and the men obligingly remove their leather jackets.

At no point in this process does it occur to us to unlock the doors or get out of the car.

'It's no good,' says the biker, finally, withdrawing his head and gingerly approaching my window. He is still frowning as if this is our fault. 'You'll have to find a garage. We'll give you a start.' The other man makes no eye contact at all. I ask the woman where they've come from, and she says, 'The rally,' and indicates vaguely behind us.

Our 'thank yous' come out half hysterical. 'Thank you! Thank you!' And to Piet: 'Thanks for saving the creature!' He stares at us blankly.

In the car we explode with the sudden relief.

'*Thanks for saving the creature?*'

'Did you see the swastika?'

'How embarrassing would it be to be murdered by a man who thinks "Can I see the front of your bottom?" is funny?'

After giving us a push start, the biker had said the only way to guarantee the car wouldn't break down again was to keep the engine running until we got to our destination and called a mechanic. An hour later, as we pull up at a dusty fork in the road, I let my foot drift off the pedal. I am preoccupied with a building to my left, a whitewashed structure with a green tin roof. There is a large, tropical tree in the front garden. The place my grandparents married is, seventy years on, as remote as it must have been then, one fork of the junction petering out into unsurfaced road, the other heading off between fields in the distance. By the time we sail around the corner, I have stalled the car. We crawl to a halt opposite the Babanango courthouse.

'FUCK.'

'Fuck.'

I have read in the guidebook of a bar called Stan's, where Michael Caine reportedly drank every night during the filming of *Zulu*. It is the only business the guide lists in Babanango. There is a single shuttered building further up the track that might be Stan's, but it doesn't look very promising. 'Maybe we can go and find coffee somewhere while the engine cools down,' I say unthinkingly, and we look at each other and burst into laughter.

As the dust settles, a car appears at the junction, draws parallel with us and stops. The driver and his passengers, all black men, peer cautiously through our window. One of them says something we don't understand and then, addressing Pooly in English, asks if she is OK.

'They think I've taken you hostage,' I say. We grin and in unison say, 'We're from England.' The entire car erupts with laughter.

As the shadows around the old courthouse lengthen, we get out of the car. One of the men comes round to the driver's side and eases himself in. The other three arrange themselves at the back and start to push. The car is on a slight incline, and after moving forward promisingly teeters and then rocks back into its groove. It is then that a 4x4 pulls up, and a white man, in mirrored aviator shades and with a large, blond moustache and short-sleeved butter-yellow shirt, takes in the scene, focuses on me and says something sharp in Afrikaans. Then, in English, 'Do you need help?' There can't have been this much excitement in Babanango since Michael Caine passed through.

As the white man gets out of the car, the black men remove their hands from the boot as if a charge has passed through it. The white man looks critically at Pooly. His wife mumbles something to him, along the lines, I imagine, of 'Do something, dear,' and in one swift movement he skirts around the car's bonnet and approaches the driver's seat.

'We broke down, and these men are kindly helping us,' I say, which he ignores, and with a flick of his head he indicates for the man who'd been helping us to get out, which he does, instantly, and goes to the back of the car to stand with his friends. Out of the 4x4's window, the wife calls to me, 'I had a Vauxhall Astra once! It was always doing this.'

In the driver's seat her husband starts whacking the gears about. Then he looks over his shoulder and shouts, 'Push!' and the men push. The car starts.

'Lucky we were passing through,' he says. 'Follow us as far as Isandlwana, and if you have any trouble, flash the lights.'

Pooly and I thank the black men. One of them asks for Pooly's number.

'Er,' she says, 'I have a boyfriend.' The white guy stares.

We get back in the car. '"I have a boyfriend"?'

'Oh, all right.'

'I think you should have given him your number.'

'I think you should go and ride in the car with your white friends.'

Down more remote roads, across a broken bridge, past endless brown land where the branches of the trees grow out flat from their shoulders, like Egyptian dancers. Occasionally the road has bright-green patches, frayed at the edges, from some bizarre aid initiative to give South African children from the rural villages artificial football pitches. When we leave the main road, the white couple drive past, and with flashing lights and a friendly salute call out, 'Take care, girls.'

It is dusk by the time we arrive, and Paul, the owner of the lodge, is pacing outside. 'I was getting worried,' he says. We tell him meekly of our engine trouble and wait on the terrace while he makes us a cheese and tomato sandwich. We chose this place for its proximity to the battlefields and its views: it is on a hill, and as advertised, the land stretches away before us on a breathtaking scale, disappearing to a blue line on the horizon. The only light is from a rival lodge twenty miles away.

Somewhere round here was the farm where my grandmother was sent during an early bout of consumption and which was left to my mother in Johanna's will. There was a photo of Sarah from this period, flanked by Johanna and Charlie in a desert landscape, and with a dog called Bill. 'Such a nice old thing,' someone had written on the back. In another shot, she stood surrounded by family, everyone in their best dress, arms slung around each other in a slouchy pose that looked modern – as if one or other of her brothers might be about to throw a V-sign behind their sister's head. The men, shirt sleeves pushed up to their elbows, look guileless, freshly baked. I had looked at this photo and wondered why these people hadn't tried harder to take their dead sister's baby, and then wondered if I was being unfair. People have their own lives to lead.

At dinner, under the influence of his wife Christine, Paul's gruffness diminishes. We are the only guests and it feels, in the candlelight and with the darkness outside pressing in, as if we are the only remaining people in the world. Christine talks of being a miner's daughter who only twigged apartheid was wrong when she was in her mid-thirties. She grew up on mine compounds where it was enough, she says, to get through one's own existence without considering what anyone else was up to. Not, she says quickly, that this is an excuse. They ask Pooly where she is from, and she says, 'Manchester,' and they say, 'Ancestrally, I mean,' and she says, 'Eritrea,' and for about ten minutes they can't get enough of this and ask her what she thinks the future holds for South Africa, until I snap, 'It's a completely different part of the world,' and they blink and say, 'We know.'

They talk about the difficulties of running their lodge in the shadow of the ritzy establishment across the valley, whose lights you can see twinkling in the darkness, a popular resort run by the well-known historian David Rattray, where the Prince of Wales has stayed. 'Although we had Christiane Amanpour once,' says Christine.

If South Africa is to have a future, she says, the different cultures will have to mix. Assimilation is the only hope of survival.

'In that case,' says Paul, 'why aren't we eating with chopsticks?'

'Don't worry about him,' says his wife. 'He says bizarre things sometimes.'

Later in the dinner, Paul says, with a sense of wonder, 'Do you know, there are rocket scientists in South Africa, and no rockets?'

Christine looks at her husband fondly. 'What you're saying is bizarre.'

The thing you do around here is take a battlefield tour. It was in this area in 1879 that the British colonial forces suffered one of their greatest defeats, at the hands of the Zulus. We ask Paul if he will oblige us the following day, and with the air of a man acting against his best interests for the greater good, he says he must point out that the lodge next door also offers a tour. 'You might prefer to go with him,' he says. 'He's probably better than I am. The market leader.'

Christine smiles tightly, and Pooly and I fall over each other to say, 'Oh, no, we'd much rather go with you. Much rather.' He smiles, cautiously.

When we tell the couple how we were nearly murdered by bikers on the road, Christine laughs and dismisses it.

'But one of them had a swastika on his jacket,' I say.

'Oh, please. He'd hardly have known what it was.'

We had drawn lots for the rooms, and I had won, so after dinner I climb the stairs to a kind of whitewashed adobe turret with views over the valley. I stand for a long time at the window. Even if you were very sick, you would, I think, have every reason to feel optimistic looking out at this landscape, its vastness on a sympathy of scale with your will to live. I think of the one surviving quote that made it down from my grandmother – 'I have everything to live for.' She had said it to her sister Kathy when the TB came back. Kathy told her daughter, Gloria, who told my mother, who told me. The notion that fiendishness can be conquered by beauty or love or good housekeeping is one that has kept women in bad marriages since the beginning of time, and yet I can't

*Mum on her second birthday, 16 December, 1934.
Her mother has written on the back: 'Doing her Daily Dozen
Exercising — To Auntie Violet and Uncle Dan with fondest love,
from Pauline'*

help thinking that they must have been happy; she couldn't
have known. They must have been happy, she couldn't have
known, because there she is in the photo, arms slung around

her loving family, who didn't knock down the door when she died to take back the child but allowed her to be transported away.

'If there had been the slightest doubt –' Gloria said to me, once.

'I know, Gloria.'

But there wasn't. There was 'we three' and Bonza the dog. There was 'Pauline, doing her daily dozen.' There was 'From Sarah with love to Johanna and Charlie.' There was 'I have everything to live for.'

From the top of the hill, the next morning, we look out across the boundless space of the valley. In the centre is the rock of Isandlwana, in the shadow of which chips of bone occasionally surface and where families still travel in order to leave markers to honour their dead. People in this part of the world have long memories. Through binoculars, I find a small group of people surrounding a single figure: the market leader and his tour group.

School trip-like, Paul has given us a work sheet with a timeline on it that explains how the morning will proceed:

– General background
  Zulu Kingdom
  British Colonies
  'Confederation' policy
– Short description of initial invasion phase
  Drive from Drift to Batshee river site
9.45 Guest go through museum (pay entrance fee)
  Explain some points of interest, weapons etc.
– Drive up to Nyoni Ridge
  Zulu manoeuvres

British manoeuvres
Durnford's arrival
Second alarm
Zulu attack
British retreat

Paul gets up from his chair and in a bravura performance over the course of the morning narrates to us, with gestures, the folly of Lord Chelmsford. He was the British commander in South Africa, ordered to expand the colony into King Cetshwayo's Zulu Kingdom. In 1879, he marched out, leaving his garrison undefended, whereupon a pincer movement of twenty thousand Zulu warriors rushed down from the hills and wiped out the encampment. When word finally reached home, London couldn't believe it, that a 'native' army with spears could defeat the colonial forces. The British won, eventually, but lost more than half of their men and killed a thousand Zulus.

Tour guides, mindful of the sensitivities of their audience, substitute the word 'arrogance' with 'foolhardiness' and 'bravery', as required. 'They must have been very hot,' say guests delicately, of the red-coated troops. At the site of the old barracks, Paul tells us the story of the British soldier who hid in a closet under a fur coat and fled the building disguised as an animal. At lunchtime, Christine drives to meet us with a home-made quiche. In the distance, the market leader can be seen, dressed in a fishing vest and surrounded by thirty people. He has a lot of equipment and hired hands, who carry chairs and folding tables and bags of provisions like something from an old-fashioned game hunt.

About a year later, there is a foiled robbery in the valley, in the course of which a famous South African historian is murdered. It is reported on widely in the British press because Prince Charles had once stayed at his lodge. Pooly rings me in excitement. 'Was that our man?' We try to remember. No. It was the other man, the market leader.

The next morning, we take leave of the couple as if they're old friends, drive on to the coast for a few days and then head home. On the road north, every motorway exit signals the proximity of small towns and outposts with names instantly and intimately familiar to me: Eshowe, where my mother was baptised; Melmoth, where her parents lived at the time; Dannhauser, where she was a young child. I take the turn-off for Dundee, a mid-sized town where she went to school, and pull in at the high school. After turning off the engine, I sit looking dumbly through the window at the shrubbery in front of a red-brick building.

'One minute,' says Pooly, and hops out of the car. A moment later, she comes back.

'It was built in the 1980s,' says my friend. 'Not one for us.' I have reached a point of exhaustion with all this. Either it will cohere at some point and turn out to have been useful, or be an odd thing I did once that made no difference at all.

'We can try somewhere else?' says Pooly, gently.

'No,' I say. It is time to go home.

*Family portrait: my mother's stepmother, Marjorie (middle),
and her three daughters.*

15

Who Wears Hats to the Dentist?

There is one last trip I need to take: back to the coast to see my mother's sister Doreen. She is house-sitting for one of her son's neighbours in the village. This time we may be able to talk.

I am listless in the days before flying and after Pooly has left. The summer has gathered itself up for one final blast and the air is glutinous and distorting, the sound of the ice-cream van, with its sinister tinkle, muffled as it drives round the neighbourhood. In the shade of the trees on Third Avenue two ladies in elegant robes and headdresses run a public telephone service – an ironing board with two old-fashioned telephones balanced on it, hooked up illegally via the junction box. When I pass them on my afternoon walks, they look like a mirage. One evening, there is a storm. I sit on the deck sipping tea and watching. It is just as my mother said: forked lightning like judgement; warm, quick snatches of wind; rain so hard it bounces off the ground and meets itself falling.

A few days before leaving, I take the car to the garage, and it stalls and dies at the end of the street, right in front of Siya. Lolling, graceful, he pushes himself upright from where he's sitting on the wall, and with a whistle summons men from the park to help out. He himself is far too grand to take part, but he organises the effort with much barking and waving of arms. A large, sullen man has to be cajoled into taking the driver's seat, and he shoots me nervous glances throughout, as if I might call the police and accuse him of car-jacking. When the engine starts, I give each of them ten rand, partly from gratitude, partly, I am aware, as some sort of insurance. Siya bows very low and gives me a glittering look, as if he has done me the favour, this fine morning, of allowing me to feel good about myself.

A few days later, I am walking down the street when peripherally I see a blurry movement: a figure crossing the park, jumping the fence and travelling towards me at speed. My heart sinks; I am going to get mugged again. Ahead of me in the road stands Siya, and when he turns, I think, 'A co-ordinated attack.' He grins broadly when he sees me, and then his focus shifts over my shoulder. The grin fades. Frowning, he lifts his hand and wags his finger, a small but unmistakable gesture: 'No.' As I draw level with him, he grabs me by the arm and pushes me roughly up the street. 'Go on,' he says. He sounds cross. 'Be more careful.' I look back, and Siya is standing in the road, all boyishness gone, staring down a man who, half turned and muttering, is dragging himself up the street and back to the park.

Without her son as an audience, my aunt seems calmer, more thoughtful. After driving the three hours from George airport, I pull up at the house, and she greets me with warmth. The house is more remote than Jason's, further up the hill and on the edge of a semi-wooded area, where a dirt track runs towards a logging facility. The lock on the front door doesn't strike me as adequate.

'Aren't you afraid up here, alone?' I ask.

My aunt shrugs. She has the blank indifference of someone inured to risk. 'Not really. I'm lonely. I'm ashamed to admit it, but it's true.'

Doreen sits smoking on the terrace most days, looking out at the view. She is dog-sitting, too, for a poodle she has no respect for and refers to scornfully as a sheep-on-stilts. The owners have asked her to de-tick it every time she comes back from a walk, but 'fuck that', says my aunt. 'I'm not killing ticks for those people when they're not even paying me.' That afternoon, we take the dog for a walk and on the way back stop in for tea at one of the prettiest cottages in the community, occupied by an elderly couple who wouldn't look out of place in a village in Kent.

My aunt shows me off; a visitor from England, just the thing to get one over on these pretentious retirees with their fussy house and superior attitude and la-di-da anglicised accents. My aunt's belligerence in the face of perceived condescension is as familiar to me as my own face; it could be my mother sitting there. When David, the husband, shows us a photo of a large puff adder which materialised on their doorstep a month earlier and which he chased off, Doreen affects boredom. When he contradicts her assertion that if you take half a banknote into the bank, they are obliged to give you a new one, she becomes furious.

'Why are you disagreeing?' she says. David looks surprised. 'Because I don't agree.'

When we get back to the house, I laugh at her. 'You got so aggressive with him!' I say, and Doreen looks mystified. 'Did I? I didn't even notice.' Anyway, she says, she isn't sure about those two, with all their knick-knacks and so pleased with themselves about the puff adder. 'They're not my bag o' laundry.'

That evening, she cooks me stew, and as I put the glasses out on the table, she jokes, 'Want to do a Ouija board?' She gives me a devilish look. 'We could call up Jimmy.'

At last, over dinner, my aunt and I talk. Like her sister Fay's recollections, Doreen's come out as sudden flashes surrounded by darkness. She guards her memories jealously in the face of her siblings' rival memories. When I tell her Fay has complete memory loss between the knife at her throat and the children's home afterwards, Doreen snorts, 'Really? Well, I don't believe that for an instant.'

When I mention Steve's decision not to marry in case he repeated the violent patterns of his father and brothers, she gives me an even more derisive look. 'No one would have him, more like.' As Doreen talks, I think how everyone in the family congratulates themselves on being simultaneously the least damaged and the most afflicted of the siblings. The ones at the top had it worst, they say, because they had it longest. The ones at the bottom say they had it worst because, as well as everything else, they were bullied by the ones at the top. Doreen tells me about a fight she once had with Tony. She had brought her first boyfriend home, a well-spoken boy who, Tony sneered after he left, 'speaks like a queer'.

'And you speak like a fucking Kaffir,' snapped his sister, and he hit her so hard across the face 'I actually saw stars, like in a cartoon.' Being no slouch in this department, Doreen ran to the kitchen, picked up a bread knife, and lunging at her brother, said, 'I'm going to kill you,' before their mother ran in and managed to pull them apart.

I had never considered this; neither the pecking order of injury, nor the possibility that the siblings were anything but a united front against a common oppressor. A lively debate still rages, says Doreen, over who in a family that large can claim rights to middle-child issues. She smiles. 'John thinks it's him, but I'm the real middle child.'

She looks at me curiously for a moment. 'Why do you want to know all this?' she says. She knows I'm a journalist, and I haven't disguised the fact that I am taking notes for a book, nor that I have been to the archive to look at the transcript. But I don't think she means that. Doreen is shrewd enough to see through the camouflage.

'Because I won't be ashamed. Fuck that,' I say, playing once more to the idea we both have of my mother.

Doreen smiles. 'Just like Paula.'

The first time my mother came back for a visit, Doreen was in her early twenties and with a failed marriage already behind her. My mother seemed a very glamorous figure, thirteen years her senior and with the worldly air of the returnee. She wanted to give Doreen the benefit of her experience in swinging London and talked frankly to her younger sister about how to improve her sex life. I am as amazed by this as by anything I've heard. My mother, for all her posturing on how sophisticated she was, could not mention sex to me without chasing it up, a second later, with the suggestion that it would in all likelihood lead to death. When she ordered me clothes from the mail-order catalogues, she invariably ordered them way too big. 'Room to grow into,' she said. It was only years later, when I found photos from a holiday we took in my teens, that I saw with sudden clarity what

I couldn't see then: a size-8 girl in a size-18 dress. If she felt the same kind of protective impulse towards her younger sisters, it was obviously outweighed by something else: a need to show off.

'Yes,' says Doreen. 'She was quite helpful. Eye-opening. You know, you could try this, or this.' She looks at me wickedly while I make involuntary retching sounds.

We continue talking as we clear the table. 'Fay was my baby, Steve was my baby' had always struck me as an odd choice of language for my mother to use. Were it not for her telling me about a small operation she had in her twenties, without which she could not have conceived, I would seriously have worried about the family tree.

'I think she told me about the operation for a reason,' I say, as we sit down for tea. 'In case I found out about all this and ever started wondering.'

My aunt looks blank.

'You know,' I say, 'is everyone related to each other in the proper way?' This seems to me such an obvious thought that I'm surprised by my aunt's shock. Doreen's jaw actually drops.

'My God,' she says. 'You poor thing.'

This is what she remembers: a gritty powder in the milk; a door opening in the night; a trip out into the country on a bicycle.

Jimmy brought them the milk before they went to sleep. Doreen noticed there was powder in it and told Fay to spit it out. She was only a child, but she had lived long enough in that household to assume it was some kind of sedative and fought to stay awake. A few hours later, her father crept into the room, and when she felt his hand go up her pyjama leg, she kicked him so hard he slunk away.

She has almost no memory of the court proceedings. There is an incident she remembers which she didn't tell the court. She tells me now. She was five years old. There was a green bicycle the children shared. Her father took her out into the country for a bike ride, and when they were sufficiently far from the house, dragged her off the bike and tried to rape her. 'I screamed so loudly,' says Doreen. 'Pure instinct. And I'm still screaming now.'

She remembers the children's home, the formal portrait of her father the staff made her put by her bed. The matron's husband was an Uncle Gussy, practically onomatopoeic for 'child molester', and sure enough, there was a scandal at the home. Fay had told me about this; that Uncle Gussy, who, with his wife Matron Flotto, left shortly afterwards, had been caught with his hand up one of the children's skirts. Fay told me she'd gone to her mother and said, 'You did nothing last time. Now do something.' Marjorie removed them from the home the next day and they went back to live with her. Family life resumed.

'I didn't blame Paula for leaving,' says Doreen. 'When my mother took the old man back, that was the end for her.'

My aunt was eleven years old when she was called upon to testify in support of the evidence of her twelve-year-old sister, in whose name the action had been brought. Her sister and her mother had already testified. Waiting to go on was her sixteen-year-old brother, Tony, and her twenty-four-year-old half-sister, Pauline. This was the preliminary hearing, to determine whether the case would proceed to the High Court for a full trial.

The magistrates' court was in a small provincial mining town, fifteen miles west of Johannesburg and a few miles from the family home, although, the court recorded, the twelve-year-old was staying at the house of friends and her mother was staying in Johannesburg, at her stepdaughter's bedsit. It took place over two weeks in November, before a magistrate called Jooste. If my mother's contention was true – that the case foundered at the High Court because her stepmother changed her testimony – there is no record of it in the archive. The only records that remain, therefore, are those from the first trial, when by all accounts everyone was telling the truth. Any frustration I have at the missing paperwork is soothed by this fact.

And so here is Marjorie, who in this first court appearance holds her nerve, despite the extraordinary provocation of being cross-examined in open court by her own husband. She was thirty-seven years old. She had been married for twenty years. When I came to look at these papers again, I saw what I had not seen the first time. That this wretched woman, as my mother came to see her, had married him when she was only seventeen.

She confirmed her address to the court – that she was staying with her stepdaughter Pauline at Soper Road – and the defendant stepped forward to begin his questioning. Only some of the transcript has survived, although enough to indicate his line of defence.

Q: I have been drinking for about 20 years. Heavily for about 15 years.
A: Correct.

Q: You have known that I get blackouts whilst under the influence of
liquor.
A: Correct.
Q: I had to ask you what had happened when I was drunk.
A: Correct.
Q: A few years ago we discovered that I was an alcoholic and I made
desperate attempts to have it cured.
A: That is correct.

She confirmed that at the time of their marriage her husband
had a daughter from a previous marriage. She told the court she
noticed nothing wrong at their first address, in Springfield, but
at the second, at Zwartkoppies, in the district of Vereeniging,
she became 'a little suspicious'. One night, she heard her ten-
year-old say the words 'Leave me alone.' She went into the
child's bedroom to discover the accused awake, the child half-
asleep, and both covered by blankets. 'I told the accused that
the child should not sleep with him, she is too big.'

When the family moved to Witpoortjie, a mining community in the district of Roodepoort, the defendant worked
shifts in the mines and would sometimes be home in the
middle of the afternoon.

One day about three months ago in September I came home early, about 6
p.m. I usually get home at 7 p.m. I went to my bedroom and found the door
locked. I called for the accused to open the door. Faith opened the door.
When she opened the door, she was tidying her clothes. She was straighten-
ing her dress. When I asked them to open the door it was done
immediately. The accused was also in the room, in bed, covered with
blankets. Faith looked upset. I said 'what is going on?' and she did not reply.
The accused was under the influence of liquor. Faith left the room.
Q: When sober I was quite devoted to you and children.
A: That is so.

Q: We were happy.
A: Apart from the drinking, yes.
Q: You had no complaints in any way.
A: Not whilst you were sober.
Q: When intoxicated there was a change of behaviour in myself.
A: Yes.
Q: I became a different person.
A: Yes, correct.

Six months later, the witness noticed a light on in the bathroom and got up to switch it off. She looked in the children's bedroom and saw her husband lying in the bed that two of his daughters shared. She told him to go back to his own bed and that he shouldn't be there. Later that month, he took the children on an outing to Robinson Lake, in Randfontein. The witness decided to stay at home. Her family returned at 5 p.m.

I noticed that Faith was upset. She came and spoke to me and said the accused took her into the trees and pushed her down on the ground. I was upset and took the children and ran out of the house. When the accused returned from Randfontein he was not sober, he could not walk straight. I told him he should leave the girls alone. He said he was lonely. When I said he must not touch them he said he was living by the laws of nature. When he said this he was drunk. Three months ago Pauline complained to me and said the children must not stay in the room alone with the accused.

Q: You forbade me to have liquor in house.
A: Yes.
Q: You warned me that unless I stopped drinking you would take action against me and have me put in an institution or a work colony.
A: I suggested treatment for alcoholism.
Q: On two occasions the children found alcohol which I had hidden.
A: I don't know.
Q: Did you know that I hid alcohol in the girls' bedroom?
A: No.

Under re-examination, the witness said the accused had assaulted her, but not in the past year. When under the influence, he was, she said, 'unreasonable with children'.

This was the sum of her testimony. It was a bare-minimum account, but it was unequivocal. A surgeon then appeared to confirm that he had examined the twelve-year-old. There were signs of haemorrhage, he said, consistent with forceful intercourse with penetration. Asked to describe the examination as either easy or painful, he replied, 'Painful.'

The twenty-four-year-old was of limited value to the prosecution, since she was far too old to provide any medical evidence, and her testimony was short. She confirmed her mother had died when she was two years old. She confirmed a series of addresses where the family had lived. 'We stayed at Dannhauser, Natal,' she said,

and whilst there, as far as I can remember, it started. I cannot say for sure. I was about 15 years old when we stayed at De Deur, Vereeniging. Whilst staying there I had intercourse with my father. It happened very often. As far as I know the accused had full intercourse with me. Whilst at Witpoortjie I stayed with my father. He was always mixing with the children and touching them. None of the children ever complained to me, but because of my experience I was suspicious of my father. Shortly before I left Witpoortjie, at the end of August, I warned my stepmother. She made a report to me. I said I was not surprised.

The accused had no questions for his adult daughter.

The defendant's eleven-year-old daughter, Doreen, was brought forth to testify. 'During July holidays I was at home one afternoon,' she said. 'Mother was working, my father was at home.' Her father called the witness's seven-year-old sister to come into the room with him.

I know the smell of liquor. Father smelt of liquor. My sister went into the room with my father and he locked the door from inside. I was in the kitchen. I heard my sister crying. I went to the door and asked my father to open it. He opened the door a bit afterwards and my sister came out. I asked her what happened and she said nothing.

We were doing homework and father told me to go to the shop. Faith followed me – she did not want to go to my father's room. One day Faith was in the room and the door was locked and I knocked at the door and said I wanted a tissue. My father opened the door and Faith came out. It looked like she was crying. Her eyes were red and she was busy fastening her shirt. I asked her what happened and she said nothing.

I woke up on several occasions and found our father in our room. I heard Faith say, 'leave me.' In my father's bedroom, when Faith was in there with him, I heard the bed squeaking. It sounded like Faith was crying.

A prior witness statement was read out to the court, in which the eleven-year-old confirmed she had never been molested. The only boy to testify was the defendant's sixteen-year-old son, Tony, who spoke plainly and matter-of-factly in defence of his sister. He said:

Whilst staying at Witpoortjie I noticed Faith used to go into the accused's room. Usually the door was locked from the inside. On one occasion I knocked at the door and asked him to open it. Faith opened the door. She looked cross. I have told my father not to take the girls in the room and lock the door. I did not want the girls to go in his room when he had been drinking.

One afternoon my mother came home early. I knew Faith was in my father's room and the door was locked. My mother went to the door and found it was locked. When I got out of the bath my mother said she wanted to speak to me. I thought she was going to speak to me about the locked door and I reported it to her.

For over two years my father had been taking the girls into his room, that is since we stayed at Zwartkoppies. Faith did not like going to my father's room. Once I asked Faith what was going on in the room. She did not reply.

The accused had no questions for his son.

Finally, it was the plaintiff's turn to testify. Fay spoke in a voice so clear and confident it is hard to believe she was only twelve years old. Her courage makes a mockery of her image as saint to Doreen's devil. Fay stood up in court, and as her older sister had urged her to, spoke up to confirm her name, her age and her temporary address – with friends on Konig Avenue – and her former address 'at Witpoortjie, Corlett Avenue, with my father and mother'.

One afternoon, she said, her father asked her to help him add up figures in the book they kept for recording the groceries. She was sitting on her mother's bed; he was dressed in his pyjamas. While she was adding up the columns, he locked the door. She tried to open the door, but he wouldn't let her. He pushed her onto the bed. The twelve-year-old told the court:

His private part was in my private part. I felt pain. He was moving his body up and down. I wanted to call my brother but he put his hand over my mouth and then left me. My mother was at work. That night I told my mother that the accused had intercourse with me. My mother went to the room of the accused. I don't know what she said.

Three weeks earlier, her mother had come home early from work. It was three or four in the afternoon. She was locked in the bedroom with her father. Her mother had shouted, 'Faith, open the door.' Her father had put his pants on and opened the door. Her mother was at the door. She told her mother he had locked the door, laid on top of her 'and then he put his private in mine. Mother went and spoke to my father.'

Three or four days later, the accused called her to help him with a puzzle. It was something, he said, you could win a car with. She said she didn't want to, but he said she must. He got up and said he was going to get something, but instead he locked the door. He pushed her onto the bed. Her fifteen-year-old brother came and said, 'Open the door.' Her father opened it and asked Tony what he wanted. Tony said he shouldn't lock the door when there was a girl in the room. She left the room. Tony told her mother, in her presence, and her mother asked her if he did anything to her. She said no.

About a week later, the ice-cream cart came by. Her father told three of her siblings to go and buy ice cream. She wanted to go, too, but her father forbade her and asked her to get tea ready. While she was pouring water into the teapot, he pulled her away from the stove and the water spilt. She put the kettle down, and the accused took her to his room, left the door open and pulled her pants down to her knees. She tried to get away. She hit him on the arm, and the accused hit her on the leg with his fist. He then let her go. The accused told her she must not be cross with him; he was not going to do anything, he was only playing.

The same night she told her mother. She told her mother on all these occasions. She could not tell the court the first time that it happened. She said she never agreed to him doing it.

On 17 November, their father took three of them – the witness, her seven-year-old sister and her eight-year-old brother – to an air rally near their house. They were playing. At some point in the afternoon, her father asked her to accompany him to where he said the airplanes landed. She told him she didn't want to go. He took her arm and pulled her away and said he didn't want to go alone.

She didn't smell alcohol on his breath. She didn't think he knew where they were going and told him to ask someone. He said he already had, and led her down a path into a wooded area, still holding her arm. He dragged her off the path and pushed her to the ground. She got up, pulled her arm away and wanted to run. He got hold of her arm again and pushed her to the ground. She told him she would tell her mother. Her father said that if she did that, she would cause a lot of trouble, and she had caused enough trouble already. She asked him to leave her alone, and he told her not to shout as someone might hear. She got up from the ground, pulled her pants up and walked away. She tried to shout, but the accused put his hand over her mouth. He asked her not to tell her mother, and she said she would. 'I am going to,' she said. He said he knew she wouldn't. He then asked her if she wanted to go and look for where the airplanes landed. She said no.

When she got home, she told her mother, and they fled the house.

The court recorded only a brief segment of the cross-examination. The transcript conflated the two opening questions, so it was unclear which one she was answering.

Q: Have I ever been unkind to you or beat you or hurt you, we have always been fond of each other until now.
A: Yes.
Q: You always asked me to join your games.
A: Yes.
Q: I always joined in.
A: Yes.
Q: I have always given you what you have asked.
A: Yes.
Q: I was nearly always drunk.

A: Lots of times.

Q: Was I just as kind then.

A: Yes.

Her father's defence, of diminished responsibility through alcohol, was not successful, and at the end of the week-long hearing the magistrate found him guilty of the charge 'that he did unlawfully assault, and then wrongfully and unlawfully, violently and against her will did ravish and casually know [the victim] and being asked what he will say in answer thereto and being at the same time cautioned that he is not obliged to make any statement that may incriminate him and that what he shall say may be used in evidence against him'.

Jimmy replied, 'I have nothing to say.'

The magistrate committed him for full trial at the High Court. The accused requested that he be tried by a judge and no jury. It took place four months later and lasted ten days.

As far as I'm aware, he was kept in jail for the entirety of those four months. He was not able personally to intimidate the witnesses. What, if anything, provoked his wife to change her testimony is unknown, although having to go through the entire ordeal again, this time before a high-court judge in full wig and robes and with journalists on the press bench, strikes me as more than sufficient. None of Marjorie's children can remember what she said; what was revoked and what of her original testimony survived. Only my mother remembered, and I had been too afraid to ask her. I can't summon any particular animosity towards Marjorie. At this distance the failure of the action seems secondary to the fact that something was said and done in the first place, that it is a matter of public record and that my aunt and I, all these years later, are having dinner tonight and talking about it.

Doreen remembers very little of the high-court trial. It's extraordinary what the mind does to protect itself. Sometimes only the smallest things stick. The strongest single image she retains is from the morning before it started. For those ten days, she says, her sisters and her mother were accommodated at the state's expense in a hostel in downtown Johannesburg, and that first morning they sat in the dining room and had breakfast. Although it was a weekday, the girls were made to wear their Sunday hats for court, and a horrible boy in the breakfast room laughed at them. 'Why are you wearing hats?' he said, and Doreen, as her mother had instructed her, replied, 'Because we are going to the dentist.'

This had made the boy laugh even harder. 'Who wears hats to the dentist?'

It was this small mortification that stayed with her; that and the memory of her father's face in court. She remembers looking up during her testimony and seeing him and feeling paralysed. All she could think was that she was letting her mother down. 'Although . . .' She bends her eyes out of focus and tries to remember.

'There was something about a tissue, wasn't there?' says Doreen.

Yes, I say. There was something about a tissue.

*Unsuitable footwear: my grandmother (centre) on a
beach in Durban in the late 1920s.*

16

Freedom Day

My aunt stands in the grass outside the small house and waves as I back the car up the track. I am sorry to be saying goodbye to her. As with all my mother's siblings, I am immensely touched by her willingness to talk to me. After my mother left South Africa, said Doreen, she was lonely for her sister and would sometimes look up her name in the Johannesburg phone book. It was listed for a long time afterwards, and she would pretend to herself that my mother still lived there. Then, one day, it was gone.

I am driving five hours north, over a mountain pass only useable in summer, down into the Karoo and a small town called Willowmore. It once took sixteen hours to get here from the coast, but it takes me five, through a semi-desert landscape of bewildering emptiness.

It was here in 1820, three years after the Voortrekkers passed through, that a man called William Joseph Moore built a farm. It is also where, as my mother had it, the good genes were from. For decades her mother's family, the Doubells, lived in Willowmore and made a living mending fences on the ostrich farms, until they moved to the coast in search of an easier life.

In his history of the town, Norrie Steyn makes the place sound idyllic, a settlement 'beside a murmuring stream, winding its way through a bush-covered, game-infested basin, flanked by low hills and lying at the foot of a mountain above which vultures hovered'. There is a certain arid beauty to it, and I stop to take photos of the deserted road cleaving through scrubland to the horizon and beyond. Ostriches are still farmed here, and the farms are so large – or there are so few ostriches – that fifty miles can pass and you will only see a couple of birds at the fence, tail feathers hanging like mud flaps, heads poking over the wire looking half daffy, half lethal. 'Welkom,' reads a sign at the turn-off from the highway. It wouldn't take much, I think, for the Karoo to reclaim this town.

The high street is empty. There is an old Methodist church with a corrugated tin roof and a coffee shop with '1906' in-scribed over the door. The only sign of life comes from a liquor store at the far end of the main strip. I can hear Elton John's 'Nikita' blasting from somewhere within. When I knock at the door of the guesthouse, a block back from the high street and in a Dutch gabled building in traditional green and white, the man that opens it blinks and looks up the street, as if to see where I have landed my spaceship.

'Have you any vacancies?' I say.

There is a long pause. 'You mean, is there anywhere for you to sleep?'

'Yes.'

Another pause. 'I wouldn't turn a pretty girl away. Follow me.'

We walk down a dim corridor, decorated with framed photos and oil lamps and oppressively silent.

'Hot,' spits the man, by way of general introduction, 'the Karoo.'

When I emerge from my room a little later, the man comes out from his office and shows me the photos on the wall. I've told him I'm here to do the family tree, and as it turns out, many of the photos are of my hatchet-faced relatives. Next to a picture of Queen Victoria and a sign that reads 'Blessed Are the Meek' is a framed sepia shot of town dignitaries from the turn of the century. A man in the middle, square-shouldered, with a brushed moustache and a cigar in his hand, holding a homburg, is identified as an Oosthuizen. The man sitting next to him is a General Louis Botha. Next to that is a photo of the United Cricket Club of Willowmore, 1919–20, with, surprisingly, a mixture of black and white players.

He asks what names I'm looking for.

'Doubell,' I say.

'Yes. There were Doubells.'

'And Oost–' I can't pronounce it. 'Oosthuizen.'

He takes this calmly. 'West-hazen. There.'

From the lounge comes the sound of a voice I recognise, although it takes a moment to place it: Geoff Boycott. The TV is tuned to a satellite sports channel and is broadcasting an England cricket match.

If I like, says the owner, he'll call his neighbour Stella and she'll drive me to the cemetery to meet the Doubells. Why not?

The *begraafplase* is up the hill. Stella says to watch out for snakes, but for once I'm not worried about the wildlife. To be bitten by a snake and keel over across the marble slab of a dead ancestor would be too contrived an ending, even by my mother's standards. It is enough that they, of the good genes, mended fences for a living. My grandmother Sarah died six hundred miles east of here in Durban, the photo of her grave offering no clues as to its whereabouts, beyond the gravestone next to it, a black marble monstrosity with the name 'Connic' chiselled onto it. I had asked Gloria, my mother's cousin and the only possible source of information, if she knew where her aunt was buried, and she had looked distraught and said, 'I never thought to ask my mother.' But it is definitely not in Willowmore.

Stella likes coming up here, she says. It's peaceful among the headstones. Looking out over the town to the desert beyond, she tells me they are trying to market Willowmore as a second-home location for rich people living on the coast. The words they are using are 'authentic desert living' and 'spiritual retreat'. She says this with enough dryness to communicate her thoughts on the matter.

'You don't mind if I look around for a minute?'

'No,' she says. 'I'm fine here.'

Every other grave is a Doubell or a Van Vuuren. The women are Magdalena Magrita or Marguerite Madeline. The men are mostly Johannes. 'God is Liefde,' it says on lots of graves, which are bleached white as bone. At the edge of the cemetery, a line of trees filters the last of the day's sun, sending fingers of shadow across the white stone. 'Did you get what you wanted?' says Stella.

I eat at the guesthouse that night, where the meat is dark like duck and chewy like car tyres. 'You still happy, lady?' says the owner. We're alone in the dining room. I nod, and he sits down to join me. He tells me how he once bought an ostrich for 110 rand and sold it for thousands, although, he says, by and large ostriches disappoint. They are temperamental, like

My mother at her mother's grave.

the women who used to wear their feathers. They die easily. I
ask him about fence-mending. '*Draad-maker* in Afrikaans. It
was a skilled job. As the farms got smaller they needed more
fences. You had to get wood from far away, to make the corner
pieces. Slate stones to plant in the ground. You had to make
them jackal-proof, with three wires along the top. A skill, a
real skill. Of course, only the blacks and the coloureds do it
now.'

After dinner, the light outside is pale mauve and the tem-
perature has come down to the mid-twenties. I walk across
the street to the only place apart from the liquor store that is
open, the Die Gert Greeff old people's home.

Outside the French windows the residents sit on benches,
so old and sand-blasted that even without the shadows you
can't tell what race or sex they are. It is a state-funded home, so
I assume they are everything. I find a nurse and ask if I can talk

to anyone about the town. She shrugs and says to try Gerty, upstairs. I climb the stairs and walk down a dim corridor. All the doors are open and the rooms mostly empty, except for one, in which a woman is awake and scrunched into a chair by the window. She could be three hundred years old. It takes a moment for us to find a common language, and then she says, in what sounds like a heavy German accent, that her name is Gerty Roux and she was born in the town in 1920, making her some ten years younger than my grandmother. I ask if I can talk to her about the town, and she nods. I mention my grandmother's name, and she says, yes, there were lots of Doubells.

'They were fence-menders,' I say. Gerty does not reply to this. It is one of those encounters that unfolds in non sequiturs, as in dreams.

'What was it like here then?' I say. It's not my finest moment in journalism, and to her credit, despite my inept questioning, she manages to dredge up a few details. They worked hard; they got up at 5 a.m.; they travelled in from the farms once a week to go to the bioscope in town. I can't think of anything else to say. I sit there with Gerty in silence for what is probably only a few minutes but feels like hours, looking, as she does, out of the window. The lace curtain flutters. If you lived here long enough, I think, the day would come when you jumped up from your chair and ran screaming down the high street in your nightgown. Or fell in love with the first person who smelt of the city.

I leave Gerty Roux and go back downstairs. On the way out of the home, I run into a young nurse. She says she is on secondment here from Cape Town. I ask if she misses the city, and she gives me a desperate look. 'God, yes.'

The next morning, I get up at 4 a.m. The drive to the airport is only two hours, on a regular road with no mountain passes, and my flight isn't till noon. But I would rather sit in the lounge for four hours than in this desiccated vacuum.

From what both Doreen and Tony said, the greater betrayal was not what happened in court, but the fact that their mother took Jimmy back afterwards. In fact, Marjorie did divorce Jimmy, two years after the court case collapsed. My mother never mentioned this, and nor did anyone else. It must have seemed a hopeless gesture, too little, too late, and then he died anyway. But I am curious to discover she took a stand at all, something I only find out about by chance. When I get back to Johannesburg, I go online for one last trawl through the archive's database, and there it is. I don't know how I missed it the first time: Marjorie Violet divorced from James Mauritz, with a shelf and reference number.

I hesitate to go back to Pretoria. The divorce is probably summarised in a single line, and what's the point of driving fifty miles for that? In the end, I go less out of curiosity than as a kind of marker for how far I've come. I drive myself this time, park in the car park, and entering the reading room, feel none of the terror of the first visit. I am so pleased with myself about this that when my phone rings as I'm putting my bag in the locker, I answer cheerfully. I must be less resolved than I think. It's my friend Sam, calling from the office in London. 'Do you want anything from the trolley?' he says, delighted by his joke – it is tea time at home – and it's all I can do not to burst into tears. 'I'll have a peppermint tea,' I say weakly, and hang up the phone.

It turns out the divorce documents are more than a line long. The restitution order was served on Jimmy personally by a deputy sheriff Lotz at no. 46 single quarters, West Rand Consolidated Mines, in Krugersdorp. He was ordered to pay £10 a month to Marjorie, plus £30 maintenance for the five children still living at home. When he didn't turn up for the hearing, the judge granted the divorce by default. The court charged Marjorie £1.50 for serving him with papers. To secure a quick settlement, the grounds on which she divorced him were, with cosmic-sized irony, 'malicious desertion'. All their lives they had tried to get rid of this man, and now his absence – in the language of the court, his failure to observe 'conjugal rights' – was the only legal way to dispense with him.

Looking at those divorce papers I feel sympathy for Marjorie, the woman about whom no one has much to say – except for Steven, protecting his mother a little, who told me she had once wanted to be a Catholic missionary. She was of Scottish origin. She got pregnant not long after meeting Jimmy. Afterwards, she would say she had always been afraid of her husband, thought him 'a devil' right from the off and was reluctant to marry, but her parents had pressured her into it. And yet, said her youngest son, there came a moment when he realised that 'at some level, she must have loved the old bugger. And I thought, "I'll be damned."'

Apart from the telegram she sent my mother telling her of her father's death, the only thing of Marjorie's I have is a note she wrote on the back of a photo, which she sent to my mother shortly after she'd emigrated. 'Dearest Pauline,' she writes, 'I wrote to you last week and very stupidly lost the letter. This is just to say thanks to you. We are very grateful

To hell with all that: my mother on the day she left South Africa for England, in November 1960.

and the money was useful. Bless you! Anyway, you can be sure of getting it back soon but that doesn't mean that I am not grateful and very touched by what you did.' There follow several paragraphs of family news. Then Marjorie writes: 'Hope you like the photo.' The photo is, incredibly, of my mother and her father, taken on the day she left South Africa, his arm around her waist while my mother stares like a statue into the distance. With lots of kisses, she signs off, 'love, M'.

As with everything else, accounts of Jimmy's death varied between the siblings. Tony thought it was my mother who was asked to identify the body, but that can't have been the case; she was already in England. Doreen said she was walking to church from the children's home with Fay when Tony pulled up on his motorbike. When he told them their father was dead, 'I was so pleased. That's all I felt. Pleased and relieved.' She said Fay started screaming and had to be calmed down. 'I couldn't stop shaking,' says Fay. 'When you've been frightened all your life, it's just such a relief. I couldn't go to school for a few days, and I didn't want to talk about it.' Steven said his mother was terrified there would be an open coffin at the funeral and she would have to see his face again.

Fay is having a little gathering at her house. It is not a reunion per se. Words like 'reunion' put too much pressure on attendees, plus the idea of togetherness in this family is so toxic as to be almost funny. 'It'd be hilarious,' said my cousin Jason while we were sitting in the garden with his mother on the coast. 'We could get all of you in a room together, get in loads of booze and invite Jerry Springer.'

'You're not big,' snapped Doreen, 'and you're not clever.'

But Fay is being optimistic. Her brother Tony is coming, whom she hasn't seen for nineteen years, and Tony's ex-wife, my aunty Liz, and some of Liz's boys, plus Fay's daughter-in-law and her husband Trevor. She invited her daughter, Victoria, whose reaction I can just imagine. Yes, says Fay, it was along the lines of, 'I'd rather stick pins in my eyes.'

At her round dining table my aunt and I excitedly plan how many sandwiches we'll need. A few days later, we drive to the shopping mall to pick them up. They are dainty white triangles with their crusts taken off – not like the huge chunky doorsteps my mother used to make – laid out on a large silver tray. Before everyone arrives, I take a photo of the fridge, which has been stripped of food to make way for a pyramid of beer bottles. We drag plastic chairs out onto the terrace. It's an overcast day, but we are in high spirits.

'Won't it be weird to see Tony?' I ask.

Fay giggles. 'Very weird.'

'Will he and Liz be all right in the same room together?'

'Oh, yes.'

Everything flows off Fay's back. It is an attitude often mistaken for passivity, but one that I have come to understand as a Zen-like transcendence. I ask her how many years it has been since all the siblings were in a room together. She supposes it was at her mother's funeral over two decades ago, although 'of course your mom wasn't there for that'. It is always Fay, the sensible one, who is called upon to break news of a death in the family. It was Fay who rang my mother with news of Mike's death, and who drove over to her own mother's house to break the same news. Marjorie had been drinking heavily for a long time by then. She came to the door, says Fay, saw her daughter's face and said afterwards, 'I knew instantly. But I thought it would be Doreen.' Marjorie put a leash on the dog and went out for a long walk. When she came back, Fay says, she said goodbye and left.

Before that, she supposes, the nearest they got to a family reunion was my mother's first trip back to South Africa in 1967, before the siblings had fully scattered to pursue their own lives. Steve had told me about this; he remembered the visit well. He remembered one incident in particular. When he told me about it, I was surprised I hadn't heard the story from my mother, since it flattered the idea she had of herself, although it was also, possibly, one of those stories she thought would set a bad example, like shooting her father. Marjorie's sister had been in town from Ladysmith, and high tea was arranged at one of the posher hotels. It was Steve's recollection that my mother reluctantly gathered those of her siblings she could lay her hands on and they all trooped along to the hotel. My mother didn't like this woman, whom she sensed had always looked down on them. She referred to her not by her name, Doreen, but as 'that frowsy old cow'.

True to form, said Steven, his aunty Doreen proceeded to patronise them over sandwiches and tea. At some point in the afternoon, my mother had enough. She suggested to Doreen they play a little parlour game popular in England at the time. Doreen was delighted. In 1967, fashions established in the old country still held sway among those who considered themselves well-to-do in South Africa. 'Yes,' said my mother, who would shout when irritated but when she wanted to do real damage would lower her voice. 'It works like this: everyone goes around in a circle and says their favourite curse word. I'll start.' And summoning her pearly new accent, she looked into the eyes of her enemy and said, 'Cunt.'

As Steve remembered it, the aunt actually screamed. In any case, she leapt from her seat, fled the room and drove the five hours back to Ladysmith in one go.

There will be no tears or ululations at the gathering today. It is not the house style. Call it repression or call it self-discipline, but when brother and sister set eyes on each other after almost two decades, it is with mild, sardonic expressions. After a brief hug, Fay tells Tony to make himself useful and get up on a stool to change a light bulb over the front door. Tony hops to it. I take a photo of him up there in canary-yellow Airtex, hands clasped together like a crumpled angel. When I get back from the kitchen, he has spotted something on the horizon. 'Look at my fat wife!' yells Tony from his vantage point, as Liz struggles up the path, carrying beer. She gives him a look to stop traffic.

She has brought a friend along, George, who has a warm, likeable air, hearty and male and smelling slightly of whisky. I give my aunt a hug, and nodding at George, say, 'I'm so glad you've got rid of that other awful man.' My aunt grins out of all proportion to the comment, and looking over her shoulder I see why. A man carrying a crate of beer emerges from between parked cars. I split my face in two to receive him. 'Johannes! How lovely to see you.'

While Tony and Liz's sons mill about on the lawn, cradling beer bottles and chatting politely, their parents sit beside each other at the table, drinks in one hand, cigarettes in the other. Tony points to Johannes and says, 'You'd better watch out, eh,' and starts going through a long list of Liz's ex-boyfriends who have one way or another come to sticky ends.

'Willem, taken by God. Andreus, taken by God,' says my uncle. Liz, smoking, looks as if at any moment she might shoot a poison dart out of the end of her cigarette and into her ex-husband's neck. 'God takes away those who deserve to be punished,' says Tony, solemnly.

'Shame God didn't take you, eh,' says his ex-wife.

Tony looks martyred. 'They persecute me in His name.'

'They persecute you because you're no bloody good and a drunk.'

'Shut up, woman, or I'll beat you up.' My uncle's verbal tic doesn't get any less startling. He sighs. 'She left me for a better man.'

'Then what are you so big-headed about?'

My uncle grins. 'It took her twenty years to find one.'

Fay turns to Liz and asks about the court case. Liz inhales deeply on her cigarette and says, 'Fourteen years commuted to six.'

'What's this?' I say. Fay says blandly, 'Oh, didn't I tell you?' Liz's sister was shot dead by her husband last year. Sentencing was this week.

'Easy on the rum and Cokes, eh, George,' says Johannes from across the table. 'I don't have a black suit for your funeral.'

'I hear you, man,' George cackles. I think, 'Johannes is afraid of George, and a good thing, too.'

Johannes rubs his hands together. Someone asks after his son. 'Holding up,' he says, and explains, for the benefit of the audience, that he is serving time for murder.

I look across the table at Trevor, who is not, by Fay's account, a very enlightened individual and who seems to be struggling with the novelty of finding himself the most liberal man at the party. When Johannes starts going on about how the blacks have trashed the country, how 'monkeys in the tree are called branch managers now' and how the crime rate is way up, Trevor clears his throat, and looking nervously at me, says, 'There was always a lot of crime, but we didn't see it because it was in the townships.'

Tony is mostly oblivious to the wider conversation. He turns to his sister, and nodding at me, says, 'I told her all about our dad.'

'It's not "dad", it's Jimmy,' she snaps, the only time I have seen Fay lose her equilibrium.

To me, Tony says, 'There was something else I meant to say to you – about the twins.'

'What's this?' says Fay.

'Yes,' I say. 'My mother spoke of them once.'

Fay turns to look at her brother.

'There were twins,' says Tony, 'between Mike and me. They either miscarried or were born dead.'

Fay says, 'I don't know anything about this.'

Tony says, '*Ja*. Mom had named them already. They were called Andrew and Trevor.'

Fay smiles in a kind of half-dazed embarrassment. 'Well,' she says. 'Well.'

There is more beer, more cigarettes. Everyone pushes their chairs back from the table and settles into them. 'You'll see,' says Johannes, to one of my younger male cousins. 'They say it's wrong to hit a woman. But if one hits you, it's within your rights to hospitalise her.' My cousin scowls across the table.

'That's right,' says Trevor. His wife, smoking stonily, turns to looks at him. 'Not that I would,' he adds quickly.

'You're very quiet,' a cousin's wife says to me. If I had the courage, I would say it is because the afternoon seems to have turned into a meeting of wife-beaters anonymous. Because I don't understand what this is, where men can say these sorts of things at the lunch table as if it were the most normal thing in the world, while their wives frown and withstand it. Instead, I say, 'I'm fine.'

Tony, on his own unique path, clears his throat. 'I come from a long line of alcoholics,' he says, before everyone at the table shouts him down. When he tries to bring up the subject of the 'human intestinal fluke', an even rowdier chorus defeats him.

'She tricked me,' he says, pointing to Liz and reaching back to some distant memory from their marriage. 'She said she needed to go to the doctor, so I took her there, and when we got to the surgery they stuck a needle in me and banged me up in the drying-out ward.'

'You needed it, eh.'

'Trickery. And then she drove me home even though she can't drive, and my head bashed against the dashboard.'

'You're such a liar.'

Liz turns to me. 'We had nothing. We were really poor. We lived near the cemetery, and in the Indian section they leave curry out on the graves, so after they'd left we'd go and steal the food.' She smiles, and taking a deep drag on her cigarette, says, 'The dead can't chase you.'

Before she leaves, Liz turns her electric-blue eyes on her ex-husband. 'Man, look at the hole in your trousers,' she says. She sighs, as if in the face of an unpleasant but irresistible force. 'Give them to me and I'll mend them for you.'

My uncle looks at her tenderly. 'She's been in this family as long as any of us, eh,' he says.

After everyone has left, I take a photo of the empty fridge. Fay and I sit side by side on the sofa, exhausted. Notwithstanding Johannes's various contributions – 'Rough,' says my aunt, shuddering, 'rough' – we declare the afternoon a success. I'm not sure what criteria we're judging this by, until the next day, when Liz rings Doreen, who rings me straight afterwards, giggling. 'Liz said you all had a nice time yesterday,' says Doreen, and flattens her accent to do the impression. '"It was nice, Dor," she said. "There were no fights and no one got drunk."' Doreen laughs uproariously.

Fay and I agree. 'It was all just so civilised.'

I have not found the prosecutor. Nor the arresting officer. And there are friends of my mother's I still haven't seen. I have reached saturation point, but there is one final connection I want to explore. The person in question is dead, but she was very important to my mother. I want to know something of her.

There are four or five Sosnoviks in the Johannesburg phone book. The first one I call says with surprise, yes, he knew a Sima Sosnovik. She was his late aunt. A couple of days later, I drive to his house, a large, imposing building in one of the nicer suburbs. He is a lawyer, I think. I say hello to his wife and we repair to his study, where I repeat what I said to him over the phone; that my mother and his aunt had worked together in the 1950s; that Sima was important to her, and I'm interested in that period. I am aware that as an explanation, it doesn't quite cover it, and he looks at me oddly but is game to help. 'I think your aunt was some kind of role model to her,' I say.

'Yes, well, she was a forceful character, in a quiet way,' he says. 'Not a shouter, but forceful.' He tells me she was born the fourth of seven children in Białystok, which at the time was part of the Russian empire. The family moved to South Africa in 1920, when she was ten. Her father was a teacher of religious studies. She started out as a bookkeeper in a fish shop in Melville. 'I wish I had a photo for you,' he says. 'She had reddish hair.'

In the late 1940s, she emigrated to Australia but returned two years later. 'She was very confident. She spoke slowly but with emphasis. She had enormous integrity and a very dry sense of humour. Dry and sarcastic. She was the brightest in the family.'

He gestures helplessly. 'She had a relative called Grevler, on her mother's side. I think he won the Delagoa Bay Lottery.'

Sima's nephew gets up and goes digging in a file. 'I can give you a copy of this,' he says. It is a short piece of writing she did when she returned from Australia.

'Thank you.'

'She died in 1958 of cancer of the liver.' The year of the High Court trial. No wonder my mother's thoughts turned to suicide that year.

That evening, I sit outside on the terrace and read the piece of writing. It is a sentimental account of her childhood, how each of the seven children had an allotted role: the mother, the baby, the rebel, the caretaker. She was the rebel, in the middle, fighting to stand out. After two years in Australia, she saw she had made the wrong decision. She came home to Johannesburg, she wrote, with the realisation that after all her protestations of independence, what mattered most in the world was family.

Steven has moved to another town further east along the coast, a not so chichi resort where he is staying with friends. I go down to see him one last time. By chance, it's 27 April, the anniversary of South Africa's first democratic elections, christened Freedom Day. We walk along the beach for an hour before sunset, the sky pink and translucent, pebbles clacking beneath our feet as Jesse and Jezebel run ahead of us. Every now and then they skid to a halt and whip over to bite themselves.

At the driftwood, we stop. It is burnt white by the sun and shaped like a bench, curving up from the beach in two ribby arcs. We sit on it and watch the dogs. Steve says, 'I was headed for a life of repressed mediocrity. I didn't want to repeat his pathology, be a drunk. I thought, "If I'm going to go wrong, let me do it my own way."' He doesn't believe in closure. 'I have sufficient healing.' My uncle smiles. 'Like sufficiently free and fair elections.' He says, 'If I hadn't had her love for the first ten years, I wouldn't have survived.'

On the last day, I drive around the neighbourhood. The trees are burnt orange at the edges. Through the flat, still air a wood pigeon calls. You could die from an afternoon like this, I think. I draw level with the car park at the end of the street and wind down the window. Siya puts his hand through it and grips mine. He is wearing black, fingerless leather gloves. 'Stay cool,' he says. His guitar is slung around his back and his beanie is as high as the Cat in the Hat's. 'Keep smelling the air and feeling the sunshine.'

'See ya, Siya,' I say. Our fingers grasp and release.

I am so sure I will be back in Johannesburg before long, I have left a large pile of books in the wardrobe of the house. I have said goodbye to Fay in a deliberately casual manner because I will be seeing her again soon. On the plane home I am ecstatic. I did it. I have done it. It is done.

I don't go back.

Baby flares: in our garden in London, 1977.

17

Afterwards

Now that I knew what she was fleeing from, those intermediary years after my mother came to London but before she met my dad and had me seemed all the more extraordinary. How did she put herself together? What did that process look like from the outside? Friends, I think, are the thing.

Recently, I attended my godfather's eightieth. At the party in London was my mother's old gang from the 1960s, people I hadn't seen for years. I arranged to interview them, these people I have known my whole life, but it was strange to come to them in her absence, as an adult and ask what they remembered of her. I had put it off for a long time, thinking she'd be angry, that she mightn't want me to reveal anything to them. And then, suddenly, it didn't matter any more.

One cold winter's day, I sit in my mother's friend Edward's apartment, where she and my dad had their wedding-day brunch; I go to the pub with her great friend Roger; I sit in the beautiful living room of her friends Bob and Nick. It is the old Thursday Night Club.

Edward is eighty. He makes me a cup of tea. The late afternoon light floods his top-floor apartment. There are paintings on the wall whose styles I recognise from our house. They are by another great friend of my mother's. 'Yes!' says Edward. 'It seems nice, somehow, that we all have these paintings by Bill Graham. We're all part of a club!' He met my mother in the early 1960s, when Britain was just emerging from post-war austerity. Edward had come to the country as a ten-year-old refugee, on the *Kindertransport* from Vienna. He knew something about what it was to be alone. They were natural allies.

'When I first met her, she was really compressed. Not depressed, but compressed. As if she had been in one of those chambers in films that gets smaller and smaller. And slowly she expanded. She had resources that were there and that she had to find in herself.'

I ask Edward if she said anything about her background before arriving in London. He tucks his chin in and smiles at me. 'There was something about a gun, I think?'

I am unexpectedly joyful – that she had a friend and that she spoke to him, and that he saw her come to life. That she didn't do all this alone. That she was not, in fact, superhuman.

Still, says Edward, those were not easy times, not for any of them. 'We were all potentially criminalised. Our lives were illegal. There was a certain danger. We all adapted to living that way, but it was a dreary time; one was oppressed. Black people were having a very tough time in Notting Hill Gate. It was volatile. Thursday nights were a lovely kind of anchor in the week.' The pretext was exercise. None of them had the cash to join a gym, so they were supposed to meet each week to work out. 'But I don't recall exercises lasting longer than a few weeks. Then it became a get-together and food.' He smiles. 'Your mother, this girl, with this odd bunch of gay guys. She embraced us. She might not have. Not everybody did.'

She was living then in a bedsit in west London. Her friend Bob was among the other tenants. It was at Bob and Nick's house, many years later, that my mother fell and cut her own throat. 'Yes,' says Bob, 'and of course you know the punch-line? That she came back from the hospital and insisted on finishing the dinner party?'

'Yes,' I say. 'She loved that story.'

We are in Bob and Nick's living room in west London. Back then, it was just Bob. 'We were all single,' he says, 'all working. Paula lived in the basement with a girl called Ann, who she didn't like, but it helped pay the rent. She'd take a book out the front of the house and would smoke a pipe out there and sometimes a cigar. She was quite eccentric. We'd sit and gossip and groan.' He pauses. 'I always had the feeling there was a father problem. I understood that it was import-ant for her to leave South Africa. That getting away from the father was a problem. I think we had heard that.' He looks at Nick, who looks blank. '*A father problem that affected girls, not boys.*'

'Oh,' says Nick. We all burst out laughing.

Bob had come from Australia, so they had a colonial back-ground in common. 'I was twenty-six and had left Australia – yippee! – and was in London, for God's sake. It was enorm-ously exciting. There was Mary Quant on the King's Road. It was the beginning of more freedom for people. The law didn't allow our lifestyle, but it went on – in the back of buses, every-where. The rent was six pounds a week. It was a nice house, although it only had one lavatory and one bathroom. We were there for two years.

'Everyone was poor but not broke. You might have to bor-row 10p for your bus fare occasionally but you didn't feel poor because everyone was in the same boat. The only people who went back to Australia were those whose family sent them money. £300. I had wobbles, and I think your mother did, too. But we didn't have the money to go back, and it passed.

'Paula was always herself. She didn't dress up for anyone. She wasn't out looking for men. She was quite lonely I think. She went to Cornwall for four days and didn't speak to anyone.'

'Was she happy?' I ask.

Bob pauses. 'I wouldn't say she was happy. But I wouldn't say she was unhappy. She was trying to work her life out. She was not depressed, not at all. She was a coper.' He looks thoughtful. 'But happy? No. She was lonely.'

In the pub around the corner from my dad's house I sit with Roger. My mother and Roger infuriated each other and would go through spells during my childhood of not being on speaking terms. There were photos from a famous holiday we all took together when I was a baby, to Majorca. Now, Roger says, 'I looked in one of the suitcases, and d'you know what was in there? Pond's Face Cream – glass, heavy as hell, like a paperweight. She'd brought two of them, and I said, "What the fuck? Where's the kitchen sink?"

'We first met in the 1960s. She was working for your god-father. There was a dinner for eight people, and Paula was on my immediate left. All of a sudden, out comes a white clay pipe, out comes a cigarette that she sticks in the end and smokes. I had never seen anything like it before. And she dropped a few words every now and then.

'She was very forthright, outgoing. She was up for a good row. It was a bit daunting at first, but you learnt to fight back, and she enjoyed that. Your dad would let us get on with it. I remember one time I went down with the two dogs, and they chased her cat and she went ballistic.

'The 1960s in London were brilliant, let me tell you. I didn't start fooling around until I was twenty-nine and I was just starting to find my feet. We used to hang out on the King's Road. Everyone down there was a bit dotty. The Markham Pub, and Mary Quant had a boutique. The Alexander was a restaurant. There was a shop opposite the World's End pub called Granny Takes a Trip. Pairing off came second to the group. It was group living. It was camaraderie.

'Paula was very spatty. These spats, I liked the spark. We liked each other. She could let go with me. We could let go with each other and get rid of a lot of crap in our veins. She once said to me "You're a fucking cunt" in front of John, a friend I went to school with, and he was really angry. He didn't know Paula.'

Did Roger know she shot her dad?

He bursts out laughing. 'I wish I had. I'd have said, "Don't you get your pistol out to me, dear." I'm lucky I'm still around – I pushed my luck! I suppose I should be surprised. But I'm not.

'I used her as my referee in my vetting. I had the highest security clearance for the MOD. Paula was my referee; they asked her, "Is he homosexual?" and I passed on both occasions. The interviewer would have been tough, but Paula was tougher. If they'd said anything nasty about me, she would have slapped them down. You couldn't get a better referee. She was as tough as they come with anyone who tried to give her the push around.

'All of us thought you were going to be a horrible kid, you

were going to be a spoilt brat – only child, older mother. We were surprised at the way you turned out. I mean,' he smiles, 'you're nasty, but not the way we expected.'

Does he think she mellowed over the years? 'Not really. Towards the end, when she'd lost her hair, we were sitting on stools in your old kitchen, and I suggested going somewhere for lunch, and she snatched the hat off her head and hissed, "What, looking like this?"'

It is wonderful talking to my mother's friends, the love they had for each other still so apparent. Out of all the conversations I have that week, it is something Edward says to me that I think most about afterwards. Of everyone, he perhaps understood her the best, having come from war-torn Europe and lost not only a family but a country and a way of life. 'When people have had an awful childhood themselves,' he says, 'it impinges later in life. At its best, it becomes an ability to make sure that your child has none of the experiences of your own childhood. Some are too wounded to do that. I was in great admiration for Paula for that reason, because of what she said about her father. She had a philosophy: always be positive, feel positive, encourage your children. That was her principle. She may have done some reading about bringing up children; she said, "People buy books on how to raise a dog, why wouldn't you for a child?"

'Bringing you up was her major point about life. Biologically – having reached a ridiculous age – I see no point in life other than nature's ability to repeat itself. She believed that was her role.'

The Thursday nights kept going all the way to 1972. And then what happened?

'After that?' says Edward. 'I took up with Louis. Paula was married. Another life began.'

Epilogue

Every year I promise to go back and don't. I adopt an attitude of 'It's no big deal.' On the rare occasions I talk about my time abroad, whom I met and what I discovered, I am flippant or evasive. I tell the peripheral story, as though I really had just been a tourist escaping the English winter. This attitude survives my move from London to New York, and is still in place when I sit down to write about my memories of it. I put off reading the transcript from the archive for as long as I can. As I start to write the book, it is my mother's cousin Gloria I am most worried about offending; that she won't want to be connected with all this; that she, and her family, will feel tainted by association.

Gloria greets my phone call as always with an outpouring of love and affection and then, as always, starts to talk about the past: her mother's stories of my grandmother; the house where both she and my mother were born; my mother's disappearance and the long search to find her; the first time Gloria set eyes on my mother, when her legs buckled at the arrivals lounge. At the end of that trip, says Gloria, they drove back to the airport. 'Your mother hadn't said anything specific, I don't think. But I had the sense . . .' She sighs. 'On that last day, she said to me, "You were obviously well cared for as a child. I wasn't. One day, when we're two old ladies, I'll tell you about it, and we'll laugh."'

To me, my mother said, 'When I'm dead and gone you will write about me,' but she would, I know, have been deeply ambivalent about it. Tentatively, on the phone to Gloria, I bring up the subject of the book. 'Am I wrong to –' I say, but before I can finish, she cuts me off.

'No,' she says fiercely, this small, kind woman, and I have a flash of her ancestors chucking underachievers from the back of the wagon. 'It is right you should say something. A crime was committed.'

I don't go back to South Africa for the books or for anything else. I speak to Fay once a year on my mother's birthday, which falls on a bank holiday in South Africa and so she is usually at home.

'I am thinking of what day it is today, as, of course, are you,' she always says.

'How is Tony?' I say.

'Tony is Tony.'

'And Doreen?'

'Doreen is Doreen.'

'And Steven?'

'Who knows?'

Her grandchildren are thriving, and she remains the rock of the family. During one of these phone calls, she tells me about a relative of ours who has long put up with bad treatment from her husband and who, when he beat up her children, failed to go to the police. 'I can't forgive her,' she says. 'If you stand by and do nothing, you're as bad as the person doing it.'

One day, I receive a message through Facebook from a

cousin, asking me to ring Fay urgently. I am on a street in Brooklyn, about to go into a fancy cookware shop, and it is too late to ring by the time I get home. I call her the next day.

'Doreen passed yesterday,' says Fay, and gives me the details. It all happened very quickly – organ failure, slippage into unconsciousness, Jason was with her, etc. To my amazement, I burst into tears and begin sobbing, loudly.

'I don't know why I'm so upset,' I say.

'Yes, you're very upset,' says my aunt, sounding bewildered.

'I don't know why,' I say, around the edges of a sob. 'It's not as if . . .'

I pull myself together. 'What did Tony say? And Steven? And Liz?'

Finally, I say, 'Will anyone tell John?' John is their brother in Florida, the only one, apart from my mother, to have left, or as my dad puts it, 'got away'. My aunt doesn't have a number for him. I say I'll find one, and since we are on the same continent, give him a call to let him know his sister is dead.

The next day, after a bit of searching online, I find a mobile number for my mother's brother, and reassured by the South African accent on the voicemail, leave him a message to call me in New York. A day later, I am having coffee with my dad at Lincoln Center when the phone rings. 'This is John,' he says. I get up and walk around the back of the serving area to a quiet zone.

'Do you know who I am?' I say. I think the English accent will tip him off.

'I haven't a clue,' says John.

'I'm your . . . niece. Paula's daughter.'

'Oh,' he says. 'Yes, I've heard of you.'

I say I wished I had a better reason for ringing. I apologise for being the one to give him the news – the weirdness of it, given we've never spoken before – but finally I get it out that his sister died on Sunday. A sharp intake of breath, as if someone has crept up behind him and performed the Heimlich manoeuvre. John and Doreen were good friends. He was the one she always fought with over which of them had greater right to middle-child status.

I tell him as much as I know. Then I say, 'Your sister Fay has more details, you can call her if –'

'No,' says my uncle sharply. 'I haven't spoken to Fay for ten years. I can't get into that.'

There is a long pause.

'How is your mother?' says John.

Now it is my turn to be shocked. 'Oh God, John. Er. She's been dead for seven years.'

'Oh my God –'

'I thought Doreen – someone – would have –'

'Oh my God –'

'I'm so sorry,' I say. I am mortified. I am also aware that Doreen would be furious that my mother's death had upstaged her own in this exchange. Meanwhile, my uncle has lost two of his four sisters in the course of a single conversation. 'Nobody told me,' he says.

He can't talk. He is driving in Jacksonville, where he sells insurance for a living. He tells me to take his email address, but I can't find a pen. I'll text him, I say, but he says the text function on his phone has been disabled by the insurance company. He pulls over, writes down my email and says he'll write at the weekend. That is his preferred medium. 'But if I don't email, please ring me again. Please.' There is an intimacy on the phone with this man I have never met or spoken to, the sibling my mother knew least of the seven but still her flesh and blood, and in that moment all I want is to fly down to Florida to see if his face is like hers.

'I have a very clear picture of your mother,' he says softly. 'She must have been eighteen or nineteen, very slender, very elegant. She had reddish blonde hair, standing there in the sunlight.'

He says, 'She knew how to take command.'

'She did,' I say. 'She could give orders with the best of them.' We laugh. That evening, I picture him in a motel somewhere in Florida, sitting on the edge of the bed dodging asteroids of memory. Neither of us follows through at the weekend.

On my last trip back to London, I packed up the storage unit. Most of it went to the dump: all the clothes and the bric-a-brac, the school projects lovingly hung onto, although, inexplicably, I still have the hideous cat magnet. It is on my fridge in Brooklyn, holding up a *People* magazine recipe for fried rice. The trunk is at my dad's house. I have kept the letters and the photos, and in tribute to the random way in which she ascribed value to things, a pink towelling dress of my mother's that, as she would have said, 'doesn't owe anyone anything'.

I sometimes wonder if the owners of our old house will one day come across one of my mother's overlooked hiding places and find an old reference of hers or a piece of gold jewellery; some onion-skin letter with her father's name on it. Now, when I look at old photos of my mother and her siblings, it is with wonder. It is an axiom of disfigurement that the courage it takes to survive is construed as a substitute beauty, more powerful than the thing it replaces. But here's the thing: they really were beautiful.

We had adhered to my mother's wishes for the funeral, but a few months afterwards, my dad and I had cracked and had organised a memorial lunch for her, at a restaurant in the village. Our neighbours came, and some of my friends from London and my dad's boss, who had been generous with time off. I was touched that Ron, her old boss from the jewellery shop, came, and his wife, Connie. I stood up and told some stories about my mother's idiosyncrasies. How she picked up rubber bands in the street. How she had threatened, shortly before her death, to remove the bollocks of someone who was bullying a friend of mine, with the proviso, 'If I can find them.'

An elderly lady from the village came up to me afterwards. She was a member of what my mother called the blue-rinse brigade, a staunch Tory and upholder of village standards. Whenever she passed the house she would always look for my mother's head in the window and wave. 'She was a different kind of person, wasn't she?' she said, looking puzzled. 'But I liked her.'

A few days later, my dad and I went for a walk through the village, down the back street past the rubbish bins behind the Chinese restaurant. 'Hang on,' I said to my dad. The owner of the restaurant had come out and was throwing rubbish in the bin. I jogged back up the hill. I'd never seen him in his own clothes before; he always wore a suit in the restaurant. I stood in front of him, and without saying anything, he held open his arms. 'She's gone,' I said – not a euphemism I ever use –

and the two of us stood there hugging by the bins, while my dad looked up the hill in amazement.

About a week after her death the heatwave was still raging. England was curling at the edges. I went into the garden to fetch the last of the containers from underneath the bird table. There were dried apple cores on the ground and a lose shale of sunflower seeds from all the years of my mother's ministrations to the birds. As I straightened and turned, something caught my eye. I sprinted back into the kitchen.

'Do you know anything about a sunflower?' I asked my dad.

'No,' he said innocently. 'What sunflower?'

I led him out into the garden. Against the wall of the shed, where my mother had grown tomatoes and taught me how to do handstands, stood a huge sunflower, stalk as thick as my wrist, head fully eight feet high, which I swear, I swear, hadn't been there the week before. It was so heavy it leant over, as if taking a concerned but rather condescending view of the rest of the garden. We stood there, my father and I, staring at the flower, blinking in the sunlight.

'It's Mum,' said my dad.

'Yes,' I said.

Enough now.

Acknowledgements

I am grateful to more people than can be named here for reasons of privacy; but biggest thanks go to my mother's siblings for their generosity in sharing their memories with me, and to their children, awesome people one and all.

To Fay, for welcoming me into her house and looking after me a long way from home, and for her extraordinary courage in blessing the writing of this book.

To Tony, for his warmth and frankness; Steven, for his kindness and incredibly thoughtful insights. To the memory of the magnificent Doreen, and to Liz, for her strength and talent for seeing the funny side.

I'm grateful to my cousin, Caroline Walker, another writer in the family, for her generosity in sharing material from her grandfather with me.

Gloria and Cyrille Motet continue to be a great source of sanity and their encouragement made all the difference.

To my mum's friends: the wonderful Joan Borrill, and in fond memory of Danny, her husband, who died in 2009; to Jennifer and Terence Zinn; Denise and Reg Lander; Bob Salmon, Nick Young, Edward Mendelsohn, Roger Hearne, Len Sash and Ken Mellor.

To Marion Smith, for kind encouragement and good advice.

To those who helped me in Johannesburg; Dee Rissik, Adam Roberts, and my late friend, Heidi Holland.

Thanks to loyal friends and early readers in London: Merope Mills, Liese Spencer, Sam Wollaston, Ian Katz.

To Jat Gill for his generous early feedback; to Kate Fawcett, with whom I seem to have been talking about this book forever; and to Hannah Pool, whose friendship, then as now, I couldn't do without.

In New York, thanks to Janine Gibson for tolerating what might generously be called my fluctuating productivity while writing the tail end of this book. Oliver Burkeman listened to more of my brain melt than most and never failed to talk me down off the ledge.

Thanks to Simon Trewin for giving me such a flying start with the book and to Sarah Ballard, at United Agents, for ongoing brilliance. Thanks also to Jessica Craig and Charles Walker, for helping the book find a wider audience. At Faber, I couldn't have hoped for a better editor than Hannah Griffiths; thanks also to Kate Ward, Anna Pallai and John Grindrod.

To the late Nora Ephron, who with characteristic generosity came up with the title of the book for me and was the kind of encourager and role model you only get once.

And with love and admiration to Carin Fox, who always saw what was missing, and who made me press send.